晚清时期外国人眼中的闽南社会状况

英汉对照

[英] 乔治·休斯（George Hughes）著
罗锦生 译

本书获厦门理工学院外国语学院资助

中国出版集团有限公司
世界图书出版公司
广州·上海·西安·北京

图书在版编目（CIP）数据

晚清时期外国人眼中的闽南社会状况：英汉对照 /（英）乔治·休斯（George Hughes）著；罗锦生译. —广州：世界图书出版广东有限公司，2023.9

ISBN 978-7-5232-0056-8

Ⅰ. ①晚…　Ⅱ. ①乔…②罗…　Ⅲ. ①社会生活—历史—研究—福建—清后期—英、汉　Ⅳ. ① K295.7

中国版本图书馆 CIP 数据核字（2022）第 252974 号

书　　名： 晚清时期外国人眼中的闽南社会状况（英汉对照）

WANQING SHIQI WAIGUOREN YANZHONG DE MINNAN SHEHUI ZHUANGKUANG (YINGHAN DUIZHAO)

著　　者： [英] 乔治·休斯（George Hughes）

译　　者： 罗锦生

责任编辑： 程　静

装帧设计： 书窗设计

责任技编： 刘上锦

出版发行： 世界图书出版有限公司　世界图书出版广东有限公司

地　　址： 广州市新港西路大江冲 25 号

邮　　编： 510300

电　　话： 020-84453623　84184026

网　　址： http://www.gdst.com.cn

邮　　箱： wpc_gdst@163.com

经　　销： 各地新华书店

印　　刷： 广州市迪桦彩印有限公司

开　　本： 787 mm × 1 168 mm　1/16

印　　张： 16.5

字　　数： 376 千字

版　　次： 2023 年 9 月第 1 版　2023 年 9 月第 1 次印刷

国际书号： ISBN 978-7-5232-0056-8

定　　价： 65.00 元

咨询、投稿：020-84451258　gdstchj@126.com

译者序

《晚清时期外国人眼中的闽南社会状况》的作者是英国人乔治·休斯（George Hughes）。休斯于1859年加入清朝海关税务司署，从普通职员做起，自1861年起先后在宁波、汕头、厦门、天津、牛庄（即辽河营口）、芝罘（即山东烟台）等地担任当地海关的正、副税务司（即海关的正、副关长）等职，直到1885年离任。休斯曾于1862年12月至1865年4月，以及1869年12月至1875年3月期间两次担任厦门海关税务司，厦门也因此而成为其海关职业生涯中最长的一站。据说休斯精通汉语，在华期间大量阅读中国各类历史著作，在厦门及其周边地区广泛游历，实地走访了当地百姓，亲自参与了当地的对外贸易活动，亲身经历了若干历史事件，掌握了众多有关当时闽南社会状况的一手资料。因此，本书为读者从另一个视角了解明清时期，特别是清朝末年的闽南社会历史面貌提供了较为丰富的素材，具有一定的参考价值。

本译著依据的英文原著是香港梳沙洋行（De Souza & Co.）1872年出版的《厦门及其周边地区：中国及其他地区的文献汇编》（*AMOY AND THE SURROUNDING DISTRICTS*: *Compiled from Chinese and other Records*），译者在此将中文译名改为《晚清时期外国人眼中的闽南社会状况》。

全书共分为三个部分。第一部分是历史篇。本部分不但概述了唐宋以来，特别是明朝至晚清年间，日本、荷兰、英国对厦门及其周边地区的入侵行为以及当地的抵抗运动，还叙述了郑成功收复台湾、清末厦门小刀会的反清斗争以及太平天国起义军在厦门的活动等一系列历史事件。第二部分是地理篇。本部分主要介绍了厦门的总体情况、农业情况和行政区划、动物资源等。第三部分是贸易篇。本部分通过详细分析1870年前后厦门的对外贸易数据，力求真实地反映出厦门的对外贸易情况，以及厦门与台湾的贸易情况。

囿于时代背景、社会环境和个人经历，休斯在向外国人介绍闽南社会文化的时候，思想不免带有历史局限性并反映出西方殖民者的立场。作者恰逢中国半殖民地半封建社会程度加深之时来到中国，其所履职的清朝海关税务司署本身就是清朝政府与列强签订的不平等条约的产物，这样的时代背景和工作经历无疑对休斯产生了深远的影响。一是书中部分朝代的起止时间和历史事件的发生年代较为混乱，这其中既有中国古代纪年法转换成西元纪年法过程中所产生的失误，也有朝代划分不统一所导致的差异；二是由于当时并无规范的汉语拼音方案，专有名词的拼写使用了威妥玛式和邮政式拼音方案，其中既有汉语普通话发音，又有闽南语，甚至是粤语的发音；三是作者使用了当时西方人的习惯表达来称呼某些人、事、物，比如郑成功、台湾和清朝等的表达法。为了保持原作的时代特性，除对少数表达方法进行必要的处理外，我们最大程度地保留了原作品的面貌，并尽量通过脚注的形式对原著加以说明。此外，原著段落划分较为随意，常常一个自然段就延续了好几页。针对这一情况，我们在翻译过程中进行了必要的分段处理，并酌情添加了标题。

本译著由厦门理工学院外国语学院出版基金资助出版，在此表示感谢。在本书的翻译过程中，厦门理工学院外国语学院院长张金生教授始终保持关心，并提供了诸多帮助与指导，世界图书出版广东有限公司的程静编辑提出了不少修改意见和建议，闽南师范大学历史地理学院副院长郑榕博士阅读了译稿，在历史文化知识方面给予具体的指导。在此，谨向所有帮助过本译著的所有专家、同仁表示诚挚的谢意。

最后，由于译者本身的水平有限，书中的错误在所难免，敬请读者不吝赐教。

译　者

2022 年 10 月

Contents 目录

Part I Historical

Early intercourse with Japan 3
Japanese descents on Coast of China 5
Japanese craft 14
Troubles with the Dutch 16
Chêng Chih Lung 19
Chêng-cheng-kung (Koxinga) 26
Loss of "Formosa" by Dutch 30
Dutch endeavour to obtain a possession on mainland 39
Capture of Amoy by British 43
Small Knife Rebels 54
Capture of Amoy 56
Recapture of Amoy by Imperialists 68
Capture of Chang-chou-fu by a remnant of the T'ai-ping Rebels 73
Burgevine 85

Part II Geographical

1.Overview 91

Amoy 91
Kulangsu 95
Amoy (continued) 99
The Climate 101
People 109
Antiquities 111

Aids to Navigation 115

2. Agriculture 117

Productions 117

Agricultural Implements 119

Farm Stocks 121

Irrigations 123

3. Regions 125

Chang chou fu 125

Chüan chou fu 150

Tung-an-hsien 160

Quemoy 166

4. Animals 168

Fauna 168

Birds 174

Fishes 176

Reptiles 178

Part III Trade

General sketch of its history 182

First arrival of European vessels 202

Trade since the establishment of the Foreign Inspectorate of Customs 223

Import trade 231

Export Trade 239

Trade between Amoy and "Formosa" 247

目录 Contents

第一部分 历史篇

与日本的早期交往……4
倭寇登陆中国沿海……9
倭寇的手段……15
荷兰人制造的麻烦……17
郑芝龙其人其事……22
“国姓爷”郑成功……28
郑成功收复台湾……34
荷兰人力图在大陆获取殖民地……41
英国人攻占厦门……48
小刀会起义……55
小刀会占领厦门……62
清廷收复厦门……70
太平军余部占领漳州府……79
美国人白齐文……87

第二部分 地理篇

一、总体情况……93
厦　门……93
鼓浪屿……97
厦门岛……100
气候特征……105
当地百姓……110

历史古迹……113
助航设施……116

二、农业情况……118

农产品……118
农　具……120
家畜家禽……122
灌溉情况……124

三、行政区划……138

漳州府……138
泉州府……155
同安县……163
金　门……167

四、动物资源……171

动物群落……171
鸟　类……175
鱼类病虫害……177
爬行动物……179

第三部分　贸易篇

对外贸易概貌……192
与欧洲国家的早期贸易关系……213
海关税务司署成立以来的贸易情况……227
输入贸易……235
输出贸易……243
厦门与台湾之间的贸易……252

Part I

Historical

Amoy and its vicinity. Troubles with Japanese, with Dutch. Ch'eng Chih Lung, Chêng Ch'êng Kung （Koxinga）. Loss of "Formosa" by Dutch.Their endeavour to obtain a possession on mainland. Capture of Amoy by British. Small knife rebels capture Amoy. History of this society. Scale of duties and charges published by rebel chief. Recapture of Amoy by Imperialists. Capture of Chang–chou–fu by a remnant of Chang mao or T'ai p'ing rebels. Connection of foreigners with them. Burgevine. Recapture of Chang–chou–fu by Imperialists.

第一部分
历史篇

厦门及其周边地区——日本人和荷兰人惹麻烦——郑芝龙与国姓爷郑成功——台湾[1]落入荷兰人之手——荷兰人力图在大陆获取殖民地——英国人攻占厦门——小刀会起义军攻占厦门——小刀会的历史——起义军首领颁布的关税和收费标准——清廷收复厦门——“长毛”，即太平军余部占领漳州府——洋人和太平军的联系——美国人白齐文——朝廷收复漳州府

① 原文为“Formosa”（音译为“福尔摩沙”），是西方殖民者对我国台湾的称呼，现不再使用，故全书原文中的“Formosa”均加双引号，中文均翻译为台湾。据李震明编著的《台湾史》（中华书局，1948 年版，第 4 页），16 世纪初，葡萄牙殖民者远渡重洋来到东方，途经台湾附近洋面时望到岛上林木苍郁，山水秀丽，故为其取名“伊拉福尔摩沙”（Ilha Formosa），有美丽岛之义。后来“福尔摩沙”便成为西方人对台湾的另一个称呼。译者注。

Early intercourse with Japan

The early Chinese records of Amoy, and its vicinity, are obscured by statements so obviously untruthful, as, at best, to be but very unsatisfactory data, from which to extract a précis of its history. The information available, presents a dreary picture of craft, aggression, and bloodshed, on the one hand, and of haughty intolerance, exactions, and misrule, ending in rebellion, and savagery, on the other. Chinese historians claim that Japan was the dependent state named Wõ（倭）; and that in the period of Han-chêng（咸亨）, of the Tang dynasty, A.D. 670, its name was changed to Jih-pên（日本）, or the day spring, from its proximity to the rising sun, in the eastern Ocean.

That up to the date of the Sung 950-1280, there had been intercourse, under every dynasty, between China and Japan, and that the latter country had paid tribute uninterruptedly; but that after this period, it was discontinued; whereupon the warrior founder of the Yuen, Kublai Khan, dispatched several envoys to demand this proof of allegiance. The proud and warlike Japanese, resenting with disdain the Mongols' attempts to induce them to pay homage, and smarting under slights and injuries, slew a tribute seeking envoy, and his entire suite. To exact vengeance for this massacre, and to subjugate Japan, Kublai Khan, sent a large fleet bearing a hundred thousand men, under the command of Fan Wan-h'u. It reached Wu-lung-shan, where it was wrecked in a storm, and most of the ill-fated troops, who escaped the fury of the sea, perished by the swords of the Japanese. Few, if any, ever returned to China. After this disaster, intercourse between the two countries was suspended until the close of the Yuen dynasty, 1366.

与日本的早期交往

早期中国有关厦门及其周边地区的记载混杂着明显不够真实、模棱两可的说法，充其量不过是些差强人意的数据而已，择其历史要点，作如下概述。现有资料向我们展示了一幅充满诡计、侵略、杀戮，目空一切、排除异己、苛税暴政并最终导致叛乱多发和野蛮相残的景象。中国历史学家声称，日本原是国名为“倭”（Wō）的属国，在唐咸亨①元年（670年）改名为“日本”（Jih-pên），也就是“日出处”，意为靠近东海太阳升起的地方。

直至宋朝（950—1280年）②，中国历朝历代同日本都相互通好，接受后者朝贡不绝。宋朝之后，两国的双边关系中断，于是能征善战的元世祖忽必烈数次派遣使者前往日本，要求日方称臣。傲慢而又尚武的日本人对蒙古人的诱降行为既愤怒又不屑，他们深感耻辱与受伤，因此处死了元朝的招安使臣及其全部随行人员。为了报此滥杀之仇，也为了征服日本，忽必烈于是命令范文虎率领一支由十万人组成的庞大舰队赴日征讨。舰队行至五龙山（Wu-lung-shan）时遇到台风，将士们即使能够幸免于海难，也难逃死于日本人刀剑之下的厄运，最终只有少数士卒得以回国。这场灾难以后，两国终止交往，直到1366年元朝灭亡③。

① 咸亨是唐高宗李治在位期间的第七个年号，使用年份为670—674年。译者注。

② 中国史学界一般认为，宋朝的起止时间为960—1279年。译者注。

③ 史学界一般以元顺帝至正二十八年（1368年）明军攻克大都（北京）作为元朝在中原统治结束的年份。译者注。

Japanese descents on Coast of China

During the Ming dynasty, in retaliation for this attempt at invasion and conquest, the Japanese made frequent raids, carrying fire and sword along the coast of China from Chê-kiang to Kwang-tung. In 1368 an envoy bearing an Imperial letter, was sent to ascertain the cause of these incursions; but he was contemptuously entreated, by the Japanese, though, curiously enough, it is stated, that, about this time tribute was frequently tendered, but as it was unaccompanied by the proper forms of vassalage, it was always rejected. In the 20th year of Hung-w'u, 1386, means were taken to put the coasts of Chê-kiang, Fuhkien, and Kwang-tung, in a state of defence. The first named province was directed to furnish one hundred war junks, and the other two, double that number. At this period an able but crafty minister of the Throne, named H'u-wei-yung, was projecting a rebellion, and sought the aid of the Japanese, who sent one Jü-yao, a Buddhist priest, at the head of four hundred men, disguised as tribute bearers, to his assistance; the supposed tribute consisted of a large mass of wax, in which were concealed arms and gunpowder, but in the meantime H'u-wei-yung, had been overthrown, and beheaded, and the contemplated treachery becoming known, the pseudo tribute bearers were seized and punished, and intercourse with Japan, was again discontinued. Subsequently, when the chronicles of the founder of the Ming were drawn up, Japan was added to the list of unconquered states, fifteen in all.

In the reign of Yunglõ, 1401, the Japanese sent tribute accompanied by the proper address, together with twenty of the chiefs of Tui-ma, and Tai-chi, who had been piratically harrying the coast of China. From this time, tribute was always accompanied by such pirates, as had been captured. The address to the Ta-hwang-té, which covered the tribute, was couched in these terms: "If on the Islands of your majesty's servant, there be persons without regular calling, who engage in piracy, it is in truth without the knowledge of your servant, and he prays your indulgence (or that their fault be not laid to his charge) . " Attacks on the Coast, were, however still rife, until 1418, when General Lui-chiang, inflicted a very severe defeat on the marauders at Wang-hai-wõ, after which there was a temporary cessation of these raids. At this time, the payment of tribute appears to have been again discontinued.

From the fourth to the eighth years of Ching tung (1459-63), the Japanese, at the instigation of two renegades, named Huan-yeu, and Lung-yeu, made several descents upon the departments of Tai-chou, and the district of Tai-ming.

There is little doubt that many of these raids were in retaliation for injustice the Japanese had received at the hands of the Chinese, for while the Government jealously sought to exclude them from their coast, the people of Chê-Kiang, and Fuhkien, welcomed them for the trade they brought, but at the same time evaded, where practicable, paying them their just dues. When the Eunuchs, who held the posts of Superintendents of Trade, at Ningpo, and at the ports in this province, whose duties were to collect the Revenue, and fix the price of cargoes, were dismissed, and their offices abolished, the control they had exercised, passed into the hands of merchants, until communication with foreigners was strictly prohibited; it then passed into those of persons, who though of birth and station, repudiated their debts to the Japanese, to a more disgraceful extent than the others had done.

In 1547, intercourse was strictly prohibited by a Hsüne-fu, or Governor, named Chü Hwang, who mercilessly beheaded those who broke the prohibition. His action entailed upon him the hate of the people of Chê-Kiang, and Fuhkien, and he was impeached by a Fuhkien man, named Chao Liang, a censor, for putting to death some ninety people as pirates, who had been made prisoners, and forced to aid their captors. He was stripped of office, and he destroyed himself; and the prohibition fell into desuetude. In 1552 the Japanese, aided by a rebellious Chinese, one Wang Chih（汪直）, and his followers, with a fleet of some hundreds of junks, made a descent on the coast. The alarm was given simultaneously east and west of the Chê river, and North and South of the Yang-tse-kiang, for several thousand li.

They stormed the fort of Chang Kwo, invaded Tai-tsang-chou, stormed the city of Shanghae, sacked Kiang-yin, and attacked Chá-pú. They plundered the station at Kin-shan, and invaded the districts of Tsung-ming, Chang-shu and Kia-ting. In the following year they marched from Tai-tsang, upon Suchow, which city they pillaged; attacked Sung-kiang, and repassing the river, rapidly, made a stand at the North of it, at Tung-chau, and Tai-chau; Kia-shen was razed to the ground, Tsung-ming stormed, and Suchow again ravaged; Tsung-teh, Wukiang, and Kia-hing, were captured. They then took up a position at Cheh-lin (the wood of Cheh), whence they moved through the country at their pleasure, as if it were uninhabited. In 1554, they seized some vessels, and made an onslaught on Chá-pú, and Haining, destroying Tsung-teh, and ravaging Tang-tseh, Sin-shè, Hung-tang, and Shwang-lin. Uniting themselves with some newly arrived Japanese, they made a sudden descent on Kia hing ; but at the river Wang-king, they met with a severe defeat from the troops of Chang-king, president of the Board of War, who had taken the field, and who had beheaded, or said he had done so, some 2,000 of them; the remainder fell back upon Cheh-lin. Again was devastation carried into the region around Suchow, and the land from thence to Kiang-yin, and Wú sih, was stained with blood. They were on an average only three Japanese in every ten, the remaining seven being Chinese. They crossed and landed from the T'ai-Hu, or great lake, without opposition.

It is bootless to follow them; although at times suffering defeat, they appear to have ravaged and destroyed, almost where they listed. In 1556, they directed their course Southward, and made their dreaded appearance at Wu-yü in this prefecture. Desolation was soon carried through the districts of Tung-an, Hwui-an, and Nan-an; Fuh-ning-chou was assaulted, and after storming and carrying Fuh-an, and Ning-teh they, in 1557, besieged and blockaded Foochow, for a month. The towns of Fuh-ch'ing, and Yung-fuh, fell before them and were destroyed, the wave of conquest rolled down to Hing-wei, whence a sudden irruption into the Chang-chou prefecture was made, and dire alarm was felt at Chao-chou-fu, and even at the distant city of Canton.①

The accounts, which should be the fullest, of these sanguinary invasions here, are, in the *Hsia-mén-chih*, and *Chúan-chou-chih*, or Chinese histories of Amoy, and Chin-chew, lamentably bald and meagre. Little else than date, place, and event being recorded.

According to these books, the first attack by Japanese, was in 1369, on Chin-chew; the result, as in most of the accounts of subsequent attacks, is not clearly stated, but it may be gathered, without difficulty, from the context. From this date, they do not appear to have

①From the *Hai-Kwó-Tú-Chih* （《海国图志》）a sort of Chinese Atlas, containing brief accounts of foreign countries.

again visited this region, until 1552, when they swept down upon Sien-yü-hsien and An-chi-hsien. In 1556-7, they committed the depredations already recorded; and in 1559, they again captured and plundered the cities, and towns, of Chin-chew, Tung-an-hsien, Wei-an-hsien, and Nan-an-hsien. In the following year, Chin-chew was again assaulted, and Wei-an-hsien fell, with the loss of the district magistrate, and many soldiers and inhabitants. In 1561, another onslaught was made upon Chin-chew, which city, from its situation, and apparent helplessness, seems to have been constantly selected for attack. Thence they fell upon Tung-an, where, this time, they seem to have met with a stout resistance, as it is stated they besieged it for four months. It was taken, however, in 1562, as was Nan-an, and both cities were given to the sword, and completely pillaged. After an occupation of forty days, they were set fire to, and abandoned.

About this time, the Japanese moved to, and occupied, Namoa（南澳）, probably for the convenience of making unexpected irruptions on the mainland. It is stated that they built themselves houses, and remained for a year there; but most likely they occupied the Islands for a much longer period. In 1563, they appear to have captured the wealthy and important city of Chang-chou-fu; again plundered Tung-an-hsien, and to have burnt a great number of houses at Chin-kiang-hsien. In 1564, they killed many mandarins, soldiers, and other people at Chin-chew, which place they again assaulted in 1567, slaughtering and looting for three days. After having harried the coast for 200 years, they were expelled from this region, by General Chi-chi-kuang（戚继光）. This general seems to have been a man of ability and valour. He repulsed, with heavy loss to the Japanese, an attack on Chin-chew in 1569; and, again, in 1572, slaying the entire assaulting party of 200 men. After this date, the Japanese do not appear in the annals of the district; but in the reign of Wan-li （1571 to 1619）, they possessed themselves of part of "Formosa", which they held until near the end of this reign, when they were driven out by the Dutch.

倭寇登陆中国沿海

明朝时期，为了报复元军的侵略与征服行动，倭人常常携带火器、刀剑窜扰袭击中国从浙江到广东的沿海地区。1368 年①，朝廷派遣使臣持国书前往日本以查清日本人袭扰中国海疆的原因，这些使臣却备受日方怠慢。奇怪的是，据记载，这一时期日本经常向中国遣使纳贡，但由于日方不持国书，朝廷总是拒绝进贡。②洪武二十年，即 1386 年③，朝廷采取措施着手整饬浙江、福建和广东沿海的防御工程，命令浙江建造百艘战舰，福建、广东两省建造两倍于此数量的战舰。此时，权倾朝野的奸臣胡惟庸策划谋反，意欲借助日本人的力量帮助其实现图谋。日本派遣僧人如瑶率领四百人诈称入贡，将刀剑、火药藏匿于巨烛等贡物当中。然而，当如瑶到达的时候，胡惟庸所发起的叛乱早已被朝廷镇压，其本人也已经被斩首。就这样，谋反一事被大白于天下，这些冒牌国使被抓了起来并受到惩处，中国与日本的交往再次中断。后来，明太祖立下祖训，把日本列入 15 个“不征之国”的名单。

永乐年间的 1401 年④，日本派遣使臣持国书赴明朝进贡称臣，并献上 20

① 应为 1369 年。《明史》卷三百二十二：“洪武二年三月，帝遣行人杨载诏谕其国（指日本）且诘以入寇之故。”洪武二年为 1369 年。译者注。

② 14 世纪，日本国内分裂为南、北两朝，洪武七年（1374 年），南、北两朝都与明朝建立了外交关系。地方豪族以及在对明走私贸易中获巨利的日本商人，常假冒日本国使赴明进贡贸易，这就是明史书中自洪武八年以后，经常载有足利幕府和怀良多次遣使进贡。而以无国书被拒绝的原因。参见张声振：《中日关系史》卷一，吉林文史出版社，1986 年，第 211 页。译者注。

③ 洪武二十年应为 1387 年。译者注。

④ 1401 年为明惠帝建文三年。相关记载如下：“（日本使臣）肥富一行于建文三年（1401 年）秋至南京，向惠帝呈国书称臣纳贡。” 参见张振声：《中日关系史》卷一，吉林文史出版社，1986 年，第 218 页。译者注。

名袭掠过明朝滨海地区的对马和壹岐[①]二岛的海盗头目。之后，日本的贡物总是同所捕海盗一起敬献明朝。随贡物所附的国书这样写道：“臣境内之人肆为鼠窃者皆无赖逋逃之徒，实非臣之所知，皇上曲赦其罪（伏望贷臣之罪）。”[②]然而，日本人袭扰中国沿海地区的活动仍然十分猖獗。1418 年[③]，总兵官都督刘江在望海埚大败倭寇后，倭寇劫掠暂时停止。此时，日本人的朝贡似乎再次中断。

明正统四至八年（1459—1463 年）[④]，日本人在来自黄岩和龙岩的两位通倭者引路下[⑤]，数次登岸袭掠台州多地以及台、明[⑥]一带。

毋庸置疑，很多时候日本人的扰袭是为了报复明朝对他们的不公正待遇。朝廷满怀戒心地驱赶他们入海，浙闽一带的百姓虽然欢迎日本人前来通商，却寻机赖掉自己应付的款项。太监曾一度掌控市舶提举司[⑦]，该司的职责是给宁波及浙江其他港口的货物抽分[⑧]、定价。市舶提举司裁撤以后，商人便取代太监开始操纵海上贸易。随着海禁政策的严格实施，操纵权又转移到达官贵人手上，这些人同日本人交易时拒不付账，所欠款项之多、所作所为之恶更甚于前者。

1547 年，巡抚朱纨严格执行海禁措施，违令者被毫不留情地予以斩首。

① 原文为 Tai-chi，即“台岐”。但是日本只有壹岐岛，属日本长崎县的壹岐市，对马岛在其西北方向，两岛之间的海峡称为“对马海峡”，故此处译为“壹岐”。译者注。

② 明永乐十六年（1418 年），日本使臣岛津所持国书原文请参见《明太宗实录》卷一百九十九。译者注。

③ 此处应为 1419 年。据《明太宗实录》卷二百一十三载，辽东总兵官左都督刘江在望海埚大败倭寇的时间为明永乐十七年，即 1419 年。译者注。

④ 明正统四至八年应为 1439—1443 年。据《明史》卷二百一十：“（正统）四年五月，倭船四十艘连破台州洮诸、宁波大嵩二千户所，又陷昌国卫，大肆杀掠。八年五月，寇海宁。先是，洪熙时，黄岩民周来保、龙岩民钟普福困于徭役，叛入倭。倭每来寇，为之乡导。至是，导倭犯乐清，先登岸侦伺。俄倭去，二人留村中丐食，被获，置极刑，枭其首于海上。”黄岩民周来保、龙岩民钟普福早在洪熙元年（1425 年）时已开始通倭。译者注。

⑤ 原文为“at the instigation of two renegades, named Huan-yuen, and Lung-yen”，即“在两位名字叫做 Huan-yen 和 Lung-yen 的通倭者唆使下”。但据前注，此处的 Huan-yen 和 Lung-yen 应为地名。译者注。

⑥ 原文为 “Tai-ming”，判断应为台州和明州（宁波的古称）。译者注。

⑦ 即“市舶司”。明代沿袭前朝之制，于洪武三年（1370 年）在明州、泉州、广州设市舶司，职能相当于海关。浙江市舶司是专为管理日本进贡贸易而设的机构。译者注。

⑧ 即“收税”。译者注。

朱纨的举措引起浙闽两地人士的不满，御史、闽人周亮弹劾其所诛杀的约 90 名海盗实为被倭寇“逼良为盗”并受迫资敌的明朝百姓。于是朝廷撤掉朱纨的职务，他随即自尽而亡，禁海之事遭到废止。1552 年①，通倭逆贼汪直率部下勾结日本人大举入侵，数百艘舰船驶进沿海地区。浙江东西、长江南北，滨海数千里范围内同时倭警四起。

这群倭寇突袭昌国卫，侵犯太仓州，进攻上海城，劫掠江阴，攻击乍浦。接着，他们洗劫金山卫，进犯崇明及常熟、嘉定。第二年，贼寇自太仓一路劫掠至苏州，进攻松江，后回马江北，劫掠通州、泰州，攻陷嘉善，大破崇明，复掠苏州，攻入崇德、吴江和嘉兴。而后，倭寇屯兵柘林，他们纵横往来，如入无人之境。1554 年②，贼寇抢夺舟船进犯乍浦、海宁，攻陷崇德，转掠塘栖、新市、横塘、双林等处。随后倭寇又纠集新来的援兵，突犯嘉兴，至王江泾，被兵部尚书张经率部迎击并斩敌（确切地说是张经自称斩敌）2,000 余人。其余贼寇逃往柘林，其他地方的倭寇则再次劫掠苏州，战火延及江阴、无锡，一路血流成河。关于贼寇的构成，真正的倭寇大抵占百分之三十，协从倭寇的明人占百分之七十。倭贼往来太湖之间，没有遇到任何抵抗。

显然，追击倭贼是徒劳无益的，他们虽然偶尔打败仗，但对所图谋的地方却能悉数予以劫掠、摧毁。1556 年③，倭贼扬帆向南，抵达浯屿，令当地顿时弥漫着恐怖的气息。他们洗劫了同安、惠安、南安一带，攻打福宁州，攻占福安和宁德。倭贼又于 1557 年④围困福州长达一个月之久，福清和永福⑤等城也都被倭寇攻毁，劫掠波及兴化，漳州府也遭到突袭。就连潮州府，

① 此处应为 1553 年。据《明史》卷二百一十载：“（嘉靖）三十二年三月，汪直勾诸倭大举入寇，连舰数百，蔽海而至。”嘉靖三十二年为 1553 年。译者注。

② 此处应为 1555 年，参见《明史》卷二百一十。译者注。

③ 此处应为 1557 年。据《明史》卷二百一十载：“（嘉靖三十六年）十一月，贼扬帆南去，泊泉州之浯屿，掠同安、惠安、南安诸县。”嘉靖三十六年为 1557 年。译者注。

④ 此处应为 1558 年。见前书。译者注。

⑤ 即福州市永泰县，宋、元、明、清时期称“永福”。译者注。

甚至是遥远的广州都倭警告急。[①]

关于发生于此地的血腥侵略，《厦门志》和《泉州府志》（即厦门和泉州的中文历史记录）的记载应该是最为详尽的，然而材料却少得可怜，除了记录日期、地点和事件之外，别无他物。根据上述两地方志的记载，倭寇第一次进犯泉州是在 1369 年[②]。如同关于后续扰袭的大多数记载一样，书中对本次战果无明确描述，然而从对前后事件的记载来看，其结果是一目了然的。自此以后，倭寇似乎没有再进犯过此地，直到 1552 年[③]，他们扫荡了仙游县和安溪县。1556—1557 年[④]，倭寇所犯罪行已如前文所述。1559 年[⑤]，倭寇再次攻打并洗劫了泉州、同安、惠安和南安诸府县。第二年[⑥]，泉州又遭攻击，惠安县沦陷，县令战死，不少兵士和百姓都在此次袭击中丧命。1561 年[⑦]，倭寇复犯泉州，从地理位置上看，泉州明显处于孤立无援之境，因此它似乎一直都是倭寇选定的攻击目标。进犯延及同安，倭贼似乎遭遇了顽强的抵抗，据记载，他们围城长达 4 个月之久。最后，同安于 1562 年[⑧]沦陷，南安也是如此，两县皆失守于刀剑之下，惨遭洗劫。两县被占领 40 天后，倭寇放火烧城，随后弃之而去。

大约就在此时，大概是为了便于突袭大陆，倭寇移至南澳。据记载，倭寇在此地建屋而居长达一年，不过他们实际占据此地的时间可能更长。1563

① 摘自《海国图志》，一部中国人撰写的包含世界各国简介和地图册的地志书。作者注。

② 此处应为 1370 年，即明洪武三年。据乾隆版《泉州府志》卷之七十三（纪兵十九）：“明洪武三年六月倭寇泉州。”译者注。

③ 此处应为 1550 年。据乾隆版《泉州府志》卷之七十三（纪兵二十三）：“（嘉靖）二十九年，倭自仙游永春突犯安溪。”明嘉靖二十九年即 1550 年。译者注。

④ 应为前文（《明史》卷二百一十）注释的 1557—1558 年。译者注。

⑤ 此处应为 1557 年。据乾隆版《泉州府志》卷之七十三（纪兵二十三）：“（嘉靖）三十六年十一月，倭泊泉州浯屿，分掠同安、惠安、南安诸县。”译者注。

⑥ 即明嘉靖三十七年（1558 年）。译者注。

⑦ 据乾隆版《泉州府志》卷之七十三（纪兵二十四）：此处应为 1559 年，即明嘉靖三十八年。译者注。

⑧ 据前书载，此处应为 1560 年，即明嘉靖三十九年。译者注。

年[①]，倭寇在占领了漳州府这一富庶的重要城市之后，再度劫掠同安县，烧毁了晋江县多处房屋。1564年[②]，倭寇在泉州杀戮官军百姓，并于1567年[③]再次攻打泉州，对当地民众连杀带劫长达3天之久。倭寇扰袭明朝沿海地区长达200年，最终被戚继光平定。戚继光兼备能力和勇气，他于1569年[④]击退进犯泉州的倭寇，给敌人带来惨重的损失，又于1572年[⑤]全歼入侵的倭寇200人。[⑥]此后，倭寇从当地府志中销声匿迹。但是万历年间（1571—1619年）[⑦]，倭寇占领了台湾的部分地区，直到万历末年才被荷兰人赶走。

---

① 据前书载，此处应为1561年，即明嘉靖四十年。译者注。

② 据前书载，此处应为1562年，即明嘉靖四十一年。译者注。

③ 据前书载，此处应为1564年，即明嘉靖四十三年。译者注。

④ 据前书载，此处应为1566年，即明嘉靖四十五年。译者注。

⑤ 据前书载，此处应为1569年，即明隆庆三年。译者注。

⑥ 据前书载，“隆庆三年四月，倭二百余人入同安界，把总王介、参将王如龙战败。分巡检事蔡惠遣指挥张奇峰督兵袭破之，斩俘无遗。”可见戚继光并未参加此次战役。译者注。

⑦ 万历年间应为1573—1620年。译者注。

Japanese craft

The Japanese seem to have excelled their foes even in craft; rude, yet cunning, artifices were resorted to bewilder and mislead them. They carried in their armed ships, articles, which, should no opportunity occur for a savage descent upon some unprotected part of the coast, enabled them to seek the shelter of a port, as the peaceful bearers of tribute. Skirmishers bobbed up and down, attempting shot, to draw their foes fire, and when their arrows and ammunition were exhausted, the enemy dashed upon them; baits of seemingly abandoned spoils, and wine, and women, were left to draw them into ambush. The beleaguered town saw the scaling ladders prepared under its walls, and the next morning found the besiegers had effected an unmolested retreat, and were committing depredations miles away. Chinese prisoners were dressed in Japanese attire, and forced to fight in the van, and their tongues were so tied that they could not articulate the sounds of their own language, thus, in the event of escape, or wound, their death, by the hands of their own countrymen, was tolerably certain. The traditions of these fierce and sanguinary descents by the Japanese, and native pirates and cutthroats, who joined them, yet live in the minds of the people here; and the Amoy matron, coerces her fractious urchin with the black bogey of Woo-jin-lai-liao, or "the Japanese have come," up to the present hour.

倭寇的手段

倭寇的计谋似乎比对手更胜一筹，他们总是以卑劣阴险的诡计来迷惑和误导对手。如果沿海非设防区不允许蛮族登陆，倭寇就在战舰上装载一些物品，把自己装扮成求和的纳贡者，这样他们就可以进港避风。倭寇以小股人马突袭敌人，放几箭就跑，诱使对手火力全开，当对方弹尽箭绝的时候，倭寇就蜂拥而上。那些看上去似乎是倭寇丢弃的物资、美酒和女人，往往是他们伏击对手的诱饵。守城将士明明看到围城的倭寇已经准备好攀墙的云梯，第二天早上却发现他们早已悄然退兵，转向几英里（1 英里≈ 1.61 千米）外的地方进行劫掠。倭寇强迫被掳掠的明朝俘虏穿着日式服装，并在战时驱使他们作为先锋。这些俘虏的舌头被绑得紧紧的，以至于连家乡话都说不出来，这样他们在逃跑或受伤的时候难免会死于同胞之手。倭寇以及通倭的明朝海盗和歹徒在上岸后残忍劫杀当地人的场面，一直烙在当地人的脑海里，以至于时至今日厦门的妇人们仍然还在使用“倭人来了”即“日本人来了”这些吓唬人的话来管教家中闹脾气的顽童。

Troubles with the Dutch

About 1622, another fruitful source of trouble sprang up, caused by the Dutch having taken possession of the Panghu islands（Pescadores，澎湖）, and commencing to build forts thereon. This step pleased no one; it threatened the commerce between Manila and China, and in this interfered with the Spanish; and it was a menace to the Portuguese trade, between Macao and Japan; and to the Chinese it was "an incessant and intolerable grievance." The Emperor peremptorily required the withdrawal of the Dutch from the island. They, on their part, required "nothing more than liberty of commerce with China, and the prohibition of it between the Chinese, and the Spaniards, in Manila." The negociations hereon entered into, fell through, and the Dutch dispatched eight ships to scour the sea and to seize, or destroy, whatever they could along the Chinese coast, in order to compel the Chinese to trade，"many cruelties were thus committed, and several villages on the coast ravaged, to the disgrace of the Christian name."①

Negociations were resumed, and the Dutch Admiral, Keizerroon, sent an envoy to Amoy, who was received with great pageantry, and some politeness, but being required to knock his head against the ground "so that the bystanders might hear the cracking of his skull", he declined this fine old custom, and the discussion was again broken off, whereupon Chinchew was blockaded to prevent junks going to Manila, and as *argumentum ad hominem*; and the Admiral repaired to Foochow, where he was told that so long as the Dutch retained possession of the Pescadores, no trade would be permitted; but permission for them to fortify themselves upon the island of "Formosa", was offered as the price of the evacuation of Panghu. This offer was accepted, and in 1624, the Dutch concluded a peace, obtaining full commercial privileges, as then existed, and, at the same time, an entrepot for their Chinese, and Japanese, trade.

① Chinese Repository, Vol. vi. p. 584.

荷兰人制造的麻烦

大约在1622年[①]，又冒出了一件原因纷繁复杂的麻烦事，起因是荷兰人侵占了澎湖列岛，即毕斯卡度雷斯（Pescadores），开始在岛上建造堡垒。荷兰人的举动引起各方不满，因为它破坏了马尼拉和中国之间的商业交往，这就妨碍到了西班牙人，也威胁到葡萄牙人在澳门和日本之间的贸易往来。而对中国人来说，这是“一个让他们永远都无法忍受的屈辱”。明朝皇帝断然要求荷兰人撤出澎湖列岛，但在荷兰人看来，他们只不过“要求同中国自由互市，并且禁止中国人和马尼拉的西班牙人通商”。双方为此展开的和谈破裂后，荷兰人便派遣八艘船舰在海上巡查，对中国沿海地区进行恣意抢劫和破坏，以迫使中国同意互市。“许多暴行就这样发生了，沿海的一些村庄惨遭劫掠，真是玷污了基督教的名声。”[②]

谈判重新开始后，厦门当局为荷兰舰队司令凯泽鲁恩（Keizerroon）[③]所派遣的特使举行了盛大的欢迎仪式，并以礼相待，但厦门当局要求特使行磕头礼，“这样，在场的人就可以听到他脑袋叩地时发出的响声”。特使婉言拒绝了这个华而不实的旧式礼节，和谈再次中断。于是荷兰人封锁了漳州，阻止船只前往马尼拉，以此作为和谈的筹码。随后，荷兰舰队司令前往福州，

① 荷兰人第一次侵占澎湖发生在明万历三十二年（1604年）8月7日。11月17日（闰九月二十六日），浯屿把总沈有容受命前往澎湖同荷兰舰队司令韦麻郎谈判，迫使荷兰人于同年12月15日（农历十月二十五日）撤离澎湖。天启二年（1622年），荷兰人再度侵占澎湖。参见田珏主编：《台湾史纲要》，福建人民出版社，2000年，第39–40页。译者注。

② 《中国丛报》第六卷第584页，作者注。《中国丛报》（*The Chinese Repository*）是由美国传教士裨治文（Elijah Coleman Bridgman,1801–1861）在广州创办、向西方读者介绍中国的第一份英文刊物。刊物创办于1832年5月，停办于1851年12月，共20卷232期。译者注。

③ 国内外史学著作一般认为此时荷兰舰队司令为雷约兹（Cornelis Reyersen/Reijersz）。除本书外，《中国丛报》第六卷第584页也记载此时的荷兰舰队司令为凯泽鲁恩。译者注。

朝廷官员告诉他，只要荷兰人占据澎湖列岛，就不准许通商。不过，作为撤离澎湖列岛的补偿，朝廷允许他们在台湾岛上构筑堡垒。荷兰人接受了这一提议，并于1624年签订了和平协议①，继续享有当时已经获得的全部商业贸易特权，同时，台湾成为荷兰人对华和对日贸易的转口港。

① 1624年5月，福建巡抚南居益命副将俞咨皋等到达澎湖，包围了荷兰侵略军，荷兰人和俞咨皋达成协议，从澎湖撤走，福建当局允许他们到台湾贸易。荷兰人对外宣称中国皇帝把台湾赐给他们，实则是俞咨皋和地方官的私下承诺，未经上报朝廷批准。参见陈孔立：《简明台湾史》，九洲图书出版社，1998年，第18-19页。

Chêng Chih Lung

From 1624 to 1644, China was convulsed with civil war, and foreign invasion. In the latter year, Peking had fallen, and a Tartar was on the throne, and in the following, twelve of the fifteen provinces had acknowledged his sway. The province of Fuhkien, however held out; and it was not until some years afterwards that it was subdued. This district bore fully its share of the miseries entailed by this long epoch of bloodshed, when according to Chinese records, "the blood of the people flowed in sounding torrents," and of 25,000 families, which fled to "Formosa", it contributed more than its full quota. These bitter years produced a host of daring, and desperate men, patriotic, perhaps, in their hatred of the Tartar usurper, who had brought desolation to their doors, and who as a mark of submission, compelled the conquered Chinese, on pain of death, to shave off the long and thick tresses they had worn from time immemorial as a cherished ornament, and adopt the Tartar fashion of a long plaited queue, or tail, as well as the Tartar costume; but piratical also, from the necessity of paying, and feeding, the forces they gathered round them, or from having put themselves outside the law, by some act against the officials, who were sometimes their colleagues, and sometimes their accusers and judges.

Amongst these men one of the most celebrated is Chêng Chih Lung（郑芝龙）, who was born of obscure parents, at a village on the seashore at the entrance of the Anhai creek, in the district of Nan-an.① There are many accounts of his life, and much of the following is abridged from Nienhoff, in the second volume of the *Chinese Repository*. He is described as having been early distinguished by a resolute and fearless disposition, good looks, and agreeable manners. According to Du Halde, when quite young he found his way to Macao, and became a Christian under the name of Nicholas Gaspard. Subsequently he was employed by the Dutch at "Formosa", where, probably for good reasons, he had changed his named to Kwan. Thence he is stated to have gone to the Dutch factory of Firando, at Japan, where he married a daughter of a Japanese merchant; amongst the issue of that marriage,

① The village of Sheh Chien（石井）, at the foot of the East Peak.

was Chêng-cheng-kung（郑成功）,[①] who received the title of Kwŏ-hsing-ah（国姓仔）, called in the Amoy dialect Te-kok-seng, which gave rise to the names Kosenga, Coshinga, and Koxinga, by which latter name, he became celebrated as a pirate, trader, general of no mean ability, and self-created sovereign.

Chêng Chih Lung (the father) was entrusted by the Japanese with a command of vessels trading to ports on the Coast of China, with instructions, probably, should occasion serve, to employ them in a less peaceful manner. It is questionable whether he ever returned with this fleet. At all events with a facility not uncommon amongst distinguished naval commanders of other nations, of the same age, he changed his role of merchant captain to that of privateer, or rover, as circumstances arose, advantageous to himself. He combined forces with another worthy of the same stamp, named Yen Chin, who possessed one of the adjacent islands, whence, for years, they plundered passing vessels. On the death of Yen, Chêng Chih Lung, was unanimously elected Pirate-in-chief, and in that capacity became the terror of these seas. The fame of his successes attracted to him a number of vessels manned by patriotic Chinese, and by the evil disposed, so that, with the prizes he took, he gradually acquired a fleet so formidable, as to bid defiance to the Imperial junks, and to give him the command of the sea coast of Chê-kiang, Fuhkien, and Kwang Tung.

The policy of the authorities was then as now, and finding that they could not defeat nor entrap, this crafty and powerful chief, they recommended their Imperial master, Tsung Ching, the last of the Ming dynasty, to purchase his allegiance by bestowing on him high rank and office. The irresistible bait, of course, took, and Chêng replied that he was ready to submit if assured of rank, security to himself and followers, the enjoyment of their wealth, and such employment in the Imperial service, as would enable them to show their devotion and valour. The Court readily acceded to these demands, and about 1636, conferred on him the office of Admiral. For the next ten years, he took a most distinguished share in the naval operations of the Chinese during the Tartar conquest. He devised a source of wealth

① Koxinga's surname was 郑, pronounced in the locality Tin or Teng. His name was originally Lin（森）, afterwards changed to Cheng-kung（成功）, by the last Emperor of the Ming dynasty. The honor in which he was held by this Emperor, led to his receiving the title Kwoh-hsing（国姓）, he having been declared by the Monarch, to be worthy of bearing the Imperial surname. Hence he became known as Chêng-kwoh-hsing（郑国姓）, locally pronounced Tin-kok-seng, which name was by foreigners converted into Koxinga. By the name of Tin-kok-seng, he is still remembered with fondness and pride, by the inhabitants, not only of his native place, but of all Tung-an, and Nan-an.

and power, by assuming a monopoly, to some extent, of the lucrative trade with the Dutch at "Formosa", the Spaniards at Manila, the Portuguese at Macao, and with the Japanese, by compelling all trading vessels to supply themselves with his permit to trade, at a heavy cost.

His retirement from the piratical command, caused great consternation, and dissatisfaction, amongst his quondam associates, who had not followed him in giving in their allegiance, and who well knew the virtuous zeal with which an official just created from out of a band of desperadoes, would root out and punish evil doers. Their convictions were quite correct. His first commission was to destroy the pirate who had succeeded him, an old comrade, who was following his profession in the neighbourhood of Chin-chew. He cheerfully and faithfully executed this commission. Shortly, after, he was despatched against another chief, named Liao Yang; after a desperate battle, which lasted all day, Liao Yang fired his magazine and blew his vessel up, in an unsuccessful attempt to destroy his enemy; many of the remaining ships were taken, and Chêng returned triumphant, and for a time there was peace upon the seas, or as the Chinese express it "the seas were free from foam."

Chêng was now at the zenith of his fame; he had attained a power little short of imperial; his wealth was enormous, and he possessed a large and powerful fleet, entirely devoted to his will, and implicitly believing in his invincibility. His favor and his aid, were intrigued for, by all the rival and contending factions of the day, and it is said that the Prince of Fuh, on ascending the imperial throne at Nanking, bestowed a princess of the blood, in marriage, on his son. On the invasion of Fuhkien by the Manchus, and their advance on Chinckew, Chêng, at the advice of his friends, and relying on the promises made him, tendered his submission. He was treated by the Tartar General, with profound respect. Subsequently on his landing, without his usual guard, to do honor to the approaching departure of that officer, for Peking, he was pressingly invited to accompany him to the Court, to receive the almost regal rewards, promised, as due to his merit. Objections were unavailing, and his attendance was compelled. From this moment he recedes into shadow, and gradually disappears. He is no more heard of as a power; and, by and by, vague rumours from the capital, reach his son, that he is in captivity, and then that he has died, but how no one can tell. He has passed away.

郑芝龙其人其事

从 1624 年到 1644 年，中国面临着内忧外患的状况。1644 年，北京失守，满族①人登上皇位，随后明朝的 15 个省级行政区域②中有 12 个宣布归顺清朝政权。然而，福建仍然在坚持抵抗。直到若干年后，这场抗争运动才被镇压下去。百姓受够了漫长的血腥争夺，因为其残酷程度正如中国史料所记载的那样，“民众血流成河”。在 25,000 个逃到台湾的家庭中③，来自福建的人员大大超出了分配给他们的全部移民配额。这些苦难的岁月造就了一群敢于冒险、无所畏惧的人，或许正是对清朝篡位者的憎恨令他们产生了爱国情怀，因为那些篡位者把他们的家园夷为了废墟。作为征服的标志，清军人强迫归顺的汉人剃掉他们自古以来就蓄留并视为珍贵饰物的浓密长发，并依从满族人的习俗，留起尾巴状的长辫子，还要穿着满族人的服装，违令者予以处死。不过，这些福建的好汉们为了给自己拉起来的队伍支付军饷、提供给养，并在与那些时而利用，时而指控、审判他们的官员作对后还能逍遥法外，他们也干起了海盗的营生。

① 此处原文为“鞑靼”。西方文化中，“鞑靼”一词在 13 世纪初期到 17 世纪之间一般用来指曾经横扫欧洲的蒙古民族。到了 17 世纪之后，随着耶稣会士深入中国内地传教，尤其是满洲的后金政权的强大，该词开始指代新兴的满族，也就是所谓的“东鞑靼”。参见张恒：《1899 年前英语文本中大连地区“鞑靼”称谓考述》，《东北亚外语研究》2015 年第 3 期，第 36–40 页。本书中，“鞑靼人”一般指满族人，“鞑靼”指清朝。译者注。

② 1428 年（宣德三年）以后，明朝统分为 2 京（京师顺天府和南京应天府）和 13 承宣布政使司（俗称 13 省）以及关西七卫、俄力思军民元帅府、斡难河卫。译者注。

③ 关于 1650 年前后台湾的大陆移民人数，有不同的说法。有人认为，居住在台湾的福建移民人数由 1644 年的几千人，很快上升到上万人，乃至数万人；有人认为，1648 年，台湾的中国人骤然增加到 2 万人；有人认为，除了妇孺外，其余人数超过 25,000；还有人认为，1644 年仅台南一地，大陆移民就有 10 万人之多。参见林国平等：《福建移民史》，方志出版社，2005 年，第 156 页。译者注。

在这些人当中，最著名的当属郑芝龙。郑芝龙出生于南安安海溪[①]入海口处的一个海滨村庄[②]，身世不详[③]。关于他的生平记述颇多，以下大部分内容节录自《中国丛报》第二卷中尼恩霍夫（Nienhoff）所记述的内容。据记载，郑芝龙很早就因为其坚毅无畏、相貌堂堂、平易近人而广受尊敬。根据杜赫德（Du Halde）[④]的描述，郑芝龙非常年轻的时候就前往澳门，在那里皈依了基督教，取教名尼古拉斯·加斯巴德（Nicholas Gaspard）。随后，郑芝龙受雇于台湾的荷兰人，在那里他可能找到充分的理由把自己的名字改为一官[⑤]。后来，据说他从台湾前往位于日本平户（Firando）的荷兰工厂，在那里娶了一位日本商人的女儿。夫妇俩所生孩子当中有一位名叫郑成功，曾受封“国姓仔”（Kwō-hsing-ah），用厦门本地话说就是“郑国姓”（Te-kok-seng），也有人称其为“国姓爷”[⑥]（Koxinga，有的拼写为 Kosenga 或 Coshinga），不过，他在作为海盗、商人、出色的将军和自封的王爷时都使用“国姓爷”这个名字，并因此而闻名于世。

郑成功的父亲郑芝龙接受日本人的指派，负责指挥一支船队前往中国沿海港口进行通商。日本人可能还指示他，如有必要，船队可以采取一定的武

① 原文为“Anhai Creek”，即安海溪，实际为石井江（大盈溪）。译者注。

② 东峰（East Peak）脚下的“石井村”（village of Sheh Chien）。作者注。

③ 据《明史纪事本末》卷七十六“郑芝龙受抚”一节，“芝龙父绍祖，为泉州库吏”。张宗治曾撰文指出：“郑芝龙的父亲象庭公名士表，字毓程，先娶徐氏，生芝龙、芝虎、芝麟、芝凤四子，后娶黄氏，生芝豹。”参见夏蓓蓓：《郑芝龙：十七世纪的闽海巨商》，《学术月刊》2002 年第 4 期，第 58–63 页。译者注。

④ 杜赫德（Jean Baptiste Du Halde, 1674–1743），法国耶稣会士、汉学家、历史学家。杜赫德尽管没有来过中国，但是他根据其他 17 世纪来华传教士的报道编辑而成的《中华帝国志》在欧洲被认为是 19 世纪以前关于中国的知识手册。译者注。

⑤ 原文为“kwan”，应为“一官”，即郑芝龙，欧洲文献中一般拼写成 Iquan。关于郑芝龙的姓名字号，史书记载颇多不同。有的记载称，郑一官继承李旦和颜思齐的产业和事业后，将手下部众分为十八锋，结为“十八芝”，并从此改“一官”为“芝龙”。据连横《台湾通史》卷二十九列传一之“颜思齐、郑芝龙”：“芝龙，南安石井人，少名一官，字飞黄”。译者注。

⑥ 国姓爷姓“郑”，当地方言发音为“Tin”或“Teng”，原名“森”，后来由明朝末代皇帝赐名“成功”。皇帝对他极为宠爱，赐予他国姓，并称其完全当之无愧。此后，郑成功变成“郑国姓”（Chêng-kwoh-hsing），当地方言发音为“Tin-kok-seng”，外国人改写为“Koxinga”。时至今日，“郑国姓”仍然受到家乡人还有所有同安人和南安人的爱戴，并为之感到自豪。作者注。赐姓郑成功的是南明隆武帝，亦即明朝京师北京失陷后，明朝宗室在南方相继建立政权的南明第二位皇帝隆武帝朱聿键。译者注。

力手段。郑芝龙是否带着船队完璧归赵尚有疑问，毕竟他与同时代的外国舰队司令一样具备过人的天赋。随着形势的发展，他做出对自己有利的选择，把自己从商船船长变成了海盗头目。他把自己的人马同另一位海盗头目颜思齐⑦的人马联合起来，后者占据了邻近的一个岛屿，多年来以劫掠过往船只为生。颜思齐死后，郑芝龙被推举为海盗盟主，从此成为海上霸主。郑芝龙声名远扬，许多具有爱国情怀的中国人驾船前来投奔，他逐渐拥有足够对抗朝廷战船的强大舰队并得以在浙江、福建和广东沿海呼风唤雨。

当时朝廷的政策和现在一样，官员们发现他们既无力剿灭也无法诱捕这位狡猾而强大的海盗头目，就上奏明朝末代皇帝崇祯，建议赐予郑芝龙高官厚禄以换取他对朝廷的效忠。朝廷的封官许愿让人无法抗拒，郑芝龙上钩了并回复说，如若朝廷能够给自己和手下一众人等加官进爵，确保他们的人身和财产安全，允许他们为朝廷报效自己的忠诚和勇气，他愿意归降。朝廷欣然应允。大约在 1636 年，朝廷下诏授予郑芝龙海防游击将军一职。接下来的 10年里，在清朝军队征伐期间，郑芝龙出色地完成了明朝海防守备的重要职责。他推行了一系列措施以积累财富、扩充权力，迫使所有商船以高价购买他签发的贸易许可证，在某种程度上垄断了与台湾的荷兰人、马尼拉的西班牙人、澳门的葡萄牙人以及日本人的贸易，并赚取了高额利润。

郑芝龙辞去海盗盟主的做法激起了众多老部下极大的惊愕和不满，他们没有随郑芝龙归降朝廷，因为他们非常清楚曾是亡命之徒的郑芝龙身上所带有的自命不凡和狂热会促使其对违法作恶之人进行严厉惩罚，甚至将其斩草除根。他们的判断非常正确。郑芝龙的第一个差使就是消灭继任的海盗盟主，这位旧伙党在泉州干着他的老行当，郑芝龙愉快而坚定地完成了这项任务。不久后，他又被指派前去剿灭另一位名叫刘香的头目。经过一整天的殊死搏斗之后，刘香消灭对手的企图未果，遂放火烧了军火库，炸毁了自己的战船，

⑦原文为“Yen Chin”，应为颜振泉，即颜思齐，振泉系其字。译者注。

剩下的许多船只也被悉数缴获。郑芝龙凯旋而归，海上一度出现了被中国人称为“海不扬波”的和平景象。

郑芝龙的个人名望达到了巅峰，拥有了一人之下、万人之上的权力。他获得了巨大的财富以及一支绝对忠诚的强大的巨型舰队，他坚信自己是不可战胜的。由于郑芝龙投向明朝并且挽救朝廷于危难之中，他的所有敌人和竞争对手便暗中策划，图谋加害于他。据说福王①在南京登基的时候，把皇族的一位公主赐给郑芝龙的儿子作为妻子②。当满人进军福建、向泉州挺进之时，郑芝龙听从朋友的劝告，相信满人给他的承诺，向清朝投降，清朝将军③也对他毕恭毕敬。后来，郑芝龙毫无防备地上岸送别那位即将回京复命的将军，将军就软硬兼施要他一同赴京接受朝廷的丰厚赏赐。郑芝龙身不由己，只得被迫随行。从那一刻起，郑芝龙逐渐走向幕后并消失在人们的视线之中，他的势力已经消失殆尽。不久以后，他的儿子隐约听到从京城传来的消息，说郑芝龙被囚禁了，后来又听说他已经死了，但是没有人知道到底是怎么回事。

①明崇祯十七年（1644年），崇祯帝朱由检在煤山自缢。同年，福王朱由崧在南京称帝，改元弘光。译者注。

②明崇祯十四年（1641年），郑森（即郑成功）18岁，娶董氏女为妻。而福王登基时已是崇祯十七年（1644年），郑成功不太可能立公主为侧室。另外，南明隆武元年（1645年）八月，郑芝龙引郑森拜见隆武帝，（帝）抚拍郑森肩背说，可惜我没有女儿配卿。参见田珏：《台湾史纲要》，福建人民出版社，2000年，第53-54页。由此可见，郑成功并未娶皇室宗亲女子。译者注。

③指清征南大将军贝勒博洛。清顺治三年，即1646年，郑芝龙向其投降。译者注。

Chêng-cheng-kung (Koxinga)

Koxinga, now took command of his father's fleet, and followers, and proceeded to exact from the Manchus, a bloody retribution for the treachery shewn his sire. He ravaged, burnt, and destroyed, on sea and land, for years, mercilessly slaying and despoiling the Manchus, and such of his own countrymen, as had submitted to them. All attempts to restrain him were ineffectual, and of the wars of the conquest, his are said to have been the most terrible. In 1650, the scattered remnants of the Chinese armies, had been gathered together in the city of Canton, to make a last stand against the Tartars. On the approach of the enemy, the assistance of Koxinga was sought by the Governor: it was willingly accorded, and his well practised fleet inflicted heavy loss on the Tartars unaccustomed to naval warfare. The siege of the city was protracted for eight months, and thrice it was on the eve of being abandoned; and it was only when the city had fallen, through the treachery of those in charge of the north gate, that Koxinga withdrew his fleet, maintaining his supremacy upon the sea, long after all the provinces of the kingdom, had submitted to the Tartar rule.

In 1653, he made a descent on Amoy, with the design of capturing Hai-têng, its then port. The Tartars went to its relief, and in a naval engagement which ensued, were worsted, with a loss, it is stated, of seven or eight thousand men. The town was then carried by assault, and all bearing arms were slain, but injury to the peaceful inhabitants was prohibited. It was at once occupied, heavy guns mounted, and its walls repaired; and it formed a base whence to attack the open country, left unguarded by the flight of the Imperialists. Chang Chou, and Chinchew, were heavily mulcted, and smaller cities, and towns, sacked, immense booty accruing to the conquerors. Subsequently, whilst pillaging the department of Chinchew, reinforcements of Tartar troops arrived, and compelled Koxinga's forces to retreat to their ships, with the loss of much of their plunder.

In 1655, he again made a descent on Chinchew, and Hsing-hua despoiling these places. The Tartars now applied for additional forces; they were granted, and the coast so strongly garrisoned, that further raids here, were unprofitable. Koxinga now conceived the project of making himself master of the province of Kiang-nan, and after seizing certain places at the entrance of the Yang-tze-kiang, proceeded up that river, with a fleet of 800 sail, and attempted the siege of Nanking, the provincial city. Some slight success attended his early efforts, but the Manchus made so fierce and determined a night attack on his forces, that they had to fly to their ships, routed, and with the loss of over 3,000 men, arms, tents, and spoils.

In 1659, the Imperial Court, resolved to equip such a fleet as would effectually destroy this desperate man. He sought it, and in the action that ensued, utterly defeated it, capturing or destroying the greater number of the ships, and making 4,000 prisoners, whom, after cutting off their noses and ears, he set at liberty. These miserable wretches were all put to death on their return to Peking, for permitting themselves to be captured. Finding, notwithstanding his successes, that his hopes of establishing a kingdom on the mainland, were frustrated, owing to a combination of circumstances, he turned his attention to "Formosa", as a suitable asylum and dominion.

“国姓爷”郑成功

至此，郑成功接管了他父亲的舰队和手下将士，并因满人对他父亲背信弃义而展开血腥报复。连续几年，他在海上和陆地烧杀抢掠，无情屠杀和劫掠满人以及归降他们的汉人。所有试图遏制他的行动都失败了，在清军所有的征服战中，与郑军（译者注：指郑成功所属军队）之战被认为是最残酷的。1650年，南明残余部队在广州城集结，准备对清军做最后一击。在敌人逼近时，南明总督向郑成功求救，后者欣然应允。郑成功训练有素的舰队给不习惯海战的清军造成了重大损失。清军对这座城市的围攻持续了八个月之久[①]，有三次几乎都已经放弃守城了，郑成功的舰队一直坚持到北门守军投降、城市沦陷才撤出战斗[②]。在明朝所有省区都归降清朝很久之后，郑成功仍然保持着海上霸权。

1653年，郑成功在厦门登陆，计划夺取港口海澄。清廷派兵前去解围，在随之而来的海战中，官兵损失惨重，据记载伤亡达七八千人。紧接着，郑成功派兵袭击海澄，他们杀掉了所有武装人员，却禁止伤害平民百姓。郑军再次占领海澄后，立即架起重炮，修复城墙，把海澄从一个官军败退后无人防守的城镇，变成郑军向城外空旷地带前进的据点。随后郑军又重创了漳州和泉州，洗劫了较小的城镇，征服者们夺取了大量的战利品。不久之后，在劫掠泉州府的时候，清廷的增援部队接踵而至，郑成功的人马只得退回船上，

① 清顺治七年、南明永历四年（1650年），清尚可喜、耿继茂统军攻打广州。自三月初九清军架梯攻打广州北城至十一月初二轰塌西北角城垣，持续近8个月。参见顾诚：《南明史》，中国青年出版社，1997年，第606-608页。译者注。

② 郑成功于顺治七年（1650年）大举进攻南明控制的潮州，由于镇守潮州的郝尚久和潮惠巡道沈时归降清朝，同年6月清军从福建漳州调兵援潮，迫使郑军退回福建铜山。参见前书，第439-440页。译者注。

被迫扔掉了大量战利品。

1655 年，郑成功再次登陆泉州、兴化进行劫掠。清军增派人马的请求得到批准，沿海有了清军重兵驻防，再次袭击已然得不偿失。此时①，郑成功图谋夺取江南省②，他占领了长江入海口的一些地方后，率领一支由 800 艘船只组成的舰队溯江而上，企图围攻省城南京。郑成功在早期的一些攻击战中取得了小规模胜利，但是满人对他的部队发起猛烈而坚决的夜袭，郑军全线溃败，不得不逃回船上。此战造成郑成功的部队伤亡 3,000 多人，损失了大量武器、帐篷以及战利品。

1659 年，朝廷决定组建舰队以有效地消灭这位亡命之徒。郑成功率先找到官军舰队的踪迹，随后发起攻击，他们彻底击败了朝廷舰队，俘获、摧毁了大量舰船，俘虏了 4,000 人。郑成功割掉俘虏的鼻子和耳朵后就将他们释放了。这些可怜的人们因为屈膝投降成为俘虏，回到北京后立即被处死。尽管郑成功取得了胜利，但是他发现在大陆上建立王国的愿望屡屡受挫，这是多种因素综合作用的结果，于是他将注意力转移到台湾，打算将其作为一个理想的避难所和独立王国。

① 指清顺治十六年，即 1659 年，郑成功北伐南京。译者注。

② 清朝江南省的范围大致相当于今江苏省、上海市、安徽省全境以及江西省部分地区。译者注。

Loss of "Formosa" by Dutch

This beautiful island, called by the Chinese Taiwan, or Terraced Bay, includes in length from North to South, over three degrees of latitude. Its greatest breadth is about eighty miles, and it is separated from the Chinese coast, by a channel varying from seventy-five, to one hundred and twenty miles, in width. It is distant from Amoy, only a day and a half, or two days' sail. The Dutch, on obtaining possession of the island in 1624, had built a strong fort named Zelandia, and a second, less strong, named Province, at the principal harbour on its southwest face, now known as Tai-wan-foo; and, in course of time, had formed settlements at Tamsui, and Kelung, and in the interior, in the neighbourhood of their principal fort. By a combination of Dutch, and native authority, and by wise laws, they succeeded in attaching the people of these districts, to them, and the long continued anarchy on the mainland of China, arising from the invasion of the Manchus, had peopled the island with thousands of fugitives, whose industry soon brought it under cultivation, and rich crops of rice and sugar, were waving over heretofore unproductive land. At first the Hollanders encouraged this immigration, and then, becoming alarmed, tried to prevent it. How far the measures taken by the Dutch, in this endeavor tended to their own downfall, by alienating the goodwill of the Chinese, it is difficult now to conjecture, but it is certain that the Chinese entered into correspondence with Koxinga, and, on his attack on the island, assisted him with hearty good will.

The Dutch Governor Coyet, marking the warlike preparations of Koxinga at Amoy, increased as far as possible, in 1650, the garrison of his forts, Zelandia, and Province. But for several years, although there was great mutual distrust and dissatisfaction, there was no hostility between the parties. However after Koxinga's defeat at Nanking, it was evident that, unless he attacked the island, his fleet and followers would be dispersed, for want of the means of subsistence; and the Dutch, aware of the correspondence between the resident Chinese and the chieftain, increased their vigilance, seized some of the most important emigrants as hostages, and arrested and tortured others on suspicion. The wise prevision of Coyet, induced him earnestly to request assistance from Batavia, and twelve ships, and large reinforcements, were despatched thence, with orders that, if the alarm at "Formosa" proved groundless, the fleet should proceed against Macao. The force at Taiwanfoo, was now augmented to 1,500 men, sufficient, the Admiral thought, to oppose any number of Chinese troops. Koxinga was asked "whether he was for peace, or war." He replied that, "he had not the least thought of war against the company," and sent some trading junks to Taiwan, but as he still continued his preparations at Amoy, and Quemoy, the Governor's suspicions were not removed.

The majority of his council, however, were of opinion that there was no present danger, and the ships were ordered to their respective destinations. The Admiral returned to Batavia, and accused the Governor of unreasonable apprehensions, and he was suspended from office, and ordered to Batavia, to defend himself. M. Clenk, his successor, sailed for "Formosa", in June 1661.

Shortly after the departure of the ships, Koxinga with a large fleet, and 25,000 of his best troops, appeared off forts Zelandia, and Province; and, assisted by thousands of his countrymen, on shore, began to land. He was first attacked by 240 Dutch soldiers, and by four ships. He met the attack of the former, with skill and bravery, and succeeded in turning their flank, on which they gave way, became panic striken, and were so routed, that only half the division regained the fort, one captain, and nineteen men, being abandoned to the enemy. The ships fared no better, they sank a few junks, but one was destroyed by a fire ship, another escaped to Batavia, and the fate of the other two is not stated.

No further opposition was offered, and in four hours the Chinese landed, cut off all communication between forts Province and Zelandia, and between the latter fort, and the open country. The instant surrender of the forts, was now demanded, under the menace that if not complied with, all would be put to the sword. A deputation from the Dutch waited on the chief, to offer, rather than lose all, the surrender of fort Province. It was received with some state, but was told that, " 'Formosa' had always belonged to China, and now that the Chinese wanted it, the foreigners must quit the island immediately. If not, let them only hoist the red flag." Next morning the red flag was flying on fort Zelandia, but fort Province, with its garrison and cannon, was surrendered. All the Dutch capable of bearing arms, were now taken into fort Zelandia, and the city fired, but not so effectually, as to prevent the Chinese from saving many buildings, which afforded them shelter. They brought up twenty-eight cannon, to bear against the fort. Its fire was, however, so sustained and well directed, that numbers were killed and wounded in this attempt, and the besiegers, making a sally spiked the guns.

Koxinga, baffled in all his attacks on the fort, began a close blockade, and vented his rage on the open country. He made prisoners of all the Dutch he could lay hands on, especially clergymen, and schoolmasters, alleging that they secretly encouraged their parishioners, to kill the Chinese residing among them; some were crucified, their crosses being erected in their respective villages, while others were put to death in a more merciful manner. One of the prisoners taken, Mr. Hambrocock, a clergyman, was sent by Koxinga, to the Governor, to propose terms for the surrender of the fort, the alternative being vengeance on the Dutch prisoners. His wife and two children were detained as hostages; and he had no hope but that death would be his portion, if he failed in his negociations. Yet instead of urging surrender, this noble man cheered the garrison on to make a gallant defence, by hopes of relief, assuring them that Koxinga had lost many of his best ships, and soldiers, and began to weary of the siege. Two of his daughters who were within the fort, flung themselves upon him, and implored him to remain; their entreaties were seconded by the council of war, but with unselfish devotion he replied that, unless he returned, his wife and children would perish, and that, he hoped to be of service to his poor fellow prisoners. So saying he left with the Governor's refusal to surrender. Koxinga listened sternly to the answer, and then ordered all the Dutch male prisoners, to the number of five hundred, to be put to death. This was done, many of the women and children were also slain, though it is stated, "some of the best, were preserved for the use of the commanders, and the rest sold to the common soldiers." Messrs Hambrocock Mus, and Winshaim, clergymen, and several schoolmasters, perished in this massacre.

Two days after the council at Batavia had censured Coyet for his fears, and despatched his successor, Clenk, to "Formosa", the ship which had escaped, arrived with the news of the attack on that place. They revoked the censure and suspension, and fitted out ten ships, with 700 soldiers, for the island, but Clenk arrived first off fort Zelandia, where he saw, instead of the rich and peaceful Governorship he had flattered himself with obtaining, the red flag flying, and hundreds of Chinese war junks anchored in the north roads. Thereupon he sent his despatches, on shore, and, without landing, sailed for Japan.

When the succours from Batavia arrived, the besieged, began to act on the offensive, and an unsuccessful attempt was made to dislodge the enemy from the town, in which two ships, and many men, were lost. The garrisons of Kelung, and Tamsui, were ordered to reinforce the besieged, and the women and children, and other helpless persons, were sent to Batavia. These preparations checked the approaches of Koxinga; but the inexplicable imprudence of the Dutch, lost them their advantage.

The Governor, received letters from the Tartar Viceroy of Fuhkien, requesting his cooperation in expelling the remains of Koxinga's forces from the coast, and promising his aid, afterwards, to the Dutch in "Formosa". Five ships were accordingly sent away for this service, but of these, three were lost in a storm, and the other two returned to Batavia. These circumstances were such, as Koxinga, in his wildest dreams, could scarcely have hoped for, while to the besieged, they brought utter despair. Desertion commenced, and a deserter pointed out to Koxinga's forces, the weakest spots; they were assailed from three batteries, a breach was made, and a redoubt gained, and the assault was evidently about to be given.

On this the Dutch held a council of war, and the majority having decided that the fort was untenable, it was surrendered, after a siege of nine months, and a loss of sixteen hundred men. The Dutch embarked for Java, where the Governor, and his council, were imprisoned, their goods confiscated, and the Governor, himself, condemned to perpetual imprisonment on one of the Banda isles. In such wise, after thirty years duration, ended in 1662, the Dutch territorial possessions in "Formosa", and in the Chinese seas.①

① According to other accounts they did not abandon possession of the port of Keelung, on the northern extremity of the island of "Formosa", until 1668.

郑成功收复台湾

中国人把这座美丽的岛屿称作台湾，即平台上的海湾（Terraced Bay），其南北跨越纬度达 3 度以上，东西最宽处约 80 英里，与中国大陆沿海地区隔着一条宽度为 75 到 120 英里不等的海峡，距离厦门只有一天半到两天的船程。荷兰人于 1624 年占据这座岛屿以后，在其西南面最重要的港口，也就是如今被人们称为台湾府[①]的地方建造了一座名为普罗民遮城[②]（Province）的坚固堡垒，以及另一座更加坚固的热兰遮城[③]（Zelandia）堡垒。随着时间的推移，他们在淡水、鸡笼[④]和岛屿内陆的重要要塞附近建立了定居点。荷兰人联合当地权势人物，通过实施开明的法律，赢得了这些地区民众的认可。满人入侵导致中国大陆出现持续混乱，成千上万的流民逃到这座岛上定居，他们的辛勤劳动使岛上的种植业快速发展起来，水稻和甘蔗在这块不毛之地上大获丰收。[⑤]起初，荷兰人鼓励移民的到来，后来，他们开始警觉起来，试图阻止这

① 清朝收复台湾后，于康熙二十三年（1684 年）在台湾设立台湾府，归福建省管辖，下设台湾县（今台南）、凤山县（今高雄）和诸罗县（今嘉义）等三县，其中台湾县为台湾府首县。光绪十一年（1885 年）清政府升台湾府为台湾省。译者注。

② 即“赤崁楼”，又称“红毛楼”。译者注。

③ 即“安平城”，又称“台湾城”。译者注。

④ 即“基隆”。光绪元年（1875 年）设基隆厅时改为现名。译者注。

⑤ 此为原著作者立场，不代表译者和出版社立场。实际情况是，中国对台湾的经营可以追溯到 1,700 多年前的三国时期。宋元之时，闽人不断移居澎湖，明崇祯元年（1628 年），福建民众第一次由政府组织向台湾移民。1646 年，清兵进入福建，此后相当长时期内，福建成为郑、清军队拉锯战的战争，福建人纷纷向外迁移，向台湾移民出现新高潮。一方面，由于岛上居民增加，粮食匮乏，同时又由于蔗糖为当时重要的贸易商品，甘蔗种植成功可以给东印度公司带来丰厚的利润，荷兰人采取鼓励农业政策，从福建招徕贫民从事水稻和甘蔗种植，移民的到来对促进台湾农业发展起了很大作用。然而，为了谋取最大利益，荷兰人往往采取极端的榨取主义，对大陆来台移民实行苛取暴敛。另一方面，移民人数日多，势力渐大，又使荷兰殖民当局感到惶恐不安，正因为如此，殖民当局除对大陆移民肆行苛敛剥削外，又对大移民的言论行为实行严格的管制。殖民者的残暴统治经常遭到大陆移民和原住民的反抗，1652 年的郭怀一起义是大陆移民抗荷斗争规模最大的一次。参见林国平等：《福建移民史》，方志出版社，2005 年，第 147–158 页。译者注。

股移民浪潮。荷兰人为了实现目的而伤害汉人感情的种种做法究竟在多大程度上导致了自身权力的垮台，现在已经很难推测了，不过可以肯定的是，岛上的汉人已经和郑成功取得了联系，并在他进军台湾时真心实意地助了他一臂之力。

1650年，荷兰的台湾长官①揆一（Coyet）注意到郑成功在厦门整军备战，便尽其所能加强热兰遮城和普罗民遮城两处要塞的防御。多年来，尽管双方严重缺乏互信，互生不满，但还未进入敌对状态。然而，郑成功兵败南京以后，形势变得非常明朗，除非他攻打这座岛屿，否则他的舰队和部下便没有立足之地，只能被清军打散、消灭。荷兰人意识到汉人居民一直和这位首领保持着联系，于是相应地提高了警惕，抓捕了一些重要的移民首领作为人质，并逮捕和拷打其他嫌疑人等。揆一很有先见之明，他郑重其事地向巴达维亚②告急，于是12艘舰船和大量增援部队奉命前来。巴达维亚同时命令，如果台湾的战事警报纯属子虚乌有，舰队应南下转攻澳门。台湾府的兵力现在已经增加到1,500人，荷兰舰队司令认为这些力量足可对抗任何数量的中国军队。荷兰人问郑成功：“要和还是要战？”郑成功回复道“自己根本从来没有想过要和东印度公司开战”，随后他还派遣几艘商船前去台湾。但是由于郑成功仍然在厦门和金门备战，台湾长官的疑虑并未消除。

然而，评议会③的多数成员认为眼前双方并无开战的危险，于是命令战舰开赴各自的目的地。舰队司令回到巴达维亚后，指责台湾长官的担心毫无根据，于是巴达维亚停了他的职，并命令他返回巴达维亚为自己辩护。他的继任者克伦克（M. Clenk）于1661年6月起航前往台湾。

荷兰战舰离开后不久，郑成功便率领一支庞大的舰队和25,000名精兵强将抵达热兰遮城和普罗民遮城外海，在几千名同胞的帮助下，军队开始登陆。起初，郑成功的部队受到一支240人的荷兰军队以及4艘军舰的攻击。郑成

① 台湾长官（Governor），又译大员长官，是指台湾在荷兰侵占时期，荷兰东印度公司委任的驻台行政长官。译者注。
② 巴达维亚即印度尼西亚雅加达，殖民时代曾为荷属东印度公司总部所在地。译者注。
③ 评议会是荷兰殖民者侵占台湾后成立的殖民统治机构。译者注。

功巧妙用兵，英勇迎战荷军，成功地包抄了他们的侧翼，迫使荷军撤退。荷军惨遭大败，形同鸟兽散，只能扔下 1 名上尉和 19 名士兵仓皇逃命，最终只有一半人逃回要塞。军舰的情况也好不到哪里去，荷舰虽然击沉了郑军的几艘帆船，但是其中 1 艘军舰被火攻船烧毁，1 艘逃往巴达维亚，另外 2 艘军舰的命运则没有被记载下来。

中国人没有再遇到任何抵抗，4 个小时之内，他们全部登陆，切断了普罗民遮城和热兰遮城之间，以及热兰遮城和城外之间的所有联系。郑成功命令城堡内的荷军立刻投降，并警告说如果负隅顽抗，所有人都将被斩于刀剑之下。荷方派出使团前去面见郑成功，表示他们只愿意撤出普罗民遮城，但是不会交出所有堡垒。郑成功某种程度上对使团以礼相待，同时告诉他们："台湾一向是属于中国的，现在中国人需要这块土地，外国人必须立即撤离该岛。如若拒绝投降，就让他们升起红旗。"第二天早上，红旗在热兰遮城头飘扬，而普罗民遮城的荷军向郑成功交出了堡垒以及工事和大炮。现在，所有能够拿起武器的荷兰人都被召集到热兰遮城堡。他们向郑成功的部队开火，但是效果不好，攻城部队还是坚守住了多个被他们作为掩体的建筑物。荷兰人架起 28 门大炮来保卫城堡，炮击持续了很长时间，火力也很有针对性，导致攻城部队出现多人死伤，郑成功此次出击遭到挫败。

攻城受阻后，郑成功开始改为近距离围城，并把怒火转向城外宣泄。他俘虏了所有他能够找到的荷兰人，尤其是牧师和教师，指控他们暗中挑唆教区内的教徒杀死当地的汉人。有些俘虏被钉死在十字架上，竖立在各自的村庄里，而有些俘虏则以较为人道的方式被处死。郑成功指派被俘的传教士哈姆布罗库克（Hambrocock）先生前往热兰遮城向台湾长官劝降，不去的话就杀死荷兰俘虏作为报复。哈姆布罗库克牧师的妻子和 2 个孩子被扣为人质，他知道如果和谈失败的话，他没有活命的希望而唯有一死。然而，这位高贵的男士并没有敦促荷兰守军投降，而是激励他们固守待援，并且安慰他们，郑成功已经损失了许多坚船精锐，对城堡久围不下也开始让他失去耐心。与哈姆布罗库克牧师同在城堡里的 2 个女儿扑到他的怀里，乞求他留下来，战争评议会也赞成他不要回去，但是他表现出了舍己的精神，回答说如果不回到普罗民遮城的话，他的妻子和孩子都会死去，而且他也希望能够为那些可怜的囚友兄弟们做点贡献。说完，哈姆布罗库克牧师带着台湾长官拒绝投降的答复，离开了城堡。郑成功听到这个答复后，神情严峻，下令处死所有的男性荷兰囚犯，总计 500 人之多。之后，许多妇女和儿童也被杀害了，不过也有记载说，郑成功"留下一些上等美女犒赏军官，剩下的则售卖给普通士兵"。哈姆布罗库克・穆斯先生和温莎姆（Winshaim）先生 2 位牧师以及其他数位教师都在这场大屠杀中丧生。

在巴达维亚评议会斥责揆一胆小怕事的两天后，克伦克受命前往台湾接替揆一的职位。克伦克所乘坐的战船正是之前逃回巴达维亚的那一艘，战船一到岸就收到城堡被攻打的消息。他们撤消了对揆一的指控，恢复了他的职位，并派遣 10 艘舰船搭载 700 名士兵开赴台湾。克伦克先是到达热兰遮城近海，在那里等待他的是飘扬的红旗以及停泊在北边锚地的上百艘中国战舰，而不是那个令他孜孜以求、沾沾自喜，能给他带来财富而又不用打仗的长官职位。于是，克伦克把士兵送上岸，自己却没有登陆，转而驶向日本。

巴达维亚的援军到达以后，被围困的荷军开始反攻，他们试图将敌人从城里赶走未果，反而损失了 2 艘战船和多名士兵。鸡笼和淡水的驻军奉命前来增援被围困的军队，妇女、儿童和其他老弱病残者则被送往巴达维亚。这些准备工作阻止了郑成功的进军，但是荷兰人莫名其妙的轻敌却使他们丧失了优势。

台湾长官收到清朝的福建总督来信，请求双方一起合作将郑成功的残余部队逐离沿海，并承诺事后将援助在台湾的荷兰人。荷方按照约定派遣 5 艘船只参与行动，但是其中 3 艘毁于风暴，另外 2 艘则返回巴达维亚。这种情况远远超出郑成功的意料，使守城的荷军感到彻底绝望。荷军内部开始有人叛变，一位降兵向郑成功的部队指出了城堡防御最薄弱的地带。于是，三个方向的炮台一起开火轰炸这些薄弱地带，把城堡炸出了一个缺口，郑成功的人马迅速夺取了一处防御工事，很明显他们即将发起总攻。

此时，荷兰人举行了一次战事评议会，大多数人认为城堡已经守不住了。就这样，经过9个月的守城之战，热兰遮城投降了，付出了1,600条生命的代价。荷兰人登上前往爪哇的船只，在那里，台湾长官和他的评议会委员被捕入狱，财物尽被没收，台湾长官本人被永久监禁在班达群岛（Banda Isles）的一个岛屿上。1662年，荷兰人对中国台湾和海域长达30年[①]的领土侵占以这样的方式结束了。[②]

① 从1624年（明天启四年）荷兰东印度公司占领台湾算起，一直到1662年（南明永历十六年、清康熙元年）郑成功收复台湾，前后一共38年。译者注。

② 也有记载说，荷兰人直到1668年才撤出台湾岛最北端的鸡笼港。作者注。1664年7月，荷兰远征舰队（从巴达维亚）第三次驶向中国，8月18–20日，荷军在澎湖打败了守岛的郑军。27日，荷军占领了无人驻守的鸡笼。由于清廷结束了荷兰人在中国沿海的贸易特权，鸡笼失去了对中国大陆的贸易中转站作用，因此1668年10月，荷兰人主动撤离了鸡笼。参见陈孔立：《简明台湾史》，九州出版社，2016年，第51–52页。译者注。

Dutch endeavour to obtain a possession on mainland

Koxinga now constituted himself king of the island, assumed sovereign style, fixed his palace and court, at Zelandia; and distributed his garrisons, with skill, over the western region of Taiwan. The island assumed a new social aspect, Chinese laws, forms of government, customs, and industry, were introduced; and at the same time, expeditions were fitted out, to lay the inhabitants of the sea coast on the mainland, under contribution for whatever supplies were necessary. The Imperial government, was utterly powerless to check these incessant, and intolerable, acts of spoliation and murder; and as the fate of the wretched 4,000, was too fresh to hope anything from the employment of military force, recourse was had to a measure peculiarly Chinese, which could not, perhaps, have been put in force in any other country in the world. In 1662, an Imperial edict came forth, commanding "all the people upon the coast of the maritime provinces, to remove themselves and their effects, into the interior, to a distance of thirty li （10 miles） from the shore, on penalty of death; also, that the islands be abandoned, and commerce utterly cease." This remarkable edict, was actually carried into effect; and for seven years, all the rich, and populous cities upon the coast, were deserted; and whole villages crumbled into ruin, and disappeared.

His possessions passed to his son, who did not inherit his father's great military ability. Ten years later, when the provinces of Kwangtung, and Fuhkien, revolted against the Emperor Kanghi, this son resolved to join the king of Fuhkien; but the latter refusing to acknowledge him as a sovereign prince, he declared war against him, defeated him in several battles, and so destroyed his power that he was compelled to tender his submission to the Emperor.

The Emperor Kanghi, abolished the title of king, and appointed a Governor over Chê-kiang, and Fuhkien, This officer seized the Pescadores, a group of islands about twenty five miles from "Formosa", and proclaimed an amnesty, to all who submitted to the Imperial rule. His policy had its desired effect, thousands of "Formosn" emigrants, being induced to return to China, thereby weakening the enemy on the island, until, finally, it could no longer be held; and "Formosa" was surrendered to Kanghi, by the grandson of Koxinga, in 1683. In their ancestral hall at Shih ching（石井）, there is a figure of Koxinga; and it is said, that the front door of the hall, is not allowed to be opened, except on New Year's day, lest the dreaded chief should go forth, and be born again, to bring trouble and disaster on the ruling dynasty.

After the loss of "Formosa", the Dutch equipped a fleet of twelve vessels at Batavia; which they despatched to Foochow, to enter into a treaty for the recovery of the island. They possessed themselves of a sea port, and being reinforced. by sixteen other ships, most of them East Indiamen, attacked, in conjunction with the Manchus, Amoy, and Quemoy, both of which places they captured, but they were not permitted by the Manchus, to retain possession of them, and after much profitless negociation, their fleet returned to Batavia, having achieved nothing.

荷兰人力图在大陆获取殖民地

此后，郑成功在岛上自立为王，打造自己的独立王国。他在热兰遮城修建了宫殿，建立了王朝，还把兵力巧妙地布防在岛屿的西部一线。岛上呈现出一派崭新的社会风貌，律法制度、官府机构、风俗习惯和工业产业全部照搬汉人的模式。① 与此同时，郑成功派兵前往大陆沿海地区，向当地的居民强行摊派各种必要物资，清政府完全无法与之抗衡。由于四千位可怜人的悲惨命运② 仍然令人记忆犹新，没办法指望部署军事力量能够带来效果，于是朝廷只得采取一种或许世界上任何其他国家都不可能实施的特殊措施。1662 年，朝廷诏令“沿海省份所有居民及其财物一律内迁三十里（十英里），违令者杀无赦；同时，朝廷放弃台湾③，完全中断双方商业贸易”。④ 这一影响广泛的诏书产生了实际效果：七年来，所有沿海富庶繁华、人口稠密的城市都被弃之不顾，许多村庄变成废墟，直至完全消失。

① 此处仅代表原著作者的立场。郑成功收复台湾后，在其领导下，台湾岛上经济和文化得到迅速发展。郑成功按照中国封建体制的机构设置，设府县，定职官，编户籍，兴办学校，将儒家王道文化传播到台湾。郑成功还在台南仿建慈济宫一座，建造圣母妈祖庙。郑成功还大力推广大陆先进技术，鼓励发展手工业和商业等。参见苏文菁：《海洋英雄郑成功》，厦门大学出版社，2014 年，第 81–84 页。译者注。

② 本书并无此次事件的详细记载。不过，清顺治十七年（1660 年）郑成功在厦门击败清军的围剿，取得“厦门大捷”。据（清）阮文锡原著，福建人民出版社 1982 年版《海上见闻录定本》第 43 页载，本次战果为：“（清军统帅）达素率残兵回省。数日，尸浮海岸万余，长发者十二三，短发者十七八。”短发者即清军，可见清军在此次战役中的损失惨重。此役后，清军的海上力量大受打击，很多年对郑军都不敢再轻举妄动。译者注。

③ 此处仅代表原著作者的立场。实际上，“清廷颁布迁海令，原来的目的是断绝郑成功义师的物资供应，以收不攻自破之效”，并非是为了放弃台湾。参见顾诚：《南明史》，北京：中国青年出版社，1997 年，第 1080 页。林国平等也认为，清廷认识到郑成功之所以能与清军顽强抵抗，主要依靠沿海人民的交通接济，实施迁界是为了有效断绝其接济，以达到打败郑成功的目的。参见林国平、邱济端主编：《福建移民史》，方志出版社，2005 年，第 162 页。译者注。

④ 清朝的迁海令经过了一个酝酿过程。清顺治十二年（1655 年）6 月，清廷就曾下令禁止“片帆入海”，但是这一禁令收效不大。1661 年（顺治十八年）清廷断然决定实行大规模强制迁徙濒海居民的政策，史称“迁海”。参见顾诚：《南明史》，中国青年出版社，1997 年，第 1059 页。译者注。

郑成功的位子传到了他的儿子郑经手上，可是郑经却没能够继承父亲的雄才伟略。十年后[①]，当广东、福建两省举旗反叛康熙帝时，郑成功的这位儿子决心联合福建的靖南王，但是靖南王拒绝向他臣服，郑经遂向其宣战。几场战役下来，郑经击败了靖南王，摧毁了他的有生力量，靖南王被迫向康熙帝投降。

康熙任命了一位总督以取代靖南王治理福建和浙江。清廷随后派员前往距离台湾岛大约25英里远的澎湖列岛，并宣布大赦所有归顺清朝的居民。康熙的政策取得了预期效果，成千上万的台湾移民被劝返大陆，岛上敌军的实力从而被削弱，敌军再也无法坚守台湾岛了。1683年，郑成功的孙子郑克塽及其明郑部队全部投降。位于石井的郑氏宗祠里有一座郑成功塑像，据说除了大年初一以外，祠堂的前门是不允许打开的，以免这位令人可怕的首领死而复生走了出去，给时下的统治王朝带来麻烦和灾难。

失去台湾之后，荷兰人在巴达维亚组建了一支由十二艘船只组成的舰队，令其北上福州，打算就重新获取台湾同清朝签订条约。他们占领了一处港口[②]，又迎来十六艘增援舰只，船上士兵大多数是东印度公司职员。他们与满洲人一起进攻厦门和金门，并占领了这两座岛屿，但是满洲人不允许他们占据金厦。经过徒劳无功的谈判后，荷兰人的舰队返回巴达维亚，一无所获。

①康熙十二年（1673年），康熙下令裁撤三藩，将平西王吴三桂、靖南王耿精忠和平南王尚可喜的权力移交至朝廷。三藩势力先后起兵反叛，史称“三藩之乱”。译者注。

②康熙三年（1664年），荷兰人趁郑经的势力还未到达台湾北部，再次占领鸡笼，直到1668年才撤军。至此，荷兰人最终退出了台湾。参见陈孔立：《简明台湾史》，九州出版社，2016年，第51–52页。译者注。

Capture of Amoy by British

After the period of internecion, and misery, narrated, the province appears to have enjoyed many years of peace, in which it recuperated itself, and regained its prosperity. The next calamity which befell it, of sufficient importance to call for note, is the capture of Amoy, by the British. This was brought about by a series of irritating grievances, under which Great Britain had been smarting for years, terminating in the troubles and complications, arising out of the Opium trade at Canton, in 1837-40, which led, as had been foreseen, to war, and on the 23rd June 1840, the van of the British naval and military forces, arrived off Macao, and a notice of the blockade of Canton, was published. Commodore Sir Gordon Bremer, in the *Wellesley*, 74, his fleet consisting of three steamers, four ships, and twenty-one transports, sailed northwards: on the 5th July, Ting-hai, was taken and occupied, and on the 6th, the joint Plenipotentiaries, Admiral Sir G. Elliot, and Captain Elliot, R.N., arrived at Chusan, in the *Melville*, 74. They sent a copy of Lord Palmerston's letter to the Emperor, setting forth the grounds of complaint, to the authorities at Amoy, and Ningpo, for them to forward to Peking, both of whom declined taking the responsibility. The visit to these two cities, shewed that the Chinese were preparing for defence, by arming the forts, making rafts, and posting troops.[1] Amoy, was forthwith blockaded. This act on the part of the British, induced an unsuccessful attack on one of the blockading ships.

Strenuous endeavours on the part of the Chinese were now made to bring their forts, and defences, into the most efficient state possible, and a large reward was offered for the heads of "rebellious barbarians" and the capture of their ships. Fourteen months later, all negociations with the Governor General of Chihli, and Imperial Commissioner, Kishên, at Taku, and Canton, having proved fruitless, and hostilities having been resumed by the Emperor, the forts of Chuenpi, Taekotan, the Bogue, and those at the First Bar, together with all the forts, rafts, batteries, camps, and stockades, between the ocean and Canton,

[1] Williams' Middle Kingdom p.529.

were destroyed, or taken by the British. The city of Canton, which lay at the mercy of the invaders, was ransomed for $6,000,000[①], on the 26th or 27th, May, 1841. The terms of abstention from aggressive acts on both sides, which had just been agreed to, was followed, on the 30th, by an attack from 1,500 villagers, and dispersed troops. The villagers having assumed a still more menacing attitude, Sir Hugh Gough, told the Prefect that if they were not instantly dispersed, he would fire on the city. On this, one of the Commissioners, and the Prefect, accompanied by an English Officer, went out and coaxed them to retire. Yih-shan, a nephew of the Emperor, and chief generalissimo, at the same time proclaimed a victory, and rewarded his troops with decorations for driving the English out of Canton; the fact being, that he was compelled by the victors, to march these same troops sixty miles into the interior, and disband them. During the war, trade at Canton continued without any serious interruption, the usual duties and charges being paid, as if the two nations were at peace.

The expedition for the capture of Amoy, and for military operations in Cheh-kiang, left Hongkong on the 21st August 1841. The attack had been anticipated here, from the visit of the *Blonde*, the year before, with the letter for Peking, which showed that the barbarians, "sneaking in and out like rats," were aware of its existence; and the fortifications had been increased, and every island and protecting headland, overlooking the harbour, had been occupied and armed. The measures taken were useless, and its capture on the 26th August 1841, is thus described in the *Chinese Repository* Vol. x. p. 621:

"The capture of Amoy, was chiefly a naval operation, and the little that was left for the troops to do, was done by the 18th Royal Irish. Scarcely had the fleet taken up their position opposite the batteries of Amoy, when a boat bearing a white flag was seen to approach the *Wellesley*. An officer of low rank, was the bearer of a paper demanding to know what our ships wanted, and directing us to make sail for the outer waters, ere the Celestial wrath should be kindled against us, and the guns from the batteries annihilate us. The line of works, certainly, presented a most formidable appearance, and the batteries were admirably constructed. Manned by Europeans, no force could have stood before them. For four hours did the ships pepper at them without cessation. The *Wellesley*, and Blenheim, each, fired

① 如无特别指出，全书中的"$"符号指银元。译者注。

upwards of 12,000 rounds, to say nothing of the frigates, steamers, and small craft. Yet the works were as perfect when they left off, as when they began, the utmost penetration of the shot being 16 inches. The cannonade was certainly a splendid sight. The stream of fire and smoke, from the sides of the liners, was terrific. It never, for a moment, appeared to slacken. From 20, to 30, people, were all that were killed by this enormous expenditure of powder and shot.

"It was nearly 3 p.m. before the 18th landed, accompanied by Sir Hugh Gough, and staff. They landed close to a high wall, which flanked the mainline of batteries, covered by the *Queen*, and *Phlegethon*, steamers. The flank companies soon got over the wall, driving the enemy before them. They opened a gate, through which the rest of our men entered, and advancing along the batteries, they quickly cleared them, killing more men, in two minutes, than the men of war did during the whole day; three of our fellows were knocked over, besides others injured. One officer (Chinese) cut his throat in the long battery, another walked into the sea and drowned himself, in the coolest manner possible. The enemy fled on all sides, so soon as our troops approached. We bivouacked, as best we could, during the night, and next morning, took possession of the city without hindrance. Much treasure had been carried away, the mob leaving only the boxes which had contained it. Immense quantities of military stores, were found in the arsenals, and the foundaries were in active operation. One two decker, modeled from ours, and carrying 30 guns, was ready for sea, and others were on the stocks. But few war junks were stationed here, the Chinese admiral being, at this time, absent with his fleet. During the engagement the *Phlegethon*, steamer, was very severely handled. She came suddenly opposite, and close to, a masked battery, the guns from which, having the exact range, opened on her. Fortunately for the steamer, the water was sufficiently deep to come close to land. Captain McCleaverty immediately landed his men, advanced directly on the battery, and took possession of it, killing a great portion of the garrison."

That gallant old fire-eater, Sir Hugh Gough, considered the resistance of the Chinese, "more feeble", than he had anticipated, yet itis stated, by others, that "the Chinese did endure the fire right manfully", standing to their guns, until they were shot down by musketry in their rear. The attacking force consisted of H. B. M.S. *Queen*, *Sesostris*,

Blonde, *Druid*, *Modeste*, *Bentinck*, *Wellesley*, and *Blenheim*, supported by seven more ships of war, and fifteen transports, bearing the 18th, and 55th, regiments, and detachments of the 49th, and 26th, regiments, with engineers, and artillery. The Chinese officer, who walked into the sea, and drowned himself, "in the coolest manner possible", was the Tsung-ping, or General, then commanding, in the absence, of Admiral Tao-chin-pin, windbound to the northward; he is described in a memorial to the Emperor, as having fallen into the water, and died, in endeavouring to drive back the British troops, as they were landing. Four other officers, Colonel Sing-chi, and lieutenants Hwa-kwo-ching, Yang-shan-chi, and Li-chi-ming, are reported killed, and two lieutenant colonels, and one major, wounded; while amongst the soldiers, " very many," are reported to be killed and wounded; and 3,000,000 taels of silver (£1,000,000), are craved, for immediate use.

Yen-pih-t'ou, the then Governor General of Fuhkien, and Chekiang, who was at Amoy at the time of the attack, gives, in a memorial to the throne, dated the 28th August 1841, a version of the affair, that is highly creditable to his imagination. This mighty man of valour, relates how, at the head of his invincible braves, he attacked and sunk, one steamer and five ships of war, killing an innumerable number of the rebellious barbarians. But, (as with the paper braves in his native fables) the more he slew, the more came on, so a strategic advance, in a direction contrary to the enemy, was necessary. This evolution, known in later days as the skedaddle, was executed with promptitude and despatch, and his seals of office saved, but only when the office had been set on fire by the rebels. He is discreetly silent about the loss of 500 guns, stores, and shipping; and adds that, matters were not to be left long in this state, as more than 100 villages had combined, and over 10,000 warriors were mustered, ready for the battle. On this is founded the inevitable demand, springing forth from every occurrence in China, and Taels 3,000,000, are asked for. His Imperial Master replies, and strips him of his rank and office, but spares his head, because Amoy had been recaptured. So its evacuation by the British forces, appears to have been represented.

The long batteries, of whose capacity for hard usage such honourable mention is made, were, according to an inscription of one Lin-mao-shih, cut into a rock at Bellamy's Dock, erected in the first moon, of the third year of the Emperor Tien-chi, or about March 1622, by Colonel Li-kung-hwa, as a defence against foreign barbarians (meaning, probably, the Japanese and Dutch). They are ordered to be fifty chang long; and the gallant Colonel is to receive nineteen taels, or about £6.6.8, for executing the work; it is naively added that, he was compelled to spend 100 taels more, out of his own pocket, to complete the battery. Why such a statement should be cut into the rock, it is impossible to say; the works being of granite, and of great extent and thickness, must have cost nearer Tls. 119,000 than Tls. 119.

Previous to this, hostile measures had been resorted to. On the 2nd July 1840, one of the boats of H. M S. *Blonde*, under a flag of truce, and bearing the letter from Lord Palmerston to the Emperor, before referred to, was warned off the beach, with haughty threats and insults, by the military authorities, and as she obeyed, was fired into. This treacherous and wanton act, was promptly responded to, by a couple of 32 pr. round shot, from the frigate into the crowd, which caused a general flight. The *Blonde*, then opened fire on the fort, and on some mandarin junks. This was kept up for nearly two hours, until the fort was unroofed and riddled. An attempt was made to set on fire a large junk, this proving unsuccessful, the *Blonde* did not take further trouble, but, thinking the lesson given sufficient, quietly departed without doing further injury. In August of the same year, the *Alligator*, and *Braemar*, sunk 16 or 17 junks in the outer harbour, with, supposed, considerable loss of life to the Chinese; but being themselves struck several times from the batteries, and one vessel having her mainyard arm shot away, and a shot lodged in her hull, they retired out of range.

英国人攻占厦门

如前所述，福建省在经历了自相残杀和种种悲惨遭遇之后，呈现出多年来难得一见的和平景象，恢复了往日的繁华景象。但下一个严重的灾难又降临了，那就是英国人攻占厦门。这次占领源自大不列颠所受的种种委曲，多年来它一直深深刺痛着英国人的神经，由此产生许多麻烦。正如大家所预料的那样，这些问题不断激化，最终以 1837—1840 年广东的鸦片贸易为导火索，引爆了战争。1840 年 6 月 23 日，英国海陆先遣队到达澳门海面，发布通告封锁广州。① 海军准将戈登·伯麦（Gordon Bremer）爵士乘坐载炮 74 门的“威里士厘”号（Wellesley），率领由三艘蒸汽舰船、四艘轮船和二十一艘运输船组成的舰队北上，于 7 月 5 日攻占定海。7 月 6 日，英国联合全权代表、海军少将懿律（G. Elliot）爵士和舰长义律（Elliot, R.N.）乘坐载炮 74 门的“麦尔威厘”号（Melville）抵达舟山。他们打算通过厦门和宁波当局把巴麦尊（Palmerston，又译“帕麦斯顿”）勋爵撰写的罗列了英方种种冤抑的信函副本转递给北京的清朝皇帝，但厦门和宁波两处均拒绝收受信函副本。与此同时，英军在这两处地方都看到中国人正在加紧备战——架设火炮、制作木筏、部署军队，② 于是前者立即封锁厦门。英军的行动激起了清军的反击，他们攻击了一艘执行封锁任务的英方船只，但是没有命中。

中国人现在正尽最大努力把他们的炮台和防御工事调整到最佳状态，对

① 1840 年 6 月 21 日起，伯麦率领的英国海军舰队先后到达广东海面。22 日，伯麦发布通告，宣布自 6 月 28 日起封锁江面和海口。6 月 28 日，英军展开封锁，鸦片战争正式开始。参见萧致治：《鸦片战争史》下册，福建人民出版社，1996 年，第 321 页。译者注。

② 见卫三畏（Williams）著《中国总论》（*Middle Kingdom*），第 529 页。作者注。

取“逆夷”人头和夺其舰船的兵士均予以重金奖赏。14个月以后，英国人与直隶总督、钦差大臣琦善在大沽和广州的数次谈判均告无果，清朝皇帝又下诏重开战端，英国人于是摧毁了穿鼻、大角头、虎门的第一防线，并攻占了这些地方的所有炮台，海面上和广东之间的所有要塞、舢板、炮台、营地和铁链钢锁也全都未有幸免。1841年5月26日或27日，任侵略者宰割的广州城被迫支付600万银元的“赎城费”。[①]5月30日，双方签订的停战协定墨迹未干，又有1,500名乡民游勇开始攻击英军。看到乡民的态度愈发强硬，卧乌古（Hugh Gough，又译“郭富”）爵士警告知府，如果不立即解散乡勇，英军将炮击广州城。为了平息事件，朝廷的一位钦差[②]连同广州知府在一位英国军官的陪同下出城劝诱村民撤退。与此同时，清军最高统帅、皇侄奕山宣告对英作战取得胜利，并对驱赶英军出城的将士论功行赏。而事实是，奕山受到获胜的英方逼迫，将清军撤往内地六十英里后遣散他们。战争期间，广东的贸易正常开展，没有受到任何严重的干扰，该交的关税和费用照常支付，就像两国和平相处时一样。

为了占领厦门，也为了便于在浙江开展军事行动，1841年8月21日，英国远征军离开香港。本次袭击早在当地的预料之中，“布朗底号”（Blonde）去年携带英方给北京的信函来到此地就是一个信号，种种迹象表明“像老鼠一样偷偷进出”的“洋夷”清楚地知道此战在所难免。厦门加强了防御工事，所有港口目视范围内的岛屿和具有防护功能的海岬都派兵驻守、配备火力。然而，所有措施都徒劳无益。《中国丛报》第10卷第621页描述英军1841年8月26日占领厦门的经过如下：

---

① 1841年5月26日，广州知府余保纯受钦差大臣奕山委派向义律投降，义律提出了包括广州当局向英方缴交600万银元“赎城费”在内的停战条件。5月27日，余保纯完全按照英文条件，在《广州停战协定》上签字。参见萧致治：《鸦片战争史》下册，福建人民出版社，1996年，第418-419页。译者注。

② 当时，受清廷指派，督办广东海防的大臣共有三位，包括靖逆将军奕山、参赞大臣杨芳以及参赞大臣隆文。译者注。

攻占厦门的行动主要由英国海军实施，陆军的皇家爱尔兰第十八团则完成扫尾工作。舰队刚在厦门炮台对面就位，就看到一艘挂着白旗的船只驶近"威里士厘"号。一位清军下级军官携带公文要求舰队表明来意，并引导英军驶向外海，如若不然，老天将降怒于英军，炮火将歼灭英军。防御工事的样子着实令人生畏，火炮的架设也令人赞叹不已，要是由欧洲人操控的话，任何军队在它面前肯定都无法屹立不倒。整整四个小时，英军战舰不间断炮轰这些工事，"威里士厘号"和"伯兰汉号"（Blenheim）各发射了超过一万二千发炮弹，更不用说护卫舰、蒸汽船和小艇了。然而，虽然炮弹的最大穿透力是十六英寸，但停止炮击后防御工事与开炮前一模一样、完好无损。炮击的景象的确非常壮观，从战舰两侧发出的炮火浓烟惊天动地，似乎连片刻都没有减弱，有二三十人死于本次大规模炮弹消耗战。

将近下午三点，卧乌古爵士及其参谋率领十八团在"皇后号"（Queen）和"弗莱吉森号"（Phlegethon）蒸汽船的掩护下于炮台主防线边上的一堵高墙附近登陆，侧翼部队很快越过高墙，逼退阵前的敌人。十八团兵士打开一处城门，剩余部队过门而入后沿炮台行进，很快全歼敌人。守军尽管尽力回击，但仍然无法抵挡英军的优势炮火，伤亡惨重。一名清军将领在炮火中割喉自尽，另一将领投海殉国，视死如归。随着英军的逼近，守军放弃阵地后撤。夜幕降临，英军停止进攻，扎营休息。第二天一早，英军发现守军已弃守厦门，于是便占领了这座城市。清军撤退时留下大量财物，火药库里则留下大量军用物资，铸炮所也在正常运转之中。一艘仿制英军载炮 30 门的双甲板船已经造好准备下水，还有一些船只正在建造之中，只有少量的戎克①战船在这里驻泊。当时清军水师提督正率领船队出海在外。②"弗莱吉森号"蒸汽船在交火时严重受损，具体情况是："弗莱吉森号"突然调头驶近一座隐蔽的炮台，正好进入

①戎克，英文"junk"的音译，即中国帆船。译者注。
②时任福建水师提督窦振彪于 1841 年 7 月上旬率领部分水师前往浙江捕盗，未参加此次战斗。译者注。

火炮的射程，清军立即朝它开火。所幸水的深度足够让这艘蒸汽船驶近陆地，麦克莱弗蒂（McCleaverty）舰长立即命令他的手下登岸，直接向炮台推进，并占领了炮台，还杀死了大量守军。

那位英勇顽强而又好战成性的老人卧乌古爵士认为，中国人的抵抗比他预想的要“更加脆弱”，然而其他人却表示“中国人勇敢地经受了这场炮火的袭击”。他们一直坚守炮台，直到被抄了后路死于英军枪口之下。英军进攻部队包括“大英帝国皇后号”（H.B.M.S. Queen，俗称“皇后号”）、“西索斯梯斯号”（Sesostris）、“布朗底号”、“都鲁壹号”（Druid）、“摩底士底号”（Modeste）、“本廷克号”（Bentinck）、“威里士厘号”和“伯兰汉号”，支援部队包括另外七艘军舰和十五艘运输船，载运第十八团、第五十五团，第四十九和第二十六两团的分遣队，以及工兵队、炮兵队。那位以“最视死如归的方式”投海自杀的中国将领是一位总兵[①]，在水师提督窦振彪溯风北上出海期间负责军事指挥，当地官府在给皇帝的奏折中称他是在阻击英军登陆时落水而亡。据传，还有 4 名将士阵亡，他们是副将凌志、把总纪国庆、杨肇基和李启明；2 名参将和 1 名游击受伤。另据传，兵丁死伤惨重。当地官府奏请朝廷拨付应急款项银 300 万两（折合 100 万英镑）。

战斗期间，闽浙总督颜伯焘正在厦门。1841 年 8 月 28 日，他把自己凭空想象、以假乱真的战况情形上奏给皇帝。这位“无所不能”的勇士奏报其如何所向无前、奋勇当先，击沉英人火轮船一艘、兵船五艘，杀死逆夷无数。只不过，（正如中国人寓言故事中的“逞口舌之勇”一样）人越杀越多，则有必要避敌锋芒，执行战略进取。这个后来被称为仓皇逃散的战略进取迅速得到实施，颜伯焘得以带走印信，但是他的衙署被洋夷纵火焚烧，他巧妙地避而不谈受到损毁的 500 门大炮、军需存贮和船只战舰。他又补充说，此种状况不会持续太久，因为 100 多个村庄已经联合起来，招募了 1 万多名乡勇，

① 此处指在水操台指挥作战的总兵江继芸。译者注。

准备进剿英军。其结果是当地官府请奏朝廷拨银三百万两，正如中国每次发生重事件后都会产生这种刚性需求一样。因为厦门业已收复，他的皇帝主子就下旨革去他的顶戴和官职，但是饶了他的性命。这样看来，被英军败退的罪责似乎算是有所交待了。

这些长列炮台威力强大，坚固耐用。根据白拉梅船坞[①]（Bellamy's Dock）内一块岩石上的林懋时[②]题刻[③]，炮台是天启三年正月，约1622年3月[④]间，由千户李逢华[⑤]修筑而成，作为军事防御要塞。奉命修筑的炮台周长50丈，这位英勇的千户收到银19两（约6.68英镑）的工程款。题刻还说，他被迫垫付银100两以完成工程。我们无法得知为什么这么天真的说法也会被刻到石壁上。这些工事由花岗岩砌成，占地面积广大，墙体厚实，花费肯定接近银119,000两而不是119两。

在此之前，中英双方已经开始采取敌对措施。1840年7月2日，“布朗底号”的一艘护卫舰悬挂着“休战旗”，携带之前提到的巴麦尊勋爵致皇帝的信函开到岸边，清军进行警告驱离时言辞不太友善[⑥]。但是当护卫舰服从指令后撤的时候，岸上却朝它开火。对这种背信弃义、肆意妄为的行径，护卫舰立即予以反击，朝一伙清军打了几发32磅重的炮弹，使得清朝士兵四处逃窜。“布朗底号”也向炮台兵房和清军戎克战船开炮。战斗持续了将近两个小时，直到炮台兵房被打到千疮百孔，连屋顶都被炮火掀翻。英军试图焚烧一艘大型戎克战船，但是没有成功。“布朗底号”见状认为已经给予清军应有的教训，便不再招惹麻烦，悄悄地离开了，因此没有造成进一步的毁坏。同年8月，“鳄

① 白拉梅船坞是1863年外商在厦门成立的一家船舶修造厂。译者注。
② 林懋时，明代万历年间厦门人。译者注。
③ 即著名的厦门港“打石字”，是进入厦门港的标志。译者注。
④ 天启三年正月是公历1623年1月31日—2月28日。译者注。
⑤ 据道光《厦门志》卷十之一，李逢华为中左所副千户。译者注。
⑥ 此处仅代表原著作者立场。译者注。

鱼号”（Alligator）和“布雷马号”（Braemar）在外港击沉了 16 或 17 艘戎克战船。据推测，此举造成清军大量人员伤亡，但是英军的两艘战船均被炮台数发炮弹击中，其中一艘舰船的主桅臂被打飞，船体上也有炮弹降落，两船于是退到炮台的射程之外。

Small Knife Rebels

These operations were followed by the opening of the port to foreign trade, by the treaty of Nanking, signed in 1842, and by the establishment of Mr. Henry Gribble, as British Consul at Amoy, on the 2nd November 1843. During the succeeding eleven years the trade of the port was gradually developed, and little occurred worthy of special record, until Saturday the 14th May, 1853, when it became known to the Mandarins, that there was an armed band of 3,000 or 4,000 men, at Hai ching hsien, about 22 miles distant, who were on their way to attack this city. At 8 o'clock on the morning of the 18th, a party of men advanced in front of the city gates, and opened fire on the soldiers on the walls. This was returned, and the firing continued, at intervals, until one o'clock, when the Mandarins and soldiers fled, and by four o'clock in the afternoon, some four thousand ill-armed men, who had been joined by about the same number of the roughs of Amoy, had taken almost unopposed possession of city.

小刀会起义

所有这些行动结束之后，1842 年中英签订了《南京条约》，开放了通商口岸。1843 年 11 月 2 日记里布（Henry Gribble）先生被任命为英国驻厦门领事。在随后的 11 年时间里，厦门港的贸易逐渐发展起来，几乎没有发生什么特别值得记录的事情。直到 1853 年 5 月 14 日星期六，官府获悉，在大约 22 英里外的海澄县，有一股三四千人的武装团伙正在赶来攻打本城。18 日上午 8 时，一伙人行进至城门前，朝城墙上的兵丁开火，守军立即予以还击。交火断断续续持续到下午 1 时，官军弃城逃跑。下午 4 时，约 4,000 名装备落后的武装人员，加上响应行动的大约相同数量的本地居民，几乎没有遇到任何抵抗就占领了全城。

Capture of Amoy

The insurgents behaved with order and moderation, doing no injury to private property, and plundering only powder magazines, and arsenals. Patrols were distributed throughout the city, to prevent pillage, and, at night, they stationed a guard for the protection of the foreign Hongs, expressing, at the same time, towards foreigners, the most pacific intentions. No vessel of war being at the port, the safety of the foreign residents, devolved on the receiving ships of Messrs. Jardine, Matheson & Co. and Dent & Co. which had, on the first note of danger, moved into the inner harbour. This step, curiously enough, was afterwards disapproved of by Sir George Bonham. No time was lost: on the 19th rebel bands were despatched for the capture of Chin-chew, and of "Formosa"; and contributions for the support of the rebel troops, were levied on the citizens of Amoy, to their great disgust; one wealthy firm being "requisitioned", to the tune of $40,000.

A glance should now be taken at the nature of the force, that had so rapidly obtained possession of the city. It was the Hsiao-tao-hui（小刀会）, or Dagger Society. There had existed for many years amongst the Chinese at Java, Singapore, Malacca, and Penang, a secret society, the ostensible object of which, was mutual assistance and protection. It contained men of all classes, and its rules were so strictly observed, that, it is said, piratical members, meeting on the high seas the vessels of trading members, were content to accept the sign of the Society, and to allow the vessels to pass on unmolested. This society was originally called San-ho-hui（三合会）, or the society of the three (persons) united, or as it has been aptly translated, the Triad Society. The three referred to "天、地、人", are t'ien, ti, jên, heaven, earth, and man, the three great powers of nature, according to the Chinese doctrine of the universe. It became the t'ien-ti-hui（天地会）, or Society of Heaven and Earth, during the reign of Chien-lung (about 1795), when it was distinctly political, and had attained such magnitude and power, as to seriously endanger that monarch's government. And it was not until eight years after, that the snake was scotched, but not killed, by the seizure and execution, of many of its members.

This society, or an offshoot of it, was introduced into Amoy, during the years 1848-9, by a Singapore Chinese, named Tan-kêng-chin（陈庆真）, a compradore in the employ of Messrs. Jardine, Matheson & Co. The society rapidly took root, and in 1857, numbered some thousands of members; when the suspicions of the provincial government at Foochow, being excited, the Viceroy despatched to Amoy to investigate its character, and to suppress it, a resolute old anti-foreign Taotai, named Chang（张）, the same who served as Wei-yuan to the Governor General Lin, when 20,291 chests of Opium were surrendered by the British, and burnt at Canton in 1839, Chang's first act was to arrest 'Tan-kêng-chin, on a charge of conspiring against the government, the only evidence against him, was a book, found in his house, containing the names and residences of the members of the society; but this was deemed sufficient, and Tan was subjected to horrible tortures, to make him confess further particulars. Meanwhile Tan-kêng-chin, being a British born subject, the English Consul, on hearing of his arrest, went, accompanied by three other gentlemen, to the Taotai's Yamen, to demand his rendition. He was told that the prisoner was at the Hai-fang-ting's (the Magistrate's), although it is said that he was then under torture at the back of the Yamên. At the Hai-fang-ting's he was told that the man was at the Taotai's. The Consul was not successful in obtaining possession of Tan, who was tortured to death. His body was found on the following morning, on opening Jardine, Matheson's hong, dressed as usual, and seated in a sedan chair, opposite his master's door.

The leadership of the society, now appears to have fallen on a man of low extraction, but of great energy and force of character, named Hwang Wei, or in the local dialect Ng-wee（黄位）. At this time there dwelt at Amoy, one Hwang-tê-mei, or locally Ng-teck-bi（黄德美）, a merchant, once possessed of great wealth. This man bore a high character for charity and benevolence, and was exceedingly popular amongst the poor classes. He had been compelled to accept the post of salt monopolist of the prefectures of Chang-chou-fu, and Chin-chew-fu, an office then greatly dreaded, on account of its holder having to return annually to the Salt Commissioner, a certain fixed sum, far above what he could collect (the Salt Commissioner, being, himself, in precisely the same position vis-a-vis the Board of Revenue, usually compelled one of the richest merchants to accept the post). This office resulted in losses to the amount of $800,000, it is said. Smarting under these, and at a second attempt to force the post of monopolist upon him, he probably, although this is not admitted by my informants, joined the society. At all events it is certain that he advanced money to it, and was on terms of intimacy with Hwang, otherwise Ng-wee.

The second attempt to impose the detested office upon Ng-teck-bi, was seized upon by Ng-wee, as a means of securely enmeshing this wealthy and influential man in the society; about 2,000 of its members, now styled the Hsiao-tao-hui（小刀会）, or Dagger society, rose under Ng-wee, at his native village, Gin-tai（沈宅）, and proclaiming that they sought to right Ng-teck-be (without his authority and against his wishes, he always declared) marched on and captured Hai-téng-hsien（海澄县）, Chioh-bei（石码）, Chang-chou fu（漳州府）, (which they only held for three days), and finally Amoy, where, soon after arrival, the society was found to consists of about 8,000 men, controlled by a Council of six persons, three of whom were Singapore Chinamen, and at whose head was Ng-wee. Many of the subordinate positions, such as centurions, and leaders of ten, were also held by Singapore Chinese. The pay of private soldiers was 100 cash, or about five pence per diem. This was the force that captured Amoy, and retained possession of it, until the 11th November following.

On the 29th May, a fleet of Imperial junks entered the port, and landed some 500 or 600 soldiers, who marched on the city. They were met by the rebels, and after a brief skirmish, driven back to their boats, which immediately left. This defeat, considered by the rebels as an auspicious omen, greatly elated them, and strengthened their numbers. Preparations for extending their conquest were made, and requisitions issued for the stores, ammunition, &c., stolen from the arsenals, at the capture of the city, for which compensation was promised to the holders. Proclamations for the repression of disorder, and the administration of justice, in which nearly all breaches of regulations were punishable by death, were put forth by the rebel T'ou or head, Hwang or Ng-wee, who now styled himself, Appointed by Imperial Decree, of the Emperor of the Han (Chinese) Ta Ming dynasty, commander-in-chief of the forces for the conquest of the Fuhkien province. As an earnest of his intention to carry out the proclamations, one Chin-kien, an educated man, the first offender, whose tongue was longer than his discretion, was promptly decapitated.

On the 4th July, the Imperialists landed between 4,000 and 5,000 men, some 10 miles to the north east of Amoy; the rebels responded by erecting a barricade at their advanced station, 6 miles from them, and on the 7th, the Imperialists having approached, a melée took place, when the Imperialists were driven back with a loss of eighteen heads. On the same day about forty-two Imperial junks, appeared off the harbour, and attacked some twenty-five rebel junks. After two hours fighting, in which it has been computed, by eyewitnesses, that about one shot in a thousand took effect, the fleets parted, the mandarins standing out to the six Islands, and the rebels returning into harbour. On the following morning the rebel junks went out to the six Islands, and engaged the Imperialists. The action was fought at a sufficient distance to avoid injury to each other, and the Imperialists left next day.

About this period the contributions to the rebel coffers falling short, an attempt was made to raise funds by the levy of port charges. As the proclamation, and tariff, are curiosities in their way, I shall perhaps be pardoned for inserting a translation of them here:

"By Kwang, appointed by Imperial decree of the Emperor of the Han, (Chinese) Ta-ming, Dynasty, Commander-in-chief of the forces for the conquest of Fuhkien province.

An order for the guidance of the Merchant Shipping, I, the Commander-in-chief, received an Imperial order to come to Amoy to relieve the people, not to harm them, to put down, not to commit, oppression, for by means of their strength, and by a display of power, these Tartar miscreants, have embittered the whole living population; people of all classes asserted their innocence to the Gods both above and below, and merchants, too, had long been suffering their cruel injuries.

In the absence of a new code of port regulations, which weightier military duties, at this pressing moment, leaves no time for framing in your behalf, I have, for present use, drawn up an abstract of the rules heretofore in force here, for the merchant shipping, which, in comparison with the port charges, levied by the Tartar brigands, will be found considerably reduced. My chief aim being to procure for the people, those benefits which are to their advantage. Accordingly I beg hereby to notify to the merchant shipping of Amoy, that all such ships as are engaged in Import, or Export, trade, are to be duly provided with passes or papers, which will enable them to leave, or enter, the port, on their voyages to and fro, without danger of obstruction.

Annexed is a scale of charges temporarily fixed upon, to which every one is called upon to obey.

Dated 癸酉年 Kwei-chow, Cycle year, 5th moon, 27th day (1st August 1853)."

SCALE OF AMOY PORT CHARGES

1.—Vessels belonging to Lung-kee, Tung-an, Hai-ching, Ma-siang-ting, Tsin-kiang, Nan-an, Hui-an, leaving Amoy and loading beancake, oil, rice, &c., at Luk-chow, Tamsui, and Woo-tiaou-kiang, in Formasa, and returning with that cargo to Amoy, for entering and leaving the port

To pay, if of 2,000 piculs and under 4,000 piculs, $60.

To pay, if of 1,000 piculs and under 2,000 piculs $30.

2.—Vessels from Lung-kee, Tung-an, Hai-ching, Ma-siang-ting, Tsin-kiang, Hui-an, Nan-an, taking in sugar and like produce, at Amoy, and going with it to Kin-chow and Kai-chow, in Tientsin, or to Keiou-chow, in Shantung, for every such voyage and back

To pay each such vessel $50.

3.— Vessels belonging to Lung-kee, Tung-an, Hai-ching, or Ma-siang-ting bound from Amoy to Tae-tsing, Wen-chow, Tai-chow, Ningpo, Shanghai, and returning to Amoy, for each such voyage, per ship $14.

4.—Vessels belonging to Lung-kee, Tung-an, Hai-ching, or Ma-siang-ting, bound from Amoy to any port of "Formosa", and thence trading to Kui-chow, Kai-chow, and Keaou-chow in Tientsin and Shantung, and returning to Amoy, for every such voyage, per ship $100.

5.—Ships from Tsin-keang, Nan-an, Hui-an and sailing from Amoy to "Formosa", and thence proceeding to Kin-chow, Kai-chow and Kiaou-chow, in Tientsin, and Shantung, and returning to Amoy, for every such voyage （inwards and outwards）, $100.

6.—Ships from Yüne-siao, Chang-poo, and Shao-an, sailing out of port to "Formosa", and returning to Amoy with a cargo of beancake, oil and rice, for each such voyage（inwards and outwards）, each ship $50.

7.—Ships from Yüne-siao, Changpoo, and Shao-an. sailing out of Amoy harbour, and returning to Amoy, with a cargo of foreign goods and sundries, from Shang-hai, Cha-poo, Wan-chow, Tai-chow, or Chan-tou, Chang-lin, for each such voyage （outwards, and inwards） each ship $20.

8.—Vessels from Yüne-siao, Chang-poo, and Shao-an, with cargoes consisting of groceries, spices, salt and dried fish, salt pomfrets, sprats, &c., for entering and leaving the port, each vessel $10.

9.—Native Amoy boats, and those of neighbouring districts, trading to Fuchow, and returning hither by way of Ning-an, or Ning-teh, for each voyage or every boat, $10.

10.—Ships, such as the Fühwan, and Sanpwan vessels, from neighbouring provinces, or the Woo-tsaou junks, from Cha-poo, or the Teen-tsaou boats from Pang-hoo, in "Formosa", and all like out province vessels, for entering and leaving the harbour, each $20.

11.—Boats from Ho-koo, of the island Tung-shih, Pang-hoo, Tsen-kiang,

For entering and leaving the port, each boat $20.

12.—Coasting junks from Canton, and Chang-lin, laden with foreign cargo and miscellaneous goods, on every junk,

For entering and leaving the port $20.

13.—Junks engaged in Foreign commerce belonging to this port, as well as the Hung-t'ow-ling vessels （with red bows） by the old tariff taxed $1,000, afterwards reduced after the barbarian（夷）disturbances to the following scale, viz.:—

For vessels of 5,000 piculs and upwards $500.

less than 5,000 piculs $250.

14.—Natives of Amoy, engaging square rigged ships from Singapore, or other foreign places, to pay for entering and leaving the harbour, port dues on every ship, according to the following rate, viz.:—

For every 3 masted vessel (ship)　$300.

For every 2½ masted vessel (barque)　$200.

For every 2 masted vessel (brig or schooner)　$150.

小刀会占领厦门

起义军纪律严明，作风严谨，他们除了抢掠火药库和军械厂外，与平民百姓秋毫无犯。起义军遣派巡逻队巡守全城各处以防范抢掠盗劫，夜间他们调遣武装人员驻守各个洋行商号，同时还向洋人表达了最诚挚的和平相处意愿。港口没有军舰驻泊，但是由于怡和洋行（Jardine, Matheson & Co.）和宝顺洋行（Dent & Co.，又译“颠地洋行”）察觉到战事临近，并将船只撤回内港，所以这两家洋行的船只便负责收容、庇护外国侨民。说来也怪，事后文翰①（George Bonham）爵士却表示不赞成采取这一措施。兵贵神速，1853 年 5 月，起义军分遣一部分队伍前去攻打泉州和台湾。让厦门居民感到厌恶的是，起义军强迫他们捐献钱粮，一家殷实的商行被“征用”的财物价值高达 4 万银元。

现在，我们应该略加考察这支迅速占领了城市的武装力量。小刀会②，又名“匕首会”，是一个在定居爪哇、新加坡、马六甲和槟榔屿的华人中存在多年的秘密结社，其成员来自社会各个阶层，表面上以互援互助为社团宗旨。小刀会具有严格的会规，据说海盗在公海上只要遇到悬挂该会会旗的船舶，都视其为该会的生意伙伴，允许船只顺利通行。这个社团最初称为“三合会”，即“三人联合”社团，有人把它译为“三人会”（the Triad Society），可谓恰到好处。此处的“三”意为天、地、人，是中国宇宙观中的三大自然力量。

① 文翰爵士（1803 年 9 月 7 日—1863 年 10 月 8 日），又译文咸，英国东印度公司及殖民地官员，1848 年至 1854 年出任第三任香港总督，并兼任驻华全权公使及驻华商务总监等职。译者注。

② 福建小刀会是道光三十年（1850 年）由福建华侨陈庆真按照天地会的组织形式在厦门创立起来的。此外，一位曾在辛亥革命期间在中国从事过会党活动的日本人说：“小刀会是 1849 年（道光二十九年）作为三合会（即天地会）支部在厦门建立的，其创建人是福建华侨陈正成（陈庆真是清朝官员由于读音相近而误记的）。”参见方诗铭：《上海小刀会起义》，上海人民出版社，1965 年，第 20-21 页，译者注。

约清乾隆六十年（约 1795 年），三合会改称“天地会”，即“天与地社团”，成为一个带有明显政治色彩的组织，其规模和权力之大，已经严重危及清王朝的统治。直到八年后，清政府缉捕并处死小刀会的众多成员后，这个社团才如同“蛇打七寸”一般遭到重大打击，可是也没有被赶尽杀绝。

1848 年至 1849 年间，小刀会也就是三合会的支部，由一位在怡和洋行担任买办的新加坡华人陈庆真传入厦门。随后，小刀会迅速在当地站稳脚跟，到 1857 年[①]，成员已达数千人，这引起了位于省城福州的巡抚衙门的担忧。巡抚派遣一位强毅果断而又仇洋排外的张姓老道台[②]到厦门调查小刀会的底细，打算将其取缔。正是这位张姓道台曾于 1839 年参与林则徐总督[③]在广州查禁、烧毁英国人交出的 20，291 箱鸦片的行动。张道台的第一个行动是以谋反罪名缉拿陈庆真，唯一罪证是在陈庆真家里搜出的一本记录着小刀会成员姓名和住所的花名册，官府认为仅凭这个证据就足够了。陈庆真经受不住严刑拷打，便供认出更多的细节。由于陈庆真是英国属民，英国领事听到他被捕的消息后，率领三位属员前往道台衙门要求引渡。衙门里的人告诉领事人犯在海防厅（同知署），尽管据传陈庆真当时正在后衙遭受酷刑。在海防厅，领事又被告知人犯在道台衙门。领事未能领回人犯，陈庆真也被活活拷打而死。第二天早上，陈庆真的东家怡和洋行开门时，有职员发现他的尸体就停放在洋行对面，衣着一如往常，而且还坐在轿子里面。

从那时起，小刀会的领导权似乎落在了一个出身低微，但精力充沛、性

① 据撰写于清咸丰元年（1851 年）正月十二日的《福建巡抚徐继畬奏兴泉永道张熙宇在厦门查获小刀会陈庆真等人片》，下文的巡抚（即徐继畬）派遣张姓老道台（即张熙宇）到厦门查获小刀会一事发生于 1851 年。根据上下文推断，此处的年代应为 1851 年，1857 年为笔误或印刷错误。参见上海师范大学历史系中国近代史研究室、中国第一历史档案馆编辑部编：《福建·上海小刀会档案史料汇编》，福建人民出版社，1993 年，第 110-111 页。译者注。

② 张姓老道台指张熙宇（1783-1853 年），四川眉山人，清道光十四年（1834 年）起历任广东揭阳、乐昌、澄海、番禺知县、南澳府同知等职。咸丰元年（1851 年）任福建兴泉永兵备道。译者注。

③ 据《清史稿》卷十八，清廷于道光十八年（1838 年）十一月任命林则徐为钦差大臣前往广东查办鸦片，道光十九年（1839 年）三月任命其为两江总督，以陈銮署之，十二月任命其为两广总督。故虎门销烟（道光十九年四月）发生时，林则徐为钦差大臣、两江总督，时任两广总督为邓廷桢。译者注。

格刚强的人身上，此人名字叫做黄位（当地方言发音为“Ng–wee”）。当时，厦门住着一位名为黄德美（当地方言发音为“Ng–teck–bi”）的豪商巨贾，此人乐善好施，在下层民众中颇受欢迎。官府曾经逼迫他从事漳州府和泉州府的食盐专营业务，这在当时是一件让人避之不及的差事，因为持有专营权的盐商必须每年向盐运使交纳一笔远远超过他所能赚取的定额款项（与户部地位完全一样的盐运使司通常强迫最富有的商人接受这一差事）。据传，这个差事给黄德美造成的损失高达八十万银元，他对此耿耿于怀。他加入小刀会可能是因为官府试图再次逼迫他接受食盐专营权，尽管给我（指原著作者乔治·休斯。译者注。全书同。）提供信息的人否认了这种可能性。无论如何，可以肯定的是，黄德美曾经垫钱给小刀会，与黄位关系密切。

得知官府企图强迫黄德美第二次接受他恨之入骨的差事后，黄位抓住这个机会，把这位有财有势的人物同小刀会牢牢地捆绑在一起。在黄位的领导下，这个如今被称作“小刀会”即“匕首会”社团的约 2,000 名成员在黄德美的家乡沈宅①起义，宣称要为他伸冤(黄德美一再声明，整件事情没有经过他的同意，也不是他所希望看到的)。他们向前推进，攻克了海澄县、石码、漳州府（仅仅占领三天），最后占领了厦门。到达厦门后不久，小刀会已经发展到拥有约八千名成员，确立以黄位为首，六名成员组成的议事会作为领导机构，其中三人是新加坡华人。议事会成员以下的许多职位，比如百夫长、十夫长等，也是由新加坡华人担任的。兵丁的报酬是每人每天 100 文铜钱，约等于 5 便士。正是这支起义军攻占了厦门，并且一直坚守到 11 月 11 日。

5 月 29 日，一支朝廷舰队开进厦门港，将大约 500 或 600 名清兵送上岸。清军向城内挺进的时候，遇到了起义军的阻击。经过短暂的交锋，清军被赶回船上，并立即驾船离开。起义军认为清军战败是一个吉祥的征兆，这极大

① 此处的汉语村名“沈宅”为原著提供，即漳州角美锦宅社。锦宅社，原名沈宅，原为沈姓居住地，以姓名社，故名沈宅。后以方言谐音雅化为“锦宅”。译者注。

地鼓舞了他们的士气，也进一步壮大了他们的队伍。为了继续攻城略地，起义军发布告示说他们征用了攻占厦门时从军火库抢掠的武器、弹药等军需物资，并承诺赔偿物主的损失。这时候，起义军首领黄位自封“汉大明皇帝敕授平闽统兵大元帅”，发布告示取缔骚乱、维护正义，违反禁令者将全部处死。为了表明自己言出必行的决心，黄位立刻把一位带头闹事、谣言惑众的陈姓童生①斩首。

7月4日，四五千名官军在厦门东北约10英里处登陆，小刀会则在离官军6英里外的前哨阵地设置路障加以应对。7日，官军向前挺进，双方展开近距离肉搏战，官军阵亡18人，被逼向后撤退。同一天，约42艘清军师船②出现在厦门海面，向约25艘起义军帆船发动攻击。据目击者计算，大约1,000发炮弹才有1枚命中。经过2个小时的交战，双方舰船离得越来越远，官船驶向六岛③，起义军驾船回港。次日上午，起义军帆船驶往六岛同官军交战，双方舰船一直保持足够远的距离以避免互相伤害。就这样，第二天官军也撤兵了。

大概就在这个时候，民众捐献不足导致起义军出现财政困难，起义军就想通过征收港口使用费来筹集资金。由于这个告示和税率世所罕见、非常珍贵，诸位请原谅我在此收录其译文④：

汉大明皇帝敕授平闽统兵大元帅黄位

谕尔商船知悉：照得本帅奉旨临厦，安民非以贱民，御暴非以为暴。清

① 指童生陈润渠。据《籀经堂类藁》卷十九之二十二“陈生润渠殉难纪遗”所述，小刀会攻占厦门后，陈润渠“撰讨贼文，满贴城市街衢，大呼于众，誓共灭贼”。译者注。

② 即兵船、兵舰，即前文所提的清军“戎克”（junk）船。译者注。

③ 指金（门）厦（门）海域之间的六座小岛。译者注。

④ 指本书作者将汉语的告示原文译为英文。本告示的汉语原文和时任英国驻厦领事官员巴克好（Backhouse）的英译文均馆藏于英国国家档案馆（The National Archives, UK），日本学者佐佐木正哉发表于1963年的《咸丰三年厦门小刀会叛乱》（见《东洋学报》第四十五卷，第520–545页），以及我国台湾学者黄嘉谟发表于1978年的《英人与厦门小刀会事件》（见“中央研究院”《近代史研究所集刊》第七期，第309–354页）各摘录了上述馆藏告示的部份内容，但两文所摘录的共同部分甚少，与此处的英译版也不全然相同。另，佐文还指出，本书录有告示的全文，可见此处的告示还是比较具有参考价值的。此处译文是基于本书的英语原文，参考上述两篇文章的相关内容回译成中文。译者注。

逆倚势作威、荼毒生灵，故并告无辜于上下神祀。尔商民罹其凶害者久矣。

兹因军中急务，仓卒之际，未暇详议条目，姑就向来旧例，定其大略。较清贼出入关口，倍觉省约，务要因民之所利而利之。合行出示晓谕。为此示，仰厦岛商船，凡有通商出入关口，任尔来往，准给船票，毋得拦阻。

酌定条例，胪列于左，各宜凛遵毋违。特示。

干支纪年癸丑六月二十七日（1853 年 8 月 1 日）①

厦门港口收费标准

一、龙溪、同安、海澄、马巷厅、晋江、南安及惠安船只，往台湾所属鹿州②、淡水及五条港，载运豆饼、油、大米等货来厦，进出港口收费为：

二千担以上四千担以下收六十元；

一千担以上二千担以下收三十元。

二、龙溪、同安、海澄、马巷厅、晋江、惠安、南安船只，在厦门装载糖以及同类产品，前往天津之锦州和盖州③，或山东胶州回厦，每次出航并返回，每船收五十元。

三、龙溪、同安、海澄或马巷厅籍船只，自厦门前往太仓④、温州、台州、宁波、上海，并返回厦门，每次出航，每船收十四元。

四、龙溪、同安、海澄或马巷厅籍船只，自厦门出发前往台湾任一港口后运货转往天津和山东的金州⑤、盖州和胶州并返回厦门，每船每次出航收一百元。

五、来自晋江、南安、惠安的船只，自厦门经由台湾前往天津和山东的锦州、

① 此处的年份中，原文英语为“Kwei-chow”，即“癸丑”，汉语为“癸酉”。不过，后面的 1853 年为咸丰三年癸丑年，故译为“癸丑”。原文的月份为“5th moon”即“五月”，但是当年公历 8 月 1 日为农历六月二十七日，故译为“六月”。译者注。

② 此处原文为“Luk-chow”。佐文和黄文均为“鹿港”。译者注。

③ 黄文为“天津、锦州、盖州”。译者注。

④ 此处原文为“Tae-tsing”，黄文为“乍浦”。译者注。

⑤ 原文为“Kui-chow”，黄文为“锦州”，参考条款二及条款五，此处应为“Kin-chow（锦州）”之笔误。译者注。

盖州和胶州，并返回厦门，每次航行（入出港）收一百元。

六、来自云霄、漳浦和诏安的船只，出港前往台湾并载运豆饼、油和大米返回厦门，每船每次航行（入出港）收五十元。

七、来自云霄、漳浦和诏安的船只，出厦门港前往上海、乍浦、温州、台州或汕头、樟林载运洋货日杂并返回厦门，每船每次航行（出入港）收二十元。

八、来自云霄、漳浦和诏安的船只，载运食品杂货、香料、盐和鱼干、咸鲳鱼、鲱鱼等货，进出港每船收十元。

九、厦门本地及邻近地区船只前往福州贸易，经由宁安①或宁德返回本港，每船或每次航行收十元。

十、来自邻近省份之玉环、三盘的船只，或者来自乍浦之乌舢船，以及来自台湾澎湖之尖舢船之类的船只，以及所有类似的外省船只，进出港各收二十元。

十一、澎湖东石岛之何厝、岑港各小船至厦，进出港每船收二十元。

十二、广州和樟林的驳船载洋货什货，进出港每船收二十元。

十三、本港从事对外贸易的船只以及红头船（船头漆成红色）原先收费一千元，鞑子进扰后收费下调为：

五千担及以上船舶收五百元。

五千担以下收二百五十元。

十四、厦门本地人从新加坡或其他番地承包横帆船，进出港每船按以下费率收取：

三桅船收三百元。

双桅半收二百元。

双桅船收一百五十元。

① 原文为“Ning-an”，黄文为“闽安”，即现福建省福清市闽安镇。译者注。

Recapture of Amoy by Imperialists

The rebels had now been in possession of the city for four months, and although foreigners were in the habit of riding, and walking, through it at all hours of the day, no case of molestation or insult had occurred. On the 9th September an intimation of the approach of a large squadron of Imperial junks, and of troops, was given, and foreign shipping moved out of the harbour, and took up a neutral and safe position, at the back of the island of Kulangsu. After some three weeks' delay, the junks and troops arrived, and a series of harassing attacks were commenced; the opposing forces chiefly using the matchlock, at some hundred paces, and being concealed behind embankments, rocks, &c., the casualties were few; but the Imperialists being assisted by the guns of their fleet, the balance of advantage of their daily fights, was theirs. At night each side retired with regularity to its quarter to enjoy the reasonable indulgence of a night's undisturbed repose, for there was an honorable abstention from night attacks, surprises, and such barbarian-like attempts to take a mean advantage of each other.

On the 12th September, the fleet of the Imperialists got under weigh, and the army advanced on the city. The wind failing, and the tide receding, the junks had to drop anchor, and the troops met with a signal defeat, a portion of their camp falling into the hands of the Siau-tao-hui. On the 15th, the Imperialist Admiral got his whole fleet of some 70 sail, under weigh, to attack the rebel fleet of 15 or 20 vessels. The attack would no doubt have been successful, but on his bearing down on his enemy, he was only supported by three or four junks, the remainder, disregarding his signals to come into action, did not fire a single gun. A precisely similar attempt on the following day, was attended with a precisely similar result.

Thus the combat continued on land, and water, with varied fortune, apparently, but in reality with steady success to the Imperialists, who were persistently carrying out their favourite ponderous stratagem of wearying out, and disheartening, their enemy, by incessant menaces and petty attacks, until their confidence in themselves failed, and obedience to their leaders was lost, when, panic, disorganisation, and flight, being the result, the

Imperialists would march on to, to themselves, a bloodless victory. On the 11th November, this end was gained. The previous night the fire on either side was heavier than usual, and at daybreak, the rebel junks were found warped out into the stream, and a cloud of small vessels, crowded with people, were already underweigh. The large junks soon joined them, and stood up the river, the Imperial junks standing down to the anchorage off the town, passed them, and a few shots were exchanged. It appears that the rebel chiefs had, the previous evening, made preparations for abandoning the place, of which the Imperialists were aware, so the troops at daybreak marched on the city, when finding no opposition, they scaled the walls, and Amoy was once more in Imperial possession.

The panic was terrible, hundreds were endeavouring to escape in all kinds of boats, some on rafts, some on boards, some even on doors. and numbers were attempting, and drowning in the attempt, to swim to the opposite island of Kulangsoo. Hwang escaped in the fleet, and is, it is said, living at Saigon at the present time; his Admirals, Ma E and Wen-kuan, also effected their retreat, with the greater portion of the fighting men in the junks, abandoning the rest of their miserable dupes to merciless slaughter. And merciless it was. Men and boys, were brought in batches of twenties, to the jetties next those opposite the foreign hongs, and decapitated, or half decapitated, and tumbled over into the mud; this process proving too tedious, they were attacked with swords, billhooks, spears and clubs, and destroyed like rats by the dozen. The same grisly work was going on in the junks, and the harbour was covered with chopped, slashed, and struggling human creatures, many of them boys of 12 years of age（I have quoted from an eyewitness）.

This monstrous inhumanity, had been going on from morning until three in the afternoon, when Mr., now Sir Harry, Parkes, Her Britannic Majesty's Consul, throwing to the winds the chafing fetters of that official Fêng-shuey, the responsibility of interference, told the officials, he had previously *begged* to desist, that he would not permit the carnage to go further. The stout words of the Christian gentleman, backed by the presence of H. M. S. *Hermes*, and *Bittern*, stopped the slaughter then, and must have saved the lives of hundreds, though on the following day the bloody work went briskly on, at the Northwest side of the city, away from European houses and shipping.

Regarding Ne-teck-be, he tried to escape, but his own relations detained, and delivered him over to the mandarins, to meet with such a death as may be imagined.

清廷收复厦门

起义军至此已经占领厦门达四个月之久，尽管外国人仍旧习惯于通过骑马和走路的方式穿行于这座城市之间，但是大家都没有受到过任何骚扰或者侮辱。9 月 9 日，在收到大批官军水师舰船和军队正在逼近的通知后，外国船只立刻驶离港口，停泊在鼓浪屿背面一个中立、安全的位置。拖拖拉拉过了约三个星期，师船和步军终于来了，一连串的扰袭随之开始。起义军主要使用火绳枪进行对抗，他们躲在几百步远外的堤坝、岩石等掩体后面，因此伤亡很少。但是官军有水师舰队炮火的支援，所以每次交战都占据优势。夜幕降临，双方总是回到各自的宿营地，享受一夜互不干扰的宁静。双方都光明磊落，不搞夜战、偷袭，也不靠野蛮卑鄙手段打败对方。

9 月 12 日，官军水师开拔，步军向城里逼进。这时，风息潮退，舰船只得抛锚，陆上官军也惨遭溃败，部分营地落入小刀会手中。15 日，清军水师提督集结全体水师约 70 艘舰船扬帆起锚，攻打起义军的 15 或 20 艘兵船。正常情况下，清军的这次袭击肯定会大获全胜，可是当水师提督向敌人逼近的时候，跟上来的师船仅有三四艘，剩下的则无视进攻信号，一炮不发。第二天，完全相同的一幕又重演了，得到了完全相同的结局。

就这样，战斗在水陆两个战场持续进行，表面上各有输赢，实际上官军节节胜利，他们一直采取拿手的消耗战术，通过不断地威胁恐吓以及小规模袭击，使敌人疲于应付、丧失斗志，直至信心瓦解、违抗军令，这种状况引起了起义军上下的恐慌、混乱，兵士开始逃跑，结果官军兵不血刃就取得了胜利。11 月 11 日，清军胜局已定。前一天夜里，双方的火力都比平时猛烈。天亮的时候，起义军把帆船拖进水流之中，而挤满了人的各式小船已经开拔，大型帆船很快赶了上去，继续驶向外海，官军师船驶进城外锚地途中与之相遇，双方互相发射了几发炮弹。看来起义军首领前一天晚上已经做好撤离该地的准备，这一点官军也知道，所以清军在拂晓时分向城里挺进的时候没有遇到任何抵抗。他们爬上城墙，再次占领了厦门。

人们惊慌失措的场面实在恐怖，几百号人涌上各式各样的船只抢着逃命，有的搭着木筏，有的趴在木板甚至门板上，很多人拼命试图游到对面的鼓浪屿，却被活活淹死了。黄位[①]与船队一起逃脱出来，据说目前住在西贡。他的水师统帅马义（Ma E）和文观（Wen-kuan），连同大部分士兵也都乘船撤退了，扔下那些受骗上当的可怜群众惨遭残忍的屠杀。场面实在非常残忍，只要是男人，不分老少，二十人捆在一起，一批批被带到洋行对面砍头，有的头还没砍断，就已经连人带头滚到泥里了。清军觉得这样杀人太单调乏味了，于是用刀剑、钩镰、长矛和棍棒刺击，把待刑之人像消灭老鼠一样一次十几个一起毁灭。同样恐怖的场面也在船上发生着，港口遍布着那些被砍、被劈以及还在挣扎中的人类，当中还有很多十二岁的男孩子（此处我引用了目击证人的原话）。[②]

这种骇人听闻的野蛮行径，从早上一直持续到下午三点。大英帝国领事、现在已经拥有爵士头衔的巴夏礼先生（Harry Parkes）把之前海防署[③]官员严厉警告他“管闲事就要承担干涉责任”的话抛到九霄云外了，他告诉在场的官员们，他早已请求清军停止屠杀，现在他不允许屠杀再继续下去了。因为拥有“皇家赫米斯号”（H.M.S Hermes）和“比登号”（Bitten）作为后盾，这位基督教绅士的强硬话语阻止了大屠杀，也肯定因此挽救了数百人的生命。

---

① 原文只有姓“Hwang”（黄），没有名字，符合英语行文的习惯。从上下文看，应为“黄位”。译者注。

② 此处仅为原著者的立场。据《闽南小刀会纪要》，清军攻入厦门，立即进行疯狂的烧杀掠夺，大肆屠戮起义军及群众，据传“割下来的人头和耳朵，多得象纽扣，比比皆是”。其凶狠残酷，令人触目惊心！《福建通志》（《总卷一福建通纪之清七》）载：“是役也，阅七十三日，历四十八战，擒斩及坠海死者以万计。”参见协文：《闽南小刀会纪要》，http://www.xmta.gov.cn/qq/rwls/wszl/201706/t20170604_187361.htm，2010-8-25. 译者注。

③ 原文为“Feng-shuey”，即防署，即海防署，实则为海防厅在厦门的衙门。译者注。

但是，第二天清军转移到远离欧洲人居住区和舰船的厦门西北边，兴致勃勃地继续着血腥屠杀。①

至于黄德美，他试图逃跑，但是被自己的族人扣押后移交给官府，他的死法也就不难想象了。

① 此处仅为原著者的立场。关于对清廷暴行的干预，我国史学家简又文在其《太平天国全史》一书中援引英人施佳士《旅华十二年》（John Scarth:*Twelve Years in China*）十九章的叙述，称"然而欧洲人愈看愈不忍，即有传教士、商人、水手、及军官，一齐拥至，停止他们继续屠杀。"参见简又文著，《天平天国全史》，简氏猛进书屋，1962 年，第 770 页。可见，不同的人记载的内容差别巨大。江林宣等认为，由于起义军遭到清政府的残酷镇压和摧残，起义军方面的原始史料几乎荡然无存，这些当时在厦门的外国人写的书信、报道，从不同的立场出发，不可避免地带有偏见和局限性。不仅如此，林江宣等还批驳了帝国主义在对待起义军方面的所谓"中立"，认为起义军对外国人实行保护政策，而外国商人却拒绝提供支持，实际上是扼杀起义军。参见江林宣、洪卜仁：《略述闽南小刀会起义的若干问题》，载洪卜仁主编《闽南小刀会起义史料选编》，鹭江出版社，1994 年，第 1–6 页。译者注。

Capture of Chang-chou-fu by a remnant of the T'ai-ping Rebels

Eleven years only, had elapsed since the suppression of the Dagger Society, when a second insurrection came, like a blight, upon this region. On the night of the 13th October, 1864, no one thought of disaster, on the morning of the 14th the passage boats from Chioh-bei （Shih-ma 石码） brought in many wounded, men, women, and children, and the news that Chang-chou-fu（漳州府）, a large walled city, distant 24 miles from Amoy, of 700,000 inhabitants, had been swept down upon, and captured, by a band of rebels, called indiscriminately Hung-t'ou-hui, and Chang-maos （the Red headed, or Long haired rebels）, who, came, no one knew whence, and of whose existence, in or about the province, no one had an idea. The rich city had fallen to a few men armed with gingalls, swords, pistols, and spears, only; little or no resistance had been offered, and the only casualty on the Imperialist side, was that of the Chên-tai, who had been shot in his chair; the Taotai, Sub-prefect, and Colonel commandant, escaped to the adjacent villages.

The inhabitants, who were either unable, or unwilling, to quit their property, suffered severely, being slain by thousands, irrespective of sex or age, the city was fired in several places, and the atrocities of the Northern insurrection, re-enacted. Day after day, came boatloads of wounded, mostly by the sword, many of whom had deep gaping wounds on the back of the neck; （which, strange to say, even then, in spite of exposure and dirt, looked healthy, and were subsequently, in most instances, rapidly cured by Dr. Jones, in his Chinese hospital.） These men said they had been led to execution, but the executioners being boys, they had escaped with a wound, on receiving which, they had fainted, or simulated death, until in the darkness, they had found an opportunity to creep away. Many of the wounded were Roman Catholic converts, and the Spanish priests, their pastors, went round and raised a subscription for their immediate necessities, and then, with a simple devotion, for which they will always be honoured by foreigners here, hurried up to the vicinity of Chang-chou-fu, to succour and save, or perhaps perish with, their flocks.

Meantime alarming rumours of the fall of the city of Yüne-siaou, 60 miles to the south of Chang-chou-fu, of the capture of many large and populous villages, and of the intention of the rebels to march on Têng-hwa, and to attack, Chin-chew, Amoy, and Foochow, were received; and the people of Têng-hwa, 16 miles from here, always a turbulent piratical set, fired with the reported gains of the rebels at Chang-chou（$20,000,000 according to the rumours）, were said to be desirous of allying themselves with them. These rumours created amongst the Chinese population here, an utter panic, no one spoke of resistance, only how to get away, vessels were chartered by the wealthy, and arrangements made for instant flight. It is tolerably certain that, if at this time two or three hundred resolute men had made a dash at this city, it would have been carried, without scarcely a single blow being struck by its 350,000 inhabitants, in its defence. The helplessness, and infirmity of purpose of the rulers, and the utter worthlessness of their system, in face of an emergency, were painfully apparent. The defensive measures adopted, were the mustering of a few hundreds of militiamen, armed with rusty bills, tridents, matchlocks, flags, and other obsolete weapons: the subsidising of two or three neighbouring villages, with Taels 600, and the distribution of a mace a day, to each of the ruffians in the city, to keep quiet, who were then, as now, numerous and greatly feared.

Their real reliance for the protection of the city, was on H. B. M. Surveying vessels *Swallow*, and *Dove*, which happened to be in harbour. Foreigners had not been idle. Kulangsu, and the settlement, were patrolled nightly, by volunteers and a hired patrol: and a small company of 25, or 80, men, had been formed out of the Customs employés, and drilled by the Commissioner, the present writer, and assistance had been written for to Hong Kong. It is to the great promptitude with which this appeal was responded to, by the instant despatch of H. B. M. Gunboats *Janus*, and *Flamer*, to the arrival of the *Bustard*, Lieut. John Tucker, from Foochow, who, on his own responsibility, brought his vessel here, on hearing that the city was menaced, and to the fortunate accidental arrival of H. B. M. S. *Pelorus*, 22 guns, that its safety may be attributed. This vessel, subsequently, by shelling the neighbouring turbulent and disaffected villages of Pan-t'oo（潘塗）, Kwan-hsüne（官浔）, and Choo-t'ou（枷头）, for firing on her boats when searching for pirates, gave a great shock to the rebel cause.

At the same time, 100 men of the Foochow Franco-Chinese force, with two guns, under Colonel de Mercy, were sent down in the armed Customs cruiser, *Vindex*, by the Tartar General, at the instigation of the Baron de Meritens, Commissioner of Customs at Foochow. This force, afterwards supplied with two more field pieces, might have done good service, but its presence evoked nothing but intrigue and jealousy, and it had to be sent back to Foochow in a few weeks.

Troops from "Formosa", under the command of the Ti-tu, Tsên, and from the North, under the command of Ti-tu's Kwõ, and Wang, also soon arrived, and were sent forward to the vicinity of Chang-chou: and now commenced a long and tedious investment of three sides of the city, during which the besiegers, were as frequently the besieged, varied by victories, or defeats, of which the following will serve as a fair specimen for all. "On the 25th February, during a fog, 2,000 rebels attacked Tang-chou, 5 miles above the city of Chioh-bei, but were repulsed with heavy loss, by the forces of Ti-tu's Tsên, Kwõ, and Wang. This repulse was greatly owing to the judgment of the Tang-chou villagers, in destroying a bridge, by which act, the rebels were caught as in a trap," and 76 prisoners, 254 heads, and 231 ears, and queues, are reported to have been the fruits of this achievement. It should be stated that the conduct of the villagers throughout contrasted favourably with that of the dwellers in cities; they were loyal, willing to fight for their poor homesteads, and they displayed considerable intelligence in cutting up roads, opening sluices, destroying bridges, and in doing all in their power to embarrass the movements of the rebels.

The rebels had with them at Chang-chou, some ten foreigners, at whose head was a Prussian, named Rhody, sometime a Colonel in the Imperial forces, under Gordon. This man succeeded in establishing communications with another Prussian, named Gerard, a storekeeper, and with another foreigner, a Swede, at Amoy, by whom he and his companions were visited, and supplied with whatever necessaries they required. These visits, although made clandestinely, were known to the authorities here, and were a cause of great disquiet, particularly as several foreigners had lately joined the rebels, and amongst them a Customs tidewaiter, named Patrick Shiel, formerly a plumber at Hong Kong, who was engaged to make shells. This man afterwards perished miserably, as did most of his companions, victims to the suspicions of their employers.

In order to put a stop to these visits, and to prevent some sixty Shanghai, and Ningpo, foreign roughs, attracted here by the rebels, from joining them, the Customs lorcha, *Kiang Hoo*, was stationed at a narrow part of the river leading to Chang-chou fu, called Tin-tou, and armed junks were placed at the entrance of the Pechuiya a river, and at other points, leading in the same direction. These measures were successful, and it was no longer found possible to pass the Imperial lines, by donning some article of naval uniform, or by flying the Union Jack, or Naval Reserve ensign（these flags were taken from foreign boats, which accompanied a rebel attack on Tang-pu, on the 25th February）. One of the first captures made, was by the. junks stationed at Pechuiya of three Americans,（one being nephew of the late Imperialists General, Ward,）and a Chinese rebel officer. They were taken at night in a sampan, in which were arms, and a rebel flag, after a sharp tussle, in which two Chinese soldiers were wounded.

The present writer had just returned to Chioh-bei, from a visit to the Imperial camp, before the walls of Chang-chou-fu, when, at 11 o'clock p.m., hearing that these men had been brought to Chioh-bei, and fearing that their lives might be in danger, he caused a letter to be written to the Tao-t'ai Tsêng, with whom, fortunately, he was intimate, urgently requesting that they should not be injured, and that he might be allowed to be present at their examination. These requests were complied with, and on the following day, the men were examined at the magistrate's Yamên, at Chioh-bei; the rebel officer, first, who crouching on his knees, coolly told his story making admissions, each of which, he must have known, would consign him to certain death, and quietly munched sugarcane, and cakes, which the Tao-t'ai, himself, strangely enough, handed him from our table. The foreigners were next separately interrogated, their statements taken down in writing, and they were then questioned together. The behavior of two of them, was so insufferably insolent, their complicity so apparent, and the falsehood of their statements, so gross, that the Tao-t'ai, touching the writer's knee several times beneath the table, made a short sharp significant chop with his hand. At last, at one outrageously mendacious and insolent statement, he sprung up saying: "If these men's ears can hear what their mouths say, they must know themselves to be liars," and again he made the significant gesture.

The writer, thoroughly alarmed, then warned the men that he had come there to endeavour to aid them, but that, beyond persuasion, he was as powerless as themselves, and that an order given to the soldiers and Yamên runners, thronging the room, would be executed before human aid could reach them, and earnestly cautioned them against the folly and danger of their behaviour. This speech had its effect on all, but particularly on young Ward, who shed tears, and acknowledged that they were, when seized, en route to join the rebels, &c., &c., and who then pleaded earnestly not to be left in the Yamên. The writer succeeded in taking this man away with him, and in obtaining a promise that no injury should be done to the other two. The three men were afterwards sent to the United States Consul General at Shanghai, to be dealt with.

On the 13th February, just four months after the occupation of the city, an official party, with whom was the man Gerard, before mentioned, left in the gunboat *Flamer*, to visit Chang-chou-fu. They were well received by the rebels, and returned on the 15th, bringing with them a rebel officer, who remained on board the *Pelorus* until the 19th, to the great consternation of the Chinese, who thought they saw in this, an intention on the part of the British government, to espouse the rebel cause. However when this man, recognised by a gentlemen here as his former chair coolie at Hongkong, was sent back in the *Flamer*, on the 19th, the feeling of disquiet abated. As Gerard's name will not be mentioned again, it may be well to state that shortly after this, when visiting Chang-chou by himself, he was, after leaving his countrymen in their employ, cruelly put to death by the rebels at one of the city gates.

About 6 o'clock on the evening of the 14th January 1865, a linguist, residing at the Custom House, noticed great excitement amongst the servants attached to the building. On enquiry he found it caused by the presence of a fine looking old man, who said he was one Chên-chin-lung, bearer of a letter from his brother by adoption Li-sze-hsün, the Tze-wang, or rebel king at Chang-chou-fu, to the Haikuan at Amoy. Her Britannic Majesty's Consul, and the Commissioner of Customs, are both called Haikuan, by the common classes, and he had mistaken the Custom House, for the residence of the Consul. The linguist did not undeceive him, but offered him all those little courtesies, usual to educated Chinese life, and ended by inviting him to dinner at his house in the city. The old, old, decoy, which like the invitation to skittles, or cards, to the British yokel, seems irresistible. The invitation was accepted, and half an hour afterwards, Chên, was walking to the Taotai's Yamên, to meet his fate. It was soon decided; the Hai-fang-ting （local magistrate） was summoned, and after a brief examination, Chên was decapitated, by torchlight.

太平军余部占领漳州府

小刀会被镇压以后，仅仅又过了十一年，第二次叛乱就像瘟疫一样降临到这个地区。1864 年 10 月 13 日晚上，没有人想到灾难即将来临。14 日上午，数艘来自石码的客运班船搭载着男女老少大量伤员抵达本市，有消息说是居民总数达 70 万人的漳州府，一座距离厦门 20 英里、筑有城墙的大城市，被一群统称为红头会或长毛的起义军扫荡并占领了，没有人知道他们来自何方，是来自本省还是邻省的团伙。这座富庶的城市落入了少数几个装备了抬枪[①]、刀剑、短枪和长矛的武装分子手中，他们几乎没有或者根本没有遇到任何抵抗。官军方面只死了镇台一人，他是坐在椅子上的时候被枪射杀的，道台、同知和总兵则逃到了邻近的村庄。

那些要么不能，要么不愿意舍弃财产的百姓们受尽了折磨，这数千人不分男女老少都惨遭屠杀，城里的多处地方同时开火，北方叛乱时的种种暴行在这里重演了。日复一日，一船又一船的伤员接踵而来，他们大部分是被刀砍伤的，许多人的脖子后面有很深的伤口（说来也怪，即使那时候伤员们挨冻受寒、蓬头垢面，但是看起来都很健康，随后他们被收容到一家中国人开办的医院，在琼斯医生的治疗下，多数人很快能够痊愈）。这些人说，他们已经被带往刑场，不过由于刽子手只是个小男孩，他们就带伤逃跑了。他们被砍头时有的晕倒过去，有的假装死去，到了晚上，他们找机会摸黑溜走了。许多伤员是罗马天主教的皈依者，跟他们信奉同一种教派的西班牙牧师四处奔走，募集捐款购买急需物品，然后带着一种朴素的奉献精神，一种让本地

① 抬枪，英文为“gingall”，是清军装备的一种武器，与步枪、马枪结构原理相同。译者注。

的外国侨民所敬佩的精神，赶到漳州府附近去援助、拯救他们的信徒们，尽管他们知道或许有可能和信徒们一起死去。

与此同时，令人担忧的各种传言正在四处传播，有的说漳州府以南 60 英里的云霄沦陷了，有的说很多人口稠密的大村庄被占领了，还有的说起义军打算进军同安，攻打泉州、厦门和福州。而距离此地 16 英里的同安民众本身就是一股强横的海盗分子，据称他们听说起义军在漳州缴获巨额战利品（传说有 2,000 万银元）后兴奋不已，希望自己能和起义军结盟。这些传言在当地的中国人当中引起了极度的恐慌，没有人谈论如何抵抗，他们只是谈论如何逃跑，富人们已经包租好船只，做好了随时离开的准备。基本上可以肯定，如果此时有两三百号果敢分子向这座城市发起冲锋的话，他们将会轻松获胜，三十五万居民中没有任何一人会为了守卫这座城市而反击一下。面对紧急情况，统治者彷徨无助、意志薄弱，他们的制度一无是处，这些都是显而易见的。官府采取的防御措施是召集数百名乡勇，为他们配备生锈的锯子、三叉戟、火绳枪、旗帜以及其他各类老式武器，给邻近的两三个村庄发放六百两银子的补贴。无论是当时还是现在，城里的流氓恶棍都为数众多，让人惶恐不安，朝廷就每人每天派发一钱银子安抚他们。

官府保卫城市的真正力量是碰巧停泊在厦门港的英国皇家海军测量船“燕子号”（Swallow）以及“和平鸽号”（Dove）。外国人也没有闲着：志愿者和雇佣巡逻队员每晚巡查鼓浪屿和居住区；海关税务司，即笔者所在单位为海关抽调的二十五或三十人组成的小分队开展军事训练；同时，我们还给香港写信求援。我们的求救迅速得到了回应，大英帝国海军炮舰“詹努斯号”（Janus）和“火焰号”（Flamer）被紧急调遣过来；驻扎在福州的约翰·塔克（John Tucker）海军上尉一听说这座城市面临威胁，自作主张就把他的“布斯达号”（Bustard）开到这里；更加幸运的是，载炮 22 门的大英帝国海军“罗盘号”

（Pelorus）炮舰不期而至，这才使厦门的安全有了保障。[①]“罗盘号”所属船队在搜寻海盗时，遭到了附近潘塗[②]村、官浔村和柚头[③]村村民的火力袭击，“罗盘”号随后炮击了这些目无王法、犯上作乱的村庄，给起义军带来巨大的震撼。

与此同时，清朝将军在福州海关税务司美理登（Baron de Meritens）的鼓动下，命令德·梅西（de Mercy）上校率领驻扎在福州的一百名中法混合军[④]携带二门大炮，乘坐海关武装巡洋舰“温德克斯号”（Vindex）南下。这支部队后来又获得了两门野战炮的补给，但是中法混合军的到来导致人们对它心生嫉妒和心怀不轨，最终部队作为不大，不得不在几周后撤回福州。

曾提督[⑤]率领台湾赶来的援军以及郭提督和王提督率领的清军也从北部火速赶到，奉命挺进漳州附近，打响了漫长而单调的三面攻城战。在此期间，攻防频繁转换，双方各有输赢，以下战役具有很强的代表性：“2月25日，大雾弥漫，2,000名起义军攻打位于石码以北5英里处的丹洲（Tang-chou），被曾、郭、王三位提督击退，损失惨重。这次失败很大一部分原因是丹洲村民果断捣毁了一座桥梁，使太平军陷入对方的包围圈”。据传，清军在这场战斗中所获的战果是：俘虏了76人，砍了254颗人头，割了231只（条）耳朵和辫子。应该说，村民与城里居民的行为形成了鲜明的对比：他们忠于朝廷、愿意为穷家陋室不惜一战，他们切断道路、打开水闸、摧毁桥梁，尽其所能阻滞起义军的前进，表现出了极大的智慧。

当时，漳州的起义军队伍中约有10位外国人，领头的是一位名叫罗迪（Rhody）的普鲁士人，他曾经在戈登指挥下的清军洋枪队担任上校。罗迪成

① 太平军同清军的战斗主要在厦门周边城镇展开，并未进入厦门，相反，侍王李世贤还从漳州致信驻厦门外国领事，表达了友好合作的希望。因此，此处的所谓英国人成为保卫厦门的“依靠力量”一说仅代表作者立场。译者注。

② 应为“潘涂”。“Pan-too，潘塗”为原著提供。译者注。

③ 应为“柏头”。“Choo-tou，柚头”为原著提供。译者注。

④ 中法混合军，又称“常捷军”“常胜军”，是清同治元年（1862年）法国政府协助清政府对抗太平天国而成立的洋枪队，由法国军官伯勒东担任统领，成员由中国人和菲律宾雇佣兵组成，同治三年（1864年）九月解散。译者注。

⑤ “曾提督”即曾玉明，其时任“台湾镇总兵”，署福建水师提督。译者注。

功地联系上了一位居住在厦门的名叫杰拉德（Gerard）的普鲁士商店老板以及另一位瑞典籍外国人，于是他们前往会见罗迪和他的同伴，提供了后者需求的所有物品。这些会面虽然是秘密进行的，但是却为厦门当局所知晓，引起了当局极大的不安，因为最近有几位外国人加入了起义军，其中一位是名字叫做帕特里克·希尔（Patrick Shiel）的海关监察员，他之前曾在香港当管道工，这次受起义军雇佣前来制造炮弹。此人后来跟他的大多数同伴一样死得非常凄惨，死于雇主对他们的猜疑。

为了阻止这些会面，也为了防止约 60 名上海和宁波的外籍暴徒受起义军招引来到此地并加入到他们的队伍中，海关所属的三桅帆船"江虎号"（Kiang Hoo）奉命驻泊在那条通向漳州的河流狭窄处一个名为镇头（Tin-tou）的地方，战船则停在名叫白嘴崖（Pechuiya）的河流入口处以及同一方向的其他地点。这些措施行之有效，之前那几位外国人只要穿戴上海军制服的某些物件，或者悬挂着 2 月 25 日起义军袭击丹洲时从外国船只抢来的米字旗、海军预备役旗就能通过清军防线，现在已经是不可能了。第一波缉捕行动中有一起是由驻泊在白水营的帆船执行，共俘获 3 名美国人（其中一人是已故清军将领沃德[1]的侄子）以及 1 名起义军首领。他们是夜间在一艘舢板上被捕获的，船上有武器和一面起义军旗帜，在激烈的厮打中，2 名中国兵士受伤。

我探访完驻扎在漳州府城墙外的清军营地后刚刚回到石码。晚上 11 时，一听说这些俘虏被带到石码，我担心他们有生命危险，我便让官府致函曾道台，急切请求衙门不能对他们动刑、允许我参加审讯等，所幸我与道台相熟，所提出的要求全部都得到了满足。第二天，这些俘虏在石码的厅署衙门接受审问。起义军头目跪在堂前，一开始便从容地供认出自己所做的一切，他一定知道，他所做的每一桩每一件事情都将置他于死地。奇怪的是，道台从我们的桌上拿了甘蔗和糕饼给他，他就悠闲地吃了起来。接下来，这些外国人先是被分

① 指清军洋枪队即常胜军统帅，官至清军副将的美国人华尔（Huaer，Frederick Townsend Ward）。译者注。

开审问，他们的供词被记录下来后，再被带到一起盘问。其中两个人的傲慢态度是如此令人无法忍受，他们共谋的事实是如此明显，他们供词的虚假是如此严重，以至于道台用手在桌子底下我的膝盖上做了好几次急快的有力劈砍。当道台再一次听到无耻的谎言和傲慢的供述时，他倏地一下站起来说："如果这些人的耳朵能听到他们嘴里所说的话，他们一定知道自己是骗子。"随后再次用力做了劈砍的手势。

我忧心如焚，便警告他们，我来衙门的目的是为了尽自己所能帮助他们，但是除了劝说，我和他们一样无能为力。兵勇和衙役已经将大堂围得水泄不通，他们接到命令，要赶在有人营救之前处决他们，我还真诚地提醒他们别做愚蠢和危险的举动。这些话对所有人都产生了影响，尤其是年轻的沃德，他一边流泪，一边供认他们被抓住的时候正在前往参加起义军的路上等，然后急切地恳求我不要把他留在衙门里。笔者成功地将这个人带走了，并且得到了官府不伤害其他两个人的承诺。这三个人后来都交给美国驻上海总领事处理。

2 月 13 日，即起义军占领这座城市四个月后，一个官方团组连同之前提到的杰拉德一起乘坐炮舰"火焰号"出发前往漳州访问。他们受到起义军的热烈欢迎，15 日返回厦门时他们带回一名起义军首领，并把他留在"罗盘号"上直到 19 日。中国人对此感到非常惊愕，认为从这件事情上能看出英国政府支持起义军的意图。然而，当有位先生认出起义军首领正是他在香港的轿夫时，这位起义军首领 19 日立即被送回"火焰号"，中国百姓的不满情绪才逐渐平息下来。由于我们不会再提及杰拉德这个名字，在此对他的下落做个交代。不久以后，当杰拉德离开他的同胞工友独自前往漳州探访时，他被起义军残忍地处死于一处城门前。

1865 年 1 月 14 日晚上 6 时许，一位住在海关大楼的通事注意到大楼内的仆役们激动不已。经过询问后，他发现这股情绪是由一个相貌堂堂的老人引起的，老人说他叫陈金龙（Chen-chin-lung），奉命向厦门海关转交他的拜把子兄弟李世贤，即起义军在漳州府的王爷侍王的信函。普通人把大英帝国领事和海关税务司统称为海关，他因此把海关大楼误认为是领事官邸。这位通事没有点破其中的奥妙，而是以中国文人的常见礼节接待了他，最后还邀请他到城里的寓所吃饭。这是一个老套得不能再老套的把戏了，就像邀请英国乡巴佬打球玩牌一样，似乎让人无法抗拒。陈金龙接受了邀请，半个小时以后，他走进道台衙门送命去了。决定很快就下了，海防厅同知也被叫了过来，经过短暂的审问，官府借着火把的光亮把陈庆龙斩首了。

Burgevine

On the 13th May 1865, an American named Burgevine, formerly in command of the Imperial disciplined Chinese troops at Shanghai, and subsequently a leader of rebels at Soochow, arrived in the *General Sherman*. As this person had been deported some three months previously by the United States Consul General at Shanghai, and as his object in coming to Amoy was sufficiently apparent, application was made to the United States Consul here, Mr. Irwin, for his arrest; and the Consul issued a warrant for the apprehension of any suspicious person, claiming to be a citizen of the United States. This warrant was taken to the *General Sherman*, where there is reason to believe Burgevine was at the time. But the master of the vessel refused to allow search to be made. A search warrant was then applied for, this, the Consul for sufficient reasons no doubt, did not see fit to grant, and Burgevine, unfortunately for himself, remained unarrested.

On the 14th it was known that Burgevine, and one or two other foreigners, had made arrangements to join the rebels at Chang-chou-fu, and orders were issued to the officers in command of the vessels stationed for the purpose of preventing supplies, and persons, reaching the rebel city, to keep a strict watch, and to examine every sampan that attempted to pass up the river; the result was that during the same night Burgevine, and an Englishman, named Crane, were found concealed under the bottom boards of a large native boat, and handed over to the safe keeping of the Commander-in-chief of the Chinese forces, Kwõ-sung-ling, who had been directed, in the event of any foreigners being captured, to have them well treated, in addition to which, an European had been ordered to see that they were properly lodged and cared for. The two men were forwarded to the Taotai of Amoy.

On hearing of their arrival, the Acting Commissioner of Customs, Mr. Porter, waited on the Taotai at midnight, and begged him to hand them over to their respective Consuls. To this he replied that he could not accede, his instructions being to forward them to the Viceroy at Foochow. Early next morning, the Acting Commissioner, hearing that they had actually left Amoy, communicated the fact to the British, and American, Consuls. In the meantime, a man supposed to be the owner of the *General Sherman*, and a friend of Burgevine, collected about twenty roughs, and proceeded to the Hai-fang-ting's Yamên, where Burgevine was supposed to be confined, fully determined to release him. Burgevine, as has been shewn, was not there, but another prisoner named Johnson, who stated that he was an American, was forcibly released. The subsequent death of Burgevine, by the capsizing of a boat, when en route to Foochow, will be fresh in the recollection of most residents in China.

Meanwhile the investment of the city, had been growing steadily closer and closer; and the rebels finding it no longer tenable, made their preparations to evacuate it, which they did, on the night of the 14th May, by the East gate. It was not, however, occupied by the Imperial troops, until the 17th, the rebels having left a small force to cover and conceal the retreat of the main body, by keeping up the usual skirmishing to the eastward of the city, on the 15th, and 16th. With the suppression, or, more properly speaking, the dissolution of the rebel movement at Chang-chou-fu, the long chapter of bloodshed in this department of the empire, for the present, closes.

美国人白齐文

1865年5月13日，一位名叫白齐文（Burgevine）的美国人来到“谢尔曼将军”号（General Sherman）船上。白齐文曾经担任过上海清军洋枪队统帅，后来投靠苏州起义军，还当了首领。由于此人大约三个月之前就已经受到美国驻上海总领事驱逐出境的处罚，而且他来到厦门的目的十分明显，因此官府向美国驻此地的领事欧文先生（Mr. Irving）申请逮捕他。领事签发了授权令，允许官府拘捕任何自称是美国公民的可疑人士。由于有充分理由怀疑白齐文当时正在“谢尔曼将军号”上，官府便带着这张授权令来到船上，但是船主拒绝接受检查，于是官府便向领事申请搜查令。毫无疑问，领事完全有理由认为不宜签发搜查令，所以白齐文没有被逮捕归案，这对于他本人的最终结局来说是非常“不幸的”。

14日，白齐文和另外一两位外国人已经做好前往漳州府参加起义军的准备。官府对此了如指掌，于是命令执行漳州府物资、人员封锁任务的舰船指挥官严加监视，严格检查每一艘试图溯江北上的船只。结果，就在同一天晚上，官军发现白齐文和一位名叫克兰（Crane）的英国人躲藏在一艘大型本地船只的底板下，于是就把他们移交给清军提督郭松林以确保万无一失，郭提督则早已接到善待任何遭到逮捕的外国人的指令。此外，一位欧洲人也接到命令，要确保被捕的外国人得到妥善的安置和照顾。随后，这两个人便被转送到厦门道台衙门。

一听说被捕的外国人已经被带到道台衙门，海关代理税务司波特先生（Mr. Porter）连夜前去拜访道台，恳求把他们交给各自国家的领事。对此，道台回答说他无法同意，他收到的指示是把他们转送到福州的巡抚衙门。第二天一早，代理税务司听说被捕的外国人真的已经离开厦门了，便把这件事告诉给英、美两国的领事。与此同时，一位应该是“谢尔曼将军号”船主的人，同时也是白齐文的朋友，纠集了大约20名暴徒来到他们认为关押着白齐文的海防厅衙门，决心要解救他。正如前面所说，白齐文已然离开，但是另一位名叫约翰逊（Johnson）的囚犯声称自己是美国人，于是就被他们强行释放出来。后来，在乘船前往福州的途中，白齐文死于翻船事故，至今大多数中国百姓仍然对此记忆犹新。

与此同时，清军的增援部队日趋逼进，起义军发现他们再也无法坚守，便开始准备撤离。5月14日晚上，他们顺利从东门撤退。但是，清军直到17日才占领城里，因为起义军留下小股部队，15日和16日继续在城东发动平时那样的小规模战斗来迷惑清军，以便掩护主力部队撤退。随着镇压的推进，或者更确切地说，随着漳州府起义运动的瓦解，这场漫长的流血冲突暂告一个段落。

Part II
Geographical

Amoy. Physical peculiarities, climate, disposition and customs of inhabitants. Aids to navigation. Chang chou fu. Chiang tang bridge. Polam. Ch'uan chou fu. Anhai. Tea plantations of Ankoi. Tung An. Quemoy. Fauna.

第二部分

地理篇

厦门——地貌特征——气候——居民性格与习俗——历史古迹——助航设施——漳州府——江东桥——浦南——泉州府——安海——安溪茶园——同安——金门——动物群落。

1.Overview①

Amoy

Hsia mên（厦门，the Gate, or Harbour of Hsia) or the Port of Amoy, is situated in Lat. 24°28' N. Long. 118°4' E. on a thickly inhabited island about twenty-five miles in circumference, and of the same name, appertaining to Fuhkien province. The city is of the third class only, but on account of the importance of the trade of the port, is the residence of a Taotai, who is Intendent of the circuit of Hsing-hua fu (兴化府) Ch'uan chou fu (泉州府) and Yung ch'un chou (永春州). It is in the district of Tung an (同安), belonging to the department of Ch'uan chou fu, and is situated on the south western corner of the Island of Amoy at the mouth of the Dragon river, leading to the city of Chang chou fu (漳州府). The approach from sea is between the Chih hsü (嵣屿) and Ching hsü（青屿）Islands,（in which passage there are from 11 to 14 fathoms of water）, two of a group called the Six Islands. On entering the bay or outer harbour, the scenery is picturesque and striking, ranges of savage grey, and brown barren, rocky hills and mountains rise on either side. One, the Nan t'ai wu （南泰武）, surmounted by a Pagoda, towers 1720 feet in the clear blue sky. A ruined fort, and a long line of stone fortifications stretch away to the right; to the left are a pagoda topped Island and chain of hills, and in front the island of Kulangsu, and the inner harbour, which is set, a sparkling gem, in a back ground of range upon range of the grey, brown, or misty blue, mountains, of the mainland.

The inner harbour extends from a rock, called the Cornwallis Stone, on the S.E. at Hsia mên chiang （厦门港，A mng kang in the native dialect）, along the N.E. face of the city until it joins a large estuary running some four miles into the island and skirting the northern side of the city, which, consisting of a citadel and a city, lies on a neck of land with one-third of its circuit protected by fortified walls. The city is about eight miles in circumference, including the outer town, and the North eastern environs; it contains about 350,000 inhabitants. The outer town is called in the native dialect A mng kang （厦门港）and is separated from the city by a chain of rocks having a fortified wall along their summit,

① 标题为译者所加，下同。译者注。

a paved pass connecting the two. Rugged and brown hills of barren rock, of from five to seven hundred feet in height skirt the city; and the dwellings and warehouses of the inhabitants are built in the valley.

Amoy was once exceedingly well fortified, as may be seen by the vestiges of batteries on the Islands of Wu su, and Ch'ing su, at the entrance of the outer harbour; on Kulangsu, at Red Point (once mounting 42 guns) , and at the White Fort; and from the strength and magnitude of the long line of sea batteries at A mng kang, 1,100 yards in length, and once mounting 96 guns, yet remaining, though denuded of their guns, and with embrasures, and even walls, fast disappearing under mounds of sand. The citadel, which is about a mile and a third in circumference, commands the inner town, and is surrounded by a turreted wall varying in height from eighteen to thirty-three feet.

What the sea batteries and fortifications once were, may be gathered from Mr. McPherson's description of them at the time of the British attack in 1841. "The defences appeared to be of vast extent and strength; every spot from whence guns could bear on the harbour was occupied and strongly armed. From the point of entrance into the inner harbour, the great sea lines of defence extended in one continued battery of granite upwards of a mile. This battery was faced with turf and mud several feet in thickness, so that at a distance no appearance of a fortification could be traced. The embrasures were roofed and the slabs thickly covered with turf so as to protect the men while working the guns." And he states, that for four hours the ships cannonaded these enormous batteries without a moment's cessation, the *Blenheim* and *Wellesley* alone firing upwards of 12,000 rounds each, and yet that the works were as perfect when they left off as when they began. The troops, however, assaulted and carried the batteries, when they, together with 500 guns, were rendered so far as then possible, unserviceable.

The outer harbour, affords a safe and commodious anchorage for ships windbound, or on the point of departure, but it is too distant for the shipment or discharge of cargo. The inner harbour, is capable of affording secure anchorage, within a short distance of the beach, to about 100 vessels. The hidden dangers, the Coker, Brown. and Harbour rocks, and Kellett spit are marked by five buoys, and the position of other rocks, by stone beacons and perches.

一、总体情况

厦　门

厦门，即厦门港，又称大厦之门、厦港，隶属于福建省，位于北纬24° 28’，东经18° 41’的厦门岛上。厦门岛人口稠密，周长约25英里。厦门仅仅属于三类城市，但是由于港口贸易的重要性，当地驻有道台，管辖兴化府、泉州府和永春州。[①]厦门属泉州府同安县辖区，地处厦门岛西南角的九龙江口，沿江可直通漳州府。海路通道位于被称为“六岛”中的蟳[②]屿和青屿二屿之间的水道（水深11至14英寻[③]）。一进入海湾或者外港，风景就变得如画般引人入胜，两岸连绵重叠着自然天成的灰色和褐色相混杂的大小石山，草木稀疏可见。湛蓝色的天空下，一座宝塔屹立在1,720英尺高的南太武山上，一座破乱不堪的堡垒和一排石头防御工事向右延伸开来。左边也有一座宝塔，这是全岛的至高点。此外还有连绵的群山，再往前就是鼓浪屿和内港。内港就像一颗闪闪发光的宝石，映衬在大陆上绵延不绝的灰色、褐色或是雾蒙蒙的蓝色山脉上。

内港从厦门港（本地话发音为A mng kang）东南面一块叫做天启石[④]（Cornwallis Stone）的地方沿着城市东北面一直延伸到一处深入岛内约四英里远、环绕在城市北侧边缘的大港湾。厦门城建筑在一块瓶颈状的陆地之上，

① 明朝中期设兴泉道，明末废除，康熙九年（1670年）恢复兴泉道，管辖兴化府、泉州府，道治驻泉州府。雍正十二年（1734年），增领永春州，更名兴泉永道，道台驻厦门，道署位于今厦门市思明区魁星岩下。译者注。

② “蟳”字为原著中原字。译者注。

③ 英寻是海洋测量中的深度单位，1英寻等于1.829米。译者注。

④ 即“打石字”，位于今厦门市厦港街道的火仔安，石头上记载着明代天启年间厦门守军打败荷兰人入侵的相关事迹，曾是厦门港的地理坐标。译者注。

由一座堡垒和城区构成，城市外围的三分之一环绕着坚固的城墙，整座城市包括外城和东北郊区，周长总计约 8 英里，居民约 35 万。外城是本地方言中被称为厦门港的地方，人们在一排岩石的顶端修筑了防护墙把外城和里城分隔开来，两城之间由一条人工铺砌的通道相连。高达五百到七百英尺、崎岖不平的褐色石山环绕着城市，居民的住所和仓储设施都建在山谷里。

厦门曾经是铜墙铁壁、固若金汤，从外港入口的浯屿和青屿以及鼓浪屿上的屿仔尾（Red Point）（曾经架设 42 门大炮）、白堡（White Ford）等处的炮台遗迹可见一斑。厦门港长达 1,100 码的海岸炮台曾经架设着 96 门大炮，规模巨大、火力威猛，现在尽管拆除了大炮，但是仍然残留着炮眼甚至护墙，它们很快将被掩埋在沙堆里。方圆约一又三分之一英里的堡垒俯视整个内城，其外墙高达 18 到 33 英尺不等，城墙上筑有塔楼。

我们或许可以根据麦克弗森（McPherson）先生就 1841 年英军进攻厦门时对海岸炮台和防御工事的描述来了解它们曾经的样子：“防御工事似乎规模庞大，火力强盛，港口上每一处可资利用起来的地方都架起了大炮，火力威猛。从外港入口到内港，花岗岩砌成的炮台群所构筑的巨大海防线绵延一英里以上，炮台上方覆盖着几英尺厚的草皮和泥土，所以从远处根本看不到任何防御工事的痕迹。炮眼用石板封顶，上面再覆盖厚厚的草皮以保护炮手。”他还写道：“连续 4 个小时，军舰不停地轰击这些巨型炮台，仅‘伯兰汉号’和‘威里士厘号’就分别发射了 12,000 发炮弹，然而当它们停止炮击后，海岸炮台仍完好无损。尽管如此，步兵还是袭击并占领了这些炮台，这样就可以尽量避免这些炮台以及 500 门大炮发挥作用。”

外港为避风或即将启航的船只提供了一个安全而宽敞的锚地，但对于货物的装卸来说则太远了。内港能够为大约一百艘船只提供离海滩不远的安全锚地。包括长羊礁、定户内礁、港口礁和尾涂礁等在内的危险隐患用了五个浮标加以标示，其他礁石的位置则以石头垒制的灯塔或高台加以标示。

Kulangsu

The rise and fall of the tide, is from 14 to 19 feet. The western boundary of the harbour, is formed by the island of Kulangsu, the channel being 675 to 840 yards wide, This island is about four miles in circumference, has two distinct ridges upon it, and is composed chiefly of granite and disintegrated granite. Its highest point is 280 feet above the sea, and it has detached rocks lying off nearly all its circuit. It is dotted about on all its best sites with handsome houses, the private residences of the Merchants, Missionaries and Officials worth, perhaps, in the aggregate $150,000. It contains four Chinese hamlets, and has an increasing population of probably 4,000 or 5,000 souls.

After the capture of Amoy in 1841, a garrison of detachments from the 18th and 26th regiments, and the Madras Artillery, occupied this island, until it was restored to the Chinese in December, 1845. They were encamped on its northern extremity in a hollow, shut out by high hills from the south west breeze, and facing a large bay, which, at low water, becomes a muddy flat. At one time the mortality amongst the troops from these causes, was so great, that Chinese watchmen were employed to guard the military stores. After the departure of the troops, the houses they had occupied were torn down, the roads they had made cut up, and every vestige of their presence obliterated by the Chinese as far as possible. On the north eastern end of the island are three ancient tombstones, bearing the following inscriptions: "Here lyeth the body of John Duffield, son of Henry Duffield, Commr. of the Trumbull obt. Sept. 6th anno œt. XIII. An. Dom. 1698."

"Here lyeth the body of Capt. Step^{n}. Baker, who was late Comm^{1}. Ofy^{2} *Success*, who departed this life Octob. ye 18th Anno Dom. 1700, aged 49 years."

"Sepultura de Domingo de Pangasinan y otros dos Indios de Filipinas que fallecieron en Octubre año 1759."

A fourth has succumbed to time, and its site only being faintly marked. These graves have in nowise been desecrated by the Chinese, and are in a good state of preservation, with perfectly legible inscriptions, due no doubt to some kindly hand. Itis to be hoped that they will not be suffered to fall into decay. In another spot a monument marks the resting place of a Roman Catholic bishop, and near are the graves of some Spaniards, buried during the early intercourse of Spain with China.

鼓浪屿

潮水的涨落幅度在 14 到 19 英尺之间，港口的西部边界是鼓浪屿，两端隔着一条宽 675 到 840 码的水道。鼓浪屿周长约 4 英里，岛上的两处山脊清晰可见，该岛的主要岩石种类是花岗岩和风化花岗岩。岛上的最高点为海平面以上 280 英尺，环岛沿线各处几乎都散落着一块块大岩石，岛上所有地理位置优越的地方都遍布着漂亮的房子，它们是商人、传教士和官员的私人住宅，总体价值约为 15 万银元。岛上共有 4 个中式村庄，人口不断增长，约有 4,000 或 5,000 人。

1841 年英军攻占厦门以后，由第十八团和第二十六团分遣队组成的守备部队和马德拉斯①（Madras）炮兵部队驻守鼓浪屿，直到 1845 年 12 月才被中国人收复。英军在岛屿最北端的一处山谷里扎营，营地背后的高山把西南风阻隔，前面则是一个大海湾，退潮时海湾变成了一片淤泥滩涂。因此，有一段时间部队的死亡率非常高，不得不雇佣中国籍警卫来守卫军械库。部队撤离后，他们住过的房屋被拆毁，修筑的道路被切断，中国人尽可能将英军存在的每一处痕迹都抹去。在岛屿的东北端有三块古墓碑，上面分别刻着以下铭文：

“特朗布尔号”（Trumbull）船长亨利·杜菲尔德（Henry Duffield）的儿子约翰·杜菲尔德（John Duffield）埋葬于此。卒于西元 1698 年 9 月 6 日。

已故“成功号”（Success）船长斯特普尼·贝克（Step^{n}.Baker）埋葬于此，

① 马德拉斯是印度东南部的港口城市，1996 年改为金奈（Chennai）。马德拉斯省及其军队原为英属东印度公司管辖，1858 年《印度政府组织法》通过后，包括马德拉斯省在内的印度归属英国统治。译者注。

卒于西元 1700 年 10 月 18 日，享年 49 岁。

1759 年 10 月去世的班诗兰省[1]籍多明戈（Domingo）以及另外两名已故的菲律宾籍印度人埋葬于此。

第四块墓地由于年代久远已经无法辨认，它的位置只是隐约地被标记出来。这些坟墓从来都没有被中国人亵渎过，它们保存完好，碑文清晰可辨，毫无疑问是好心的人们不希望它们破烂损坏。在另一处地方，坟墓边的纪念碑表明此处是一位罗马天主教主教的安息地，附近是一些西班牙人的坟墓，埋葬着在西班牙与中国的早期交往中逝去的人们。

① 班诗兰省位于菲律宾北吕宋地区的西南部沿海。译者注。

Amoy （continued）

The centre of the island of Amoy is in lat. 24°30’N. Long. 118°7 E. It is of an irregular oblong square form, intersected on its south west face, by a deep estuary; its greatest length from North to South is somewhat under eight miles; its extreme breadth from east to west is about six and a half miles; and its circumference, measured from point to point, is twenty-five miles. Eight insignificant streams called the Kwei hsing ho（魁星河）,Woong chai‘ho （瓮菜河）, Kwan tao ho（关刀河）, Yen ts‘ao ho（盐草河）, Hsi ma ho（洗马河）, Hwang choo ho（黄厝河）, Kuai chih ho（鬼仔河）, and Hsi pu ho（洗布河）, form its water supply; and it possesses, besides the city of Amoy, one hundred and eight villages and hamlets; the principal of which are Hou cho（后厝）T’sêng cho an（曾厝垵）,Mu hou（墓后）, Tien chien（店前）, Lew pan（刘坂）, Ma chou（麻灶）, Wu hoo（五后）, Fêng shan hsê（凤山社）and Pan wei hsê（坂尾社）. Its population has been variously estimated at from 350,000 to 800,000; but, including that of Amoy city, 550,000 persons will probably be about the correct number.

厦门岛[1]

厦门岛中心位于北纬 24° 30’，东经 118° 7’，岛屿呈不规则长方形，西南面有一处深水港湾贯穿入岛，南北最长距离不到八英里，东西最大宽度约六点五英里，岛的点到点周长是 25 英里。岛上的供水系统来自八条毫不起眼的小溪，分别是：魁星河、瓮菜河、关刀河、盐草河、洗马河、黄厝河、鬼仔河和洗布河。辖区除了厦门城以外，还有 108 个村庄，主要有后厝、曾厝垵、墓后、店前、刘坂、麻灶、五后、凤山社以及坂尾社。根据不同资料的估算，厦门的总人口在 35 万到 80 万之间，不过，包括厦门城在内，总人口可能是 55 万。

[1] 此标题为译者根据内容所拟。原文标题翻译为“厦门（续）”。译者注。

The Climate

The climate, I notice, is described by several writers, and in a recent Blue book, as highly insalubrious. From the personal experience of myself and other residents here, I think this is a mistake, and that, although the length of the summer is trying, the climate is exceedingly healthy, and that from the beginning of November to the end of March, it is equal to any in China. The highest temperature during 1871 in the shade, in the verandah of the Custom House, was 96° Fahr., on the 31st Aug. and the lowest 37° Fahr., on the 13th December, when there was ice half an inch thick on certain spots on the island of Kulangsu. To find ice here is very rare however, for although it is not unfrequently piercingly cold, it seldom freezes. Little rain usually falls, but the past year was exceptionally wet, the heaviest falls were on the 7, 8, 9 and 10th October.

Doctors Müller and Manson in their report on the health of Amoy for the half year ended 30th September 1871, write as follows:

"This part of the province of Fokien is very hilly. The hills are of granite and partly from the want of soil, but principally from the false economy of the people, who cut down nearly every tree and shrub, and grup up the natural grass, they leave a bleak and uninviting appearance. Enormous masses of granite absorb and radiate the heat, storing it up during the day, to return it to the air during the night. Fortunately several large rivers and estuaries intersect the country, and open a road through the hills for the sea breezes and monsoons. These and the great rise and fall of tide facilitate the circulation of air, rendering what would otherwise be a hot and unhealthy country, comparatively mild and salubrious. By the industry of the people every available spot has been brought under cultivation. The alluvial flats along the banks of the rivers and the narrow gorges among the hills, where water can be obtained, are occupied by rice fields, while in the drier soils, sweet potatoes, ground-nuts, sugar cane and a variety of suitable crops are raised.

The rain fall is very capricious. For the most part the climate is dry, frequently several years passing without a sufficiency of rain, famine or great distress is the consequence, and epidemic disease of some form is sure to follow in their train. After three years of drought we have this summer had abundance of rain; and tanks and wells are again filled, after remaining useless or stinking for a long time. The following table will give an idea of the temperature for the summer months, though perhaps it represents a lower range than generally obtains for the season:

Table of Temperature during Six months, April to September. Instruments on a wall facing N.E. on Kulangsu.				
April	Max.82° Fah.	Min.60° Fah.	Aver.69° 7 Fah.	3 days of rainfalls.
May	Max.89° Fah.	Min.67° Fah.	Aver.77° 5 Fah.	13 days of rainfalls.
June	Max.91° Fah.	Min.75° Fah.	Aver.79° 3 Fah.	14 days of rainfalls.
July	Max.82° Fah.	Min.76° Fah.	Aver.83° 3 Fah.	3 days of rainfalls.
August	Max.88° Fah.	Min.78° Fah.	Aver.82° 7 Fah.	11 days of rainfalls.
Sept.	Max.89° Fah.	Min.72° Fah.	Aver.81° 3 Fah.	7 days of rainfalls.

During the other half of the year the climate is much cooler. Then the clear cool air goes far to reinvigorate the victim of the summer heats, outdoor exercise is possible, and the high living usually indulged in by Europeans can be borne with comparative impunity. The people though industrious are poor in the extreme, and their earnings small. From 60 to 100 cash a day for an ordinary labourer, to 120 to 150 cash a day for a mechanic are about the general wages. To support a wife and family on this, must be a hard task even for the most economical. Very little can be saved against the rainy day, and sickness or a rise in the price of rice, must cause incalculable distress. Rice, or a mixture of rice and sweet potatoes, flavoured with pickled vegetables or salt fish, is the staple food; pork and beef are the luxuries of the few. In the country the people are chiefly agricultural: along the coast they employ themselves in fishing and are sailors, occasionally combining these occupations with farming.In Amoy and other large towns, manufactures of various kinds engage large numbers.

Typhus, and typhoid, are not the only fevers whose absence we have remarked. Indeed, with the exception of small pox, we have met with no representative of the class of continued fevers which claims so large a number of victims in Europe. We have never met a case of scarlet fever, measles, or relapsing fever, either here or in "Formosa". Diphtheria, so common in Peking, does not exist, or is very rare, yet other diseases of an epidemic character, such as mumps and whooping cough, are common enough. The petechial fevers are, we think, with the exceptions mentioned, entirely wanting. Considering this, and reflecting on the rarity of the atheromatous and fatty degenerations with the numerous dangerous diseases they entail, one may be at a loss to account for the mortality. When we consider, however, the prevalence of small-pox in a population completely unprotected by vaccination, and learn that almost every one, should he live long enough, is sure to contract the disease, while the mortality from the unmodified form is about one in three, we dispose at once of a part of the difficulty. Then, as second in fatality, we might rank malarial diseases, as remittent fever, ague, diseases of the spleen and liver, anaemia and their consequences. Cholera might come next; then perhaps leprosy. These are the principal causes of death, but ordinary diseases of neither an epidemic nor endemic character are common here as in Europe. Phthisis, bronchitis, pneumonia, cancer, &c., are rife enough.

For Europeans, as they are now housed, the climate cannot be considered unhealthy. Their places of business, and a few of their residences, are situated along the foreshore of the town,—rather a hot locality, but for the most part they have their private houses on Kulangsu. This, a small rocky island quite close to Amoy, affords excellent situations for building. These have been carefully selected by the residents, and houses in every way suitable to the climate built upon them. In the summer they have the full benefit of the strong sea breezes blowing during the greater part of the day, and of the land winds at night. The cold of winter is never so intense as to make their exposed situations uncomfortable. Did the residents display as much wisdom in the furnishing of their tables as they have in the building of their houses, they might live as comfortably here—as far as health is concerned—for eight or ten years, as they could in Europe.

The inevitable sherry and bitters, brandy and soda, and full animal diet indulged in three times a day, combined with want of exercise, and a rather high temperature, induce disease which is hardly climatic, although the victim may call and think it so. All do not err in this way, but most of those who sicken, have indulged in too high living. Those who are temperate and exercise discretion in exposing themselves to the sun and rain keep their health. A little languour by the end of summer, becoming more pronounced, as a rule, the longer one stays here, is perhaps the only climatic disease a sensible man need suffer from."

气候特征

我注意到，在几位作家的笔下以及最近的一本蓝皮书描述中，这里的气候对人们的健康非常不利。从我自己和在此居住的其他居民的个人经历来看，我认为这是错误的。尽管厦门的夏季很长、令人难熬，但是气候却非常有利健康，从 11 月初到 3 月底，此地的气候与中国其他任何地方并无二致。1871 年海关大楼走廊背阴处的最高温度是 8 月 31 日所记录的 96 华氏度，最低温度是 12 月 13 日所记录的 37 华氏度，当时鼓浪屿的一些地方结有半英寸厚的冰。结冰在这里是非常罕见的，虽然这里不乏刺骨之寒，不过极少有冷到结冰的情况。虽然厦门通常只会下小雨，但是去年的降雨量却异常偏大，最大降雨量出现在 10 月 7 日、8 日、9 日和 10 日。

穆勒（Müller）医生和曼森（Mansion）医生在截止日期为 1871 年 9 月 30 日的《厦门半年健康状况报告》中写道：

福建省的这部分地区山势起伏，山体由花岗岩构成。也许是出于对土壤的渴求，但更多是由于人们杀鸡取卵的短视，当地人几乎砍光了所有的乔木和灌木，掘除了天然草地，留下了一副满目荒芜、人见人厌的样子。量多块大的花岗岩石吸收和辐射热量，白天储存起来，晚上再释放到空气中。幸运的是，几条大河和若干港湾在乡间横穿交错，为海风和季风的进入开辟了一条翻山越岭的通道。上述因素再加上潮汐的大幅度涨落促进了空气的循环，使原本因炎热不堪而不利健康的地方变得相对温和舒适。由于人民的辛勤劳作，每一处可资利用的土地都得到了开垦。河边的冲积平地和山间的狭窄峡谷因为临近水源，所以全部开辟出来作为稻田，而在较干旱的土地里则种上红薯、花生、甘蔗以及其他各种适合生长的作物。

厦门的降雨量非常不稳定。大多数情况下，这里气候干燥，经常因为连续几年没有足够的雨水而出现饥荒，给当地人带来巨大的痛苦，随之而来的肯定还有某种疫病的流行。经历了三年的旱灾，今年夏天厦门雨水充沛，水箱和水井在经过长时间闲置或变得发臭以后，又被填满了。下表展示了夏季几个月份气温的大致情况，虽然这些数值有可能低于该季节的正常水平：

4 月至 9 月气温表

（鼓浪屿上东北朝向墙壁上悬挂的仪器测量所得）

4 月	最高 82 华氏度	最低 60 华氏度	平均 69.7 华氏度	降雨 3 天
5 月	最高 89 华氏度	最低 67 华氏度	平均 77.5 华氏度	降雨 13 天
6 月	最高 88 华氏度	最低 75 华氏度	平均 79.3 华氏度	降雨 14 天
7 月	最高 91 华氏度	最低 76 华氏度	平均 83.3 华氏度	降雨 3 天
8 月	最高 88 华氏度	最低 78 华氏度	平均 82.7 华氏度	降雨 11 天
9 月	最高 89 华氏度	最低 72 华氏度	平均 81.3 华氏度	降雨 7 天

在一年的另一半时间里，厦门的气候要凉爽得多。此时，清新凉爽的空气会让备受炎炎夏日煎熬的人们精神焕发起来，并走出户外做做运动，欧洲人也因此能够继续享受奢华的生活。人们虽然勤劳肯干，却极其贫穷。他们收入微薄，普通劳力每天收入 60 到 100 文钱，工匠每天 120 到 150 文钱，一般工钱差不多就是这个标准。靠这点钱养家糊口，即使对最节省的人家来说，也是一项艰巨的任务。人们很难存点钱以备不时之需，即使是一场疾病或是米价上涨也必然会带来无法忍受的痛苦。大米或者大米加红薯，配腌菜或者咸鱼是人们的主要食物，猪肉和牛肉只是少数人的奢侈品。在农村，人们主要从事农业生产；在沿海地区，他们以捕捞为业，讨海为生，个别情况下，也有人既从事渔业又种植庄稼。在厦门和其他大城镇，大量民众从事各种作坊加工业生产。

我们不仅注意到这里没有斑疹伤寒和伤寒这两种发热类疾病，事实上，除了天花之外，我们也还没有遇到过造成欧洲人大规模死亡的那种持续发热的典型疾病。无论在这里还是在台湾，我们从未遇到过猩红热、麻疹或回归热的病例。北京很常见的白喉在这里并不存在，或者说非常罕见。其他流行性疾病，比如腮腺炎和百日咳却很常见。我们认为，除了某些例外情况，这里完全没有脑脊膜炎。正因为这样，同时考虑到动脉粥样硬化和脂肪变性及其并发的多种危险疾病的罕见性，人们可能不知道如何解释这里的高死亡率。然而，当我们考虑到天花会在完全没有接种疫苗的人群中盛行，同时我们也知道几乎每个人，如果他活得足够长的话，肯定会感染这种疾病，那么我们立刻就能够部分理解原始表格[1]中约为三分之一的死亡率这个难题。我们认为排在第二位的致命性疾病是疟疾，因为该病会引起间歇热、寒战、脾肝受损和贫血。接下来可能是霍乱，再然后可能是麻风病，这些疾病是造成死亡的主要原因。像欧洲一样，既不是流行病也不是地方病的普通疾病在这里也很常见。肺结核、支气管炎、肺炎、癌症等疾病都很盛行。

以当地欧洲人现在的居住条件来看，我们就不能说此地的气候有害健康。欧洲人的工作场所和部分住宅位于城里的海滨地带，这些地点相当炎热，但是他们大多数人在鼓浪屿有着自己的私人住宅。这个非常靠近厦门的基岩岛是建房造屋的绝佳地点，岛上居民精心挑选建造地点，房屋的每一个细节都和这个地点的气候特点相适应。在夏季，一天的大部分时间强劲海风吹向陆地，到了晚上，风则从陆地吹向海上，他们都能够充分享受这种清爽。冬季的天气从来不会冷到让待在室外的人们感到不舒服。如果居民们在三餐饮食时表现出和他们建造房屋时一样多的智慧，他们可能会如同住在欧洲一样，在这里健健康康、舒舒服服地待上个十年八年。

可是，他们的生活少不了雪利酒和苦味酒、白兰地和苏打水，以及一日

[1] 此处所说的表格推测为穆勒医生和曼森医生在截止日期为 1871 年 9 月 30 日的《厦门半年健康状况报告》中所附的表格，本书作者并未引用。译者注。

三餐的全肉类食物，加上缺乏锻炼和高温天气，这些因素所诱发的疾病几乎与气候无关，但患者往往归咎于此。当然，不是所有的患者都会犯下这种错误，但是大多数病人却是因为过度沉溺于奢华生活而病倒的。那些生活有度、尽量避免日晒雨淋的人们总能保持健康。到了夏末，通常人们待在这里的时间越长，就越会有倦怠的感觉，这也许是一个理智的人唯一需要忍受的与气候有关的不适了。

People

The characteristics of the people have by some been described to be boldness, pride, and generosity; and by others, to be quarrelsomeness, rudeness, and intense dishonesty. My own experience of them is that they differ but little from their fellow countrymen generally. I have ever found them civil, industrious and, according to the Chinese standard, honest; they are certainly keen in pursuit of the dollar, and sight that coin from afar, leading up to it with unerring accuracy. They are shrewd traders, bold and fearless fishermen, good sailors, and they emigrate freely; tens of thousands going annually to Manila, Singapore, Penang and elsewhere. Most of the Chinese in Java, Siam, and the Straits Settlements, are Amoy, or Fohkien men, and, in proof of their character for energy and ambition, I have somewhere read that, during the last century, a Fuhkien man ascended the throne of Siam. In appearance they are middle sized, and well built, strong, active and hardy, and they endure the extremes of temperature with, apparently, no discomfort.

当地百姓

有些人把当地百姓的性格特征描述为勇敢、自尊和慷慨，另一些人则认为他们喜欢争吵、粗鲁无礼，而且阴险狡诈。我的亲身体验是，当地人与他们的同胞大体上没有多大不同。我发现他们彬彬有礼、勤劳肯干，并且按照中国的标准，他们是诚实正直的。他们当然热衷于追逐钱财，甚至达到了见钱眼开的地步。他们是头脑精明的商人、勇敢无畏的渔夫、技术娴熟的水手。他们可以自由地移居海外：每年都有成千上万人前往马尼拉、新加坡、槟榔屿和其他地方；爪哇、暹罗和海峡定居点的中国人多数都是厦门人或福建人。我在某本书里看过，为了证明自己的能力和抱负，上个世纪有个福建人登上了暹罗的王位。从外表上看，他们中等身材，体格健壮，意志坚定，积极活跃并且吃苦耐劳，他们能忍受极端天气而不会感到明显的不适。

Antiquities

Amongst the still existing antiquities in this neighbourhood, there are, so far as I am aware, but few anterior to the present dynasty, if inscriptions on rocks, temples, memorial arches, and graves be excepted. Many of these inscriptions, date from the Mongol, and some from the Southern Sung, dynasty. On the island of Amoy, on the Chin-pang-shan（金榜山）, are inscribed on the rock （金榜石） from which the hill takes its name. The following characters （谈立石）, which are said to have been written by the celebrated Confuciancommentator, Chu-hsi （朱熹）. Belonging to the present dynasty are several inscriptions of some historical importance. In front of the Nan-pu-tó（南普陀）, a Buddhistic temple of great beauty, though falling into decay, at Hsia mên chiang, are a series of large stone tablets, on which is engraved in Chinese and Manchu, an account of the subjugation of the Pescadores. Near here on the Ching nan kuan（镇南关）, road is also a tablet containing some account of the expulsion of the Dutch from "Formosa" by Coxinga. A large grave on the same road, ornamented with stone figures of men and horses, as of a high military official, is that of a cousin of Coxinga; and a yet more elaborate tomb of the same description, on the road from Tung-an to Chin-chew between Ta ying （大营） and Wuling（武陵） is the final abode of one of Koxinga's uncles.

Scattered over the island are some sixteen Joss-houses, several of which possess considerable beauty, particularly the already mentioned Nan pu to. This building contains some charming octagon shaped temples of stone, covered with carvings of most delicate tracery and exquisite finish. The Tiger's Mouth, the Hsin tung yén, or Grotto of the Hill fairies, the Temple of Ten thousand rocks, and the White stag temple, which is said to be the oldest here, are all noteworthy as fine, well preserved temples, nestling in picturesque Banyan shaded nooks far up the rocky hills. Tung lai yén, another temple, bases what claim it has to celebrity, on a hazy story of an Emperor of the Tung dynasty, having drank at a pool in its close vicinity. Many of the inscriptions in these temples enjoin the reader in phrases such as the following: "Live well and die happy" "The chief aim of life should be the practice of virtue" &c., all highly moral sentiments, and no doubt very improving to the artless beings to whom they are addressed.

During the cool season these temples are a favourite resort of the Barbarian for the performance of his rife of the picnic: here in the courts of Buddha, amidst the images of Wu Jai shen, the scowling god of Thunder, Kuan yin, the goddess of Mercy, or the simpering Tien how, empress of heaven, appear the long table and gay guests looking so incongruous and out of harmony with all their surroundings, except, perhaps, with the effigy of jovial old Buddha, himself, who, in easy sitting posture, with vinous leer and ample stomach, looks, as I have sometimes thought, no unfitting presiding deity: the effect may be somewhat marred by his ears hanging down to his shoulders and his toes being as long as his fingers, but who has not seen other presiding deities who have, or ought to have, very long ears. It is only in the direction in which they grow that his are singular.

历史古迹

据我所知，这一带现存的历史古迹中，除了碑文、寺庙、牌坊和坟墓外，几乎没有其他早于本朝的文物了。很多碑文的年代可以追溯到元朝，也有一些是南宋的。厦门岛的金榜山，因为山上的一块石头上刻有“金榜石”而得名，而“谈立石”三个字相传是由著名的儒学家朱熹书写的。有几块本朝的文碑具有一定的历史意义，在那座虽已破败但风景秀美的佛教寺庙——南普陀寺前面的厦门港（Hsia men chiang）一带有一排大石碑，碑上用汉语和满语镌刻着征服澎湖列岛纪事。距离此处不远的镇南关路上也有一块石碑，上面记载了郑成功把荷兰人逐出台湾的事迹。这条路上还有一座大坟墓，墓区排列着与高级将领墓葬规格一样的石人石马，墓主是郑成功的同族兄弟。从同安往泉州的路上，在大营（Ta ying）和五陵（Wuling）之间有另一座同等样式的坟墓，但是比前者要精巧多了，这是郑成功一位叔叔的最后安息地。

岛上各处散布着约 16 座寺庙，其中几座相当漂亮，特别是刚才提到的南普陀寺，寺里筑有几座让人叹为观止的八角形石殿，大殿的顶部是经过细腻抛光处理而显得精美无比的雕花石饰。虎溪岩、仙洞岩、万石岩寺以及据说是此地最古老的白鹿洞寺，都是值得关注的风景优美、保存完好的寺庙，它们都坐落于岩石山顶、掩蔽在风景如画的榕树树荫里。另一座名为“董内岩”[1]的佛寺，相传因唐朝（原文如此，据上注应为“宋朝”）的一位皇帝曾经饮过该佛寺旁边一处水池里的水而出名。这些寺庙中的许多碑文向读者宣扬诸如“乐生而善终”“行善积德”之类具有高度道德情感的信条。毫无疑问，

[1] 即“紫竹林寺”，旧称“宝山岩”，俗称“董内岩”。据薛起凤等《鹭江志》：“宝山岩中建寺，有泉名圣泉，相传宋幼主掬饮之。”译者注。

这些碑文会使站在石碑前面的那些天真淳朴的人获益良多。

在凉爽的季节里，这些寺庙是乡野粗人野餐聚会最喜欢去的地方。就在佛殿里，身处于怒目而视的雷神、大慈大悲的观音，或者带着淳朴笑容的天后塑像之中，摆好的长桌子旁边围着一群充满欢乐的客人，也许除了笑容可掬的弥勒佛像之外，此情此景显得与周围的一切那么格格不入、互不协调。弥勒佛带着醉人的斜睨，挺着大肚子舒舒服服地坐着，正如我有时所想的那样，弥勒佛看上去完全无愧于主宰一方的神明之尊，只是这种效果可能会因为他的耳朵垂到肩膀上，他的脚趾和他的手指一样长而稍有受损，可是谁没见过长着或者应该长着长耳朵的主宰神明呢，只不过因为弥勒佛耳朵垂下来的方向才使其独一无二吧。

Aids to Navigation

Premising that Chapel Island Lighthouse and buildings, were erected by Captain Bisbee, Divisional Inspector, and myself, by order of the Inspector General of Customs, and the Light exhibited for the first time on the 16th November 1871, I, on the following page, annex a List of aids to Navigation in the Amoy district.①

① 表格略。译者注。

助航设施

东椗岛（Chapel Island，又译“教堂岛”）灯塔及其相关建筑物是由比斯比（Bisbee）船长、分区督察和我本人承海关总税务司之命建造的，灯塔的灯光于 1871 年 11 月 16 日首次点亮。以下将附上一份厦门地区的助航设施一览表[1]。

①表格略。译者注。

2.Agriculture

Productions

Its surface is very uneven, huge and fantastic boulders frequently cropping out of the earth; and bluffs, hills, and brown arid granite mountains abounding. All the valleys are most carefully cultivated, indeed no spot capable of production is wasted, and cultivation is carried, terrace above terrace, far up the sides of the rugged mountains; or if there be a natural ledge a few feet long and broad, its poor soil of sandy earth and disintegrated granite, will surely be found to be planted with sweet potatoes. Rice, wheat, barley, maize, sugar cane, groundnut, beans, peas, sweet potatoes, yams, cabbages, turnips, onions, carrots, radishes, lettuce, melons and other vegetables are tended with the greatest care; not a weed is to be seen, and the system of manuring with human ordure （for which there is a regular market, and market day here） is to judge by results as perfect, as it is offensive to the nose. Pomeloes, pineapples, mangoes, oranges, grapes, bananas, limes, arbutus, plums, peaches, lichies, lungngans, pears, persimmons and other fruits are cultivated here and in the surrounding districts.

二、农业情况

农产品

厦门岛的地表凹凸不平，巨石嶙峋，峭壁、山冈和草木稀疏的褐色花岗岩山体随处可见。所有的山谷低地都精耕细种，事实上，可以说当地人没有浪费任何一寸可耕地，他们沿着陡峭山坡层层向上开垦梯田种植庄稼，甚至在岩石凸出部几英尺见方的贫瘠沙地和风化石头上也必定种上红薯。稻米、小麦、大麦、玉米、甘蔗、花生、豆荚、豌豆、红薯、山药、卷心菜、芜菁、洋葱、胡萝卜、萝卜、莴苣、瓜类和其他蔬菜都得到悉心栽培，一根杂草都不见。以人类粪便作为肥料虽然刺鼻难闻，但是效果特别好，为此这里还开设固定市场，设定圩日从事人粪买卖。此地以及周边地区还栽种柚子、菠萝、芒果、芦柑、葡萄、香蕉、酸橙、杨梅、李子、桃子、荔枝、龙眼、梨子、柿子以及其他水果。

Agricultural Implements

The agricultural implements are few and rude, a strong hoeshaped pick serves as a spade; an iron sharepoint, attached to a rough piece of bent wood, without colter or wheel, and drawn by a pretty little Amoy cow or bullock, and not by an ass and two women as I have seen at Peking, serves as a plough; and a large tub, against the edge of which the stalk of the cereal is beaten, with a mat screen to keep off the wind, takes the place of the flail or threshing machine. The winnowing apparatus, where one is used, is on the same principle and not unlike in form, that in use in England some twenty years ago. Notwithstanding these rude implements, the appearance of the crops and land, and the absence of waste of space or material, denotes excellent agriculture, such as would gladden the heart of Mr. Mechi, or any other scientific farmer. Grain is not cut but pulled up by the roots.

农　具

农具种类稀少而且简陋。结实的扁嘴镐头被当作铁锹使用。耕田的方法是在铁铧上绑着一段粗制的弯曲木头，不用马拉也没有轮子，而是直接由一头俊俏的厦门本地母牛或公牛拉着，这种情况不像我在北京看到的两名妇女驱使一头驴的样子。打谷的工具是一个大桶，把谷物的茎干放在谷桶的边缘拍打，再装上一个筛网挡风，以此代替连枷或打谷机。使用的扬谷设备同英格兰大约二十年前使用的机器原理相同，不过形状却各异。尽管工具简陋，但是从庄稼的外观和土地的样貌，以及当地人惜土如金、物尽其用等方面来看，厦门的农业都是一种会让梅奇先生（Mr. Mechi）[①] 或者任何其他崇尚科学种田的农民兴奋不已的优质农业。此外，谷物并非用刀收割，而是连根拔起。

① 指约翰·约瑟夫·梅奇（John Joseph Mechi，1802–1880），英国发明家、银行家和银匠，曾经改进农田水利方法。译者注。

Farm Stocks

The farm stock consists of very small and beautifully shaped cows and bullocks, hideous water buffaloes, pigs and goats, geese, ducks, and fowls, and, created by a local want of the foreigner, on Kulangsu, &c. a fine breed of turkeys, which however are not indigenous, but were imported from Manila. The Amoy horse is a very small, and handsome pony, it is never used for agricultural purposes.

家畜家禽

家畜的种类包括个头小巧、体态优美的母牛和公牛，丑陋的水牛，猪和山羊。家禽有鹅、鸭和鸡。为了满足鼓浪屿等地外国侨民的需求，当地还从马尼拉引进品种优良的火鸡进行饲养，以弥补本地所缺。厦门马是一种体型小巧，漂亮、健美的矮种马，这种马从不用于农业生产。

Irrigations

Irrigation is carefully attended to where streams are absent, wells are sunk, and a simple contrivance, an upright post, crossed see saw fashion by a long bamboo, with another at right angles, a bucket at one end and a heavy stone at the other, enables a single man to rapidly fill the little artificial channels leading to his rice or other field. If the water is to be conveyed up from a stream over the high embankment, wherewith the thrifty agriculturist has reclaimed his rich land from the river, an equally simple, efficacious and inexpensive wooden chain pump, fitted upon two cylinders and worked by one, two or three men, is used.

灌溉情况

当地人精心设计灌溉系统。他们在远离河流的地方打水井，先是竖起一根长长的竹竿作为支柱，与另一根竹竿横向交叉成直角，然后利用跷跷板原理，让竹竿的一端吊着水桶，另一端吊着大石头。有了这种简单巧妙的装置，即使一个人也能独自快速灌满一条通向稻田或其他田地的小型人工沟渠。如果需要把河水引上高处堤岸以灌溉岸边这片勤俭的农民可资开垦的沃土，他们就制作一个同样简单、有效和廉价的木制链式水泵，装上两个圆筒，这样一个、两个或三个成年男子都可以操作使用。

3.Regions

Chang chou fu

Proceeding from Amoy by water in a South westerly direction, past Pagoda Island, topped with a crumbling ruin, that gives it its name, and entering a passage formed by the mainland and a small island, a view, equal to some in the Highlands of Scotland is disclosed. It is a large oblong bay, perhaps six miles long, by four broad, whose margin is fringed with thriving and pretty looking villages embowered in fine trees, and whose boundaries are highly cultivated plains, most of which have been reclaimed from the river, stretching to the base of blue and grey mountains. In the season this bay abounds with geese, teal, widgeon, ducks of almost every description, pelicans, herons and other wild fowl. It is the favourite shooting ground of the sportsmen of Amoy. Into this bay are discharged two branches of the Dragon river, and the North river. Following the course of the Chang chou river for about three miles, a large walled town called Hai têng hsien（海澄县）, is reached, and two miles further on, a second, larger, and more busy, more prosperous town or city, called in the local dialect Chioh bei （石码 Shih ma）, which is densely populated ashore and afloat, and maintains a large and brisk foreign and native trade, with Amoy.

Winding through a charming, thriving and well populated country, rich in corn, rice, and sugar cane, and in hill and plain, for ten miles further, the city of Chang chou fu is reached.

The prefecture of Chang chou fu(漳州府), contains seven districts or Hsiens, namely Lung chi（龙溪县）, Chang pu（漳浦县）, Hai têng（海澄县）, Ping ho（平和县）, Chao an（诏安县）, Chang tai（长泰县）, and Nan ching（南靖县）.

Its chief city Chang chou, is in lat. 24°31’12 N. and long. 117°59 E. of Greenwich, or 1°24’ E. of Peking. It is approached by several broad and well made, partially paved roads, and by a bridge some 750 feet long, built upon 25 piers about 30 feet apart, and 25 feet in height; pieces of heavy timber stretch from one abutment to another, and are again crossed by smaller pieces, which are covered with earth and paved with brick and stone: some of these stones are over 40 feet long.

The entire structure is of the rudest description, and at either extremity there are hucksters' shops extending, perhaps, one-fourth of the length of the bridge.

Chang chou fu, following the course of the river, is distant 24½ miles due west from Amoy, and is situated upon the banks of the Lung or Dragon river. It must have been a very fine city, it is walled, and is described as having been well built, and its streets paved with granite, some of the slabs being twelve feet wide. It is now a picture of the abomination of desolation: literally a heap of bricks and charred ruins. When the city fell into the hands of the Chang mao rebels in 1864, from 200,000, to 250,000, persons, are said to have perished by the sword, or from disease: and some $20,000,000 worth of coin and property, to have been the spoils of the rebels. It was vacated by them in May 1865, and during the succeeding seven years, sufficient energy has been found to repair or rebuild, one long straggling street along the river front of the city. The surrounding scenery, as in many other spots in this district, is really beautiful. It is thus aptly described by Mr. Lourie in the *Chinese Repository* Vol x1 p. 506:

"Imagine an amphitheatre 30 miles in length and 20 in breadth, hemmed in on all sides by bare, pointed hills, a river running through it, and an immense city at our feet, with fields of rice, and sugar cane, noble trees, and numerous villages, stretching away in every direction. It was grand and beautiful beyond every conception we had formed of Chinese scenery. Beneath us lay the city, its shape nearly square, curving a little on the river's banks, closely built, and having an amazing number of very large trees within and around. The guide said that in the last dynasty, it had numbered 700,000 inhabitants, and now he thought it contained a million, probably a large allowance. The villages around also attracted our attention. I tried to enumerate them, but after counting twenty-nine of large size, distinctly visible in less than half the field before us, I gave over the attempt. It is certainly within the mark to say that within the circuit of this immense plain, there are at least one hundred villages, some of them small, but many numbering hundreds and even thousands of inhabitants."

This city was, prior to its capture, famous for its sugar, and sugar candy, manufactures, tea, silk, velvet, silk and cotton manufactures, and iron manufacture; and was the richest and most important in this vicinity.

Itis the residence of a Taotai, Prefect, the Magistrate of Lung Chi（龙溪县）, a Chen-t‘ai or General, a Colonel, and other military mandarins. On the north, and northeast, is the district of Chang-t’ai（长泰）, Tiohto‘a, locally, in which exists coal in undeveloped abundance. The specimens seen are very poor. This is no doubt owing to the fact that the people are allowed only to use what may be easily procured on the surface; and are not permitted to open mines. Quantities are brought down in baskets to Chioh-bei（石码）Shib-ma for sale, and are purchased by native blacksmiths.

To the northwest, is the district of Nan-ching. The district of Hai-téng, is between Lung-chi and the sea, and its chief city stands upon an island. Nearest to Chang-t‘ai on the coast, is the district of Chang-pu, next to Yune siau, while Chao an, lies to the extreme south. North of the last named district, is that of Pingho.

The prefecture of Chang-chou, constitutes the southern portion of the province of Fuhkien, and is of a triangular shape, having the departments of Ting-chou（汀州）, Lung Yen（龙岩）, and Chuan-chou（泉州）, for the northern line, the sea coast for the southern, and the department of Chao-chou-fu（潮州府）, in Kwang-tung, for the western. The line of coast stretches from Namoh（南澳）, to Amoy.

Chiang tang bridge

In the district of Lung-chi, is one of the curiosities of this neighbourhood; it is the Chiang-tung-chiao（江东桥）, or Polam bridge（浦南桥）. This bridge is distant nineteen and a half miles from Amoy; through it must come all the Teas destined for the Amoy market. It is very picturesquely situated at a sharp angle of the North River, where it turns into a savage, rocky, gorge, with seemingly, no outlet. The approach to it is for miles charming. Rich alluvial plains, bright with young paddy, wheat, and sugar cane, dotted about with numerous large, prosperous-looking villages, set generally in clumps of venerable banyan trees, greet the eye on every side, and in the distance the plains swell up, with easy sweep, to the base of a chain of fantastic and many-hued mountains.

The bridge is 354 paces long, by 6 broad, and has a small building on its centre, it is built of stone on 20 buttresses; three grouped together to form two small arches, while the fourth is placed at nearly treble the distance, and forms an arch of good span; these buttresses are spanned by huge blocks of roughly hewn granite, mostly from 54 feet to 66 feet long, and from 3 to 6 feet thick. The largest block, from a rough measurement, we calculated to weigh 80 tons. By what means these enormous stones, were got into their position, it is difficult to imagine. Although they are polished with the footsteps of seven centuries, much of their original inequalities yet remain. The ends of the arkshaped buttresses, are being forced upwards by the enormous weight resting on their centres, and two huge cross blocks of stone, have already slipped from off one of their end supports into the water.

The bridge was once defended at its southern end, by a well built stone battery, and by a circular stone fort, on the top of a steep bluff some 350 feet high, covered at its base with handsome copperbeech, banyan, lung-ngan, and other trees, festooned, here and there, with gorgeous red hued creepers. No guns are now in these fortifications. It is the station of a small military mandarin, and of a taxing establishment, at either end there are a few wretched shops and houses. On the occasion of the visit of myself and party, the inhabitants, both male and female, told us, with much gesticulation, that large tigers frequently crossed the bridge at night, perhaps as often as 40 or 50 times a year; that one carried off a dog two nights before from the house against which we were standing, and also that a short time previously, a man had been killed near there, and they urgently begged us to come and shoot them, offering the use of a small temple, and to tether a young goat near it, to attract the tigers by its bleating.

They also stated that there are wild pigs in the adjacent mountains.

Polam

Ten miles beyond this bridge, is the town of Polam, which is under the jurisdiction of the magistrate of Chiang-tung-ss'u（江东司）, and is the residence of a military mandarin.

The number of its inhabitants, is estimated to be from two to three thousand. Its principal articles of trade, are those produced in the neighbourhood, and surrounding districts, namely: tea, sugar, paper, oranges, and pomeloes; the two latter are celebrated for a peculiarly delicious flavour, and form one of the articles of tribute sent hence, annually, to the throne. Before its capture by the rebels, this place was said to contain a population of about 10,000 inhabitants. It is now in ruins, and its formerly fine warehouses, have never been rebuilt. The greater part of the place is still desolate and uninhabited.

Twenty-five miles distant from Polam, is the commencement of the Tea district. No less than seventy rapids have to be ascended in this region, and the richly wooded highland scenery, has been described to me as beautiful in the extreme. I have not yet had an opportunity of exploring this part of the country, but when I do so, it will form the subject of another paper.

The following interesting account of the Prefecture of Chang chou, has been kindly furnished me by the Rev. John Macgowan.

"The region embraced under this name was known to exist as far back as the time of the Hea dynasty (B.C. 2169-1756.) At that period it was a wild uncultivated district, inhabited mainly by the natives of the country, who, like the aborigines of 'Formosa', were altogether uncivilised, and who maintained themselves by the chase. Very few of the Chinese had penetrated thus far, and we may presume they were the more daring and adventurous spirits of the age, who acting as pioneers had pushed their way into the wild and unexplored regions that lay to the South.

The history of these early times is necessarily of the vaguest possible character. The accounts of them are scanty, and, moreover, mixed up with so much that is fabulous, that we cannot rely upon them very much for giving us an insight into the state of things then existing, or of the process by which the country finally became cleared. All we know for certain is that the Chinese, for century after century, continued to spread themselves further and further Southwards, driving the aborigines before them, till, at the commencement of the Tsin dynasty (B.C. 243-201), we find them occupying the district of Chang chou. At this time vast numbers of the natives had retired further South and West, whilst a good number of them had submitted to their conquerors, and were quietly adopting their manners and customs. Mandarins were appointed by imperial authority, so that this region became, to all intents and purposes, a portion of the kingdom of Tsin. Matters continued in this state until the time of Woo te, (B.C. 81) of the western Han dynasty, when a change in the mode of government took place. The people of Chang chou region, like most people inhabiting a frontier country, were of a turbulent and independent character. The fierce conflicts in which they were continually involved with the original inhabitants, had necessarily developed a spirit within them, that made them very unwilling to submit to the control of the law. The region, moreover, was nothing like it is now. Many parts were still uncleared. Very little comparatively had been done to develop the resources of the country. The soil was considered poor and unfruitful, and the country instead of producing the rich harvests that now sustain millions of people, was so poorly cultivated, that the vast resources that lay dormant within it, had not yet even been suspected. In consequence of the character of the people, whom it was found almost impossible to restrain, and of the fact that the revenue to be derived from the district was almost nothing, Woo te determined to relinquish the direct government of it by himself. He consequently selected a man belonging to one of the principal families in the district, and appointed him Prince, giving him the provinces of Fohkien, and Canton, as the territory over which he was to reign. He allowed him the fullest control within his dominions, and excepting that he was obliged to pay tribute to the Emperor, as his liege lord, he was to all intents and purposes an independent sovereign.

The Prince thus appointed, proved before long to be an ambitious, and unscrupulous character. Before many years had elapsed, he had not only determined to ignore the allegiance he had promised the Emperor, but he had also formed a bold scheme for invading his dominions, in order, if possible, to gain possession of his kingdom. The Emperor when he became aware of his designs, assembled an army, and having utterly routed the forces of his antagonist, carried off by main force no less than six tenths of the inhabitants of the whole district. These he distributed, in various directions, throughout his own dominions. He was prompted to this act, by the utterly unruly character of the inhabitants, and because he deemed that nothing but an utter depopulation of the country, would secure the safety of his own dominions. Those of the inhabitants who had escaped this wholesale seizure, had taken refuge amid the hills, and forests, where the soldiers of Woo te, could not follow them. After the departure of the invading forces, the people ventured out from their hiding places, and gathered once more around their former homes. Little indeed was now left them. Their houses had been burned, their property had been either plundered or destroyed, and their friends and kindred, had been ruthlessly carried off, without the remotest hope that they should ever see them again. The destruction had been very thorough and complete. The Imperialists, indeed, were under the impression that they had cleared the whole region of inhabitants, for they relinquished the government of it, and abandoned it to the care of itself for the future. The miserable remnant that had escaped, being unmolested from without, began again to grow and flourish. During the two succeeding dynasties, viz. the Eastern Han (A. D. 30-226), and the later Han (A. D. 226- 260), we have very few authentic details concerning them. Whatever rulers they may have had must have been of their own election, for none of the sovereigns of the above two dynasties, claimed allegiance from them in any respect.

At the beginning of the Western Tsin dynasty (A. D. 260-313), the place had grown so much in importance, and the inhabitants had become so numerous, that it was deemed valuable enough to be once more annexed to the empire. It was accordingly taken possession of by the emperor, who delegated suitable men to take charge of its government. During this, and the succeeding, dynasty, the country remained in quiet submission to the supreme authority: nothing of any special note occurred, sufficient to attract the notice of the historian: for we have no record beyond the simple statements regarding its internal regulations, which are of no interest to the general reader.

At the commencement of the Tang dynasty, (A.D. 622-897) we find the whole region involved in civil war. This was waged between the purely Chinese inhabitants, and the civilized natives of the country. The war continued for upwards of thirty years, with varying success, but in the end, the Chinese were beginning to find themselves unable to cope with their half civilized antagonists. In this emergency they prayed the emperor Tae tsung (A. D. 654), to appoint a wise and powerful mandarin, who would have authority to put an end to the intestine struggle going on, and who would be able, by his wise measures, to restore peace and tranquillity to the country. The Emperor consented and nominated Chèn chêng (陈政) to be a Prince, with the same powers, and under the same conditions, that governed the appointment of the first Prince during the Han dynasty. The man appointed, proved to be one of great wisdom and firmness. The civil war was put an end to, and the internal resources of the country, under his wise management, were gradually developed. He gained such a strong hold upon the affections of the people, that the supreme government seemed by right to be securely vested in his family. For a period of three hundred years, his descendants ruled as Princes in the country. At the end of that time their incapacity, and their corruption, became so marked, that the people chose a prince from another family. From the time that this change occurred, there began to be dissensions in the state. Political parties gradually arose in the country. The most powerful families, naturally, thought that they had as much right to rule, as the one that had lately been selected. The consequence. of all this was that the minds of men were exceedingly unsettled, and the aspect of affairs was anything but satisfactory.

Chên hung chin（陈洪进）, who happened to be Prince at the beginning of the Sung dynasty (A. D. 950-967), seeing that a struggle was inevitable, and that he would have to succumb before the various powerful parties that were aiming at dominion, placed his territories at the disposal of the Chinese emperor. He proposed that they should no longer be held independently of the empire, but that they should come under its direct government. The proposition was accepted by the emperor, and Chên hung chin was reinstated in his authority, with powers very similar to those of a Governor General. At once peace was restored to the country. The various parties, seeing that they would now have to cope with the whole force of the empire, silently melted away, and during the next two dynasties, no serious event marks the history of this region. After it came under the control of the Sung dynasty, the present city, which up to that time had been an open town, was surrounded with a mud wall, four li in circumference. One hundred and fifty years after, the mud walls, which had fallen into serious decay, were replaced by stone ones, which for purposes of defence and general utility, must have been a vast improvement upon the old ones.

Nothing eventful occurred in the history of Chang-chou till the beginning of the present dynasty (A. D.1643). At that time Amoy, and the surrounding districts, were held by Koxinga, who was in open rebellion against the rulers of the new dynasty. In the 12th year of Shun che (1655), Koxinga attacked Chang-chou, and took it with the greatest ease. He was not destined, however, to keep it long. Hearing that large bodies of troops were on their way from Foochow, for the purpose of attacking him, and knowing that he was in no condition to withstand them, he demolished the city walls, and, it is said, carried the stones of which they were built, and threw them into the sea. The Imperalists rebuilt the walls again next year, but on a much larger scale than previously, Formerly they had a circumference of only four li, now they extended to between nine and ten li. Twelve years after, it was again besieged by Koxinga, who, however, was unable to make any impression on the place. The early soldiers of this dynasty, have the reputation of having been exceedingly skilful in repelling attacks upon their walled towns. The ability with which they successfully defended two or three places in the Chang-chou prefecture, would seem to prove that their reputation on this point, was well deserved. It is said that, during this last siege, no fewer than 700,000 persons, died of starvation within the city. I fancy that these numbers are greatly exaggerated. Still they imply that there must have been an unprecedented degree of distress and mortality, to have given rise to such a statement.

Again the tide of history rolls on till 1864, when the prosperity of Chang-chou, again received a sudden shock, from the capture of the city by the long haired rebels. During their occupation of it, they seem to have been filled with a spirit of destruction. Temples, public buildings, and official residences, were the first to feel the effect of their presence. Large portions of the town were reduced to ruins. The population, which was reckoned at 400,000, was scattered in every direction. Immense numbers of them were murdered, and the whole business of the place was completely paralysed. It will be long before the town will recover its old prosperity. Even now (1872) it is in many places a vast heap of ruins, The former inhabitants have either been killed, or they have been so impoverished, that they have not the means of rebuilding. It is only in the more business quarters, that there is any sign of a return to the state of things that existed before its capture by the rebels.

Size.—In reference to the size of the Chang-chou prefecture, it is difficult to speak with extreme accuracy. I should say, that it is about 70 miles in length, and 240 miles in circumference. Very much of this area, however, is unavailable for the cultivation of the cereals. It is intersected in every direction, by ranges of hills, some of them rising to a considerable height. Many of these are exceedingly barren, and are comparatively of little value to their owners, others, again, are covered with trees, which are specially cultivated, with the object of being cut down for firewood, to be sold throughout the prefecture. In this latter case, the hills are a very fruitful source of gain to great numbers of the population.

Products.—The people of this prefecture, seem, on the whole, to be much better off than those outside of it. In the neighbouring prefecture of Chinchew, the people are much poorer, and seem to have a harder struggle for life, than their more favoured neighbours. This is owing, no doubt, to the fact that the Chang-chou region, is an exceedingly productive one. Most of the most important articles of general consumption, are produced in it, and the revenue derived from their sale, brings in wealth to vast numbers of the community. Its chief products, are as follows: rice, wheat, tea, sugar, oil, ginger, honey, hemp, tobacco, paper, varnish, dyestuffs, camphor, timber, charcoal. The fruits are very abundant, viz: laichi, dragon's eye, oranges, melons, plantains, persimmons, peaches, pears, olives, dates, grapes, mulberries, pomeloes, pomegranates, &c.

Population.—The population of the entire district, is estimated at between three and four millions.

Antiquities.—In the prefecture of Chang-chou, there are scarcely antiquities of value. Indeed, it is a remarkable feature in the Chinese empire, that so few remains of the past, exist. There seems to have been no care taken to preserve anything that would have explained the customs of the past, or that would have served to illustrate any peculiar fact, or feature, of their remote history. In Chang-chou, we seem to have absolutely no relics of anything in existence before the time of the Sung dynasty, and those that do remain, have escaped the general decay, simply because they were essential to the general community, and, therefore, must be preserved. I refer to their cities, and bridges. Anything that the public could get along without, has been allowed to fall into ruin, and decay. Wherever the conservation of anything interesting, or curious, has been left to private enterprise, the result has been most disastrous. The only relic in the prefecture, really worth mentioning is the very fine bridge called the Chiang-tung-chiao, or Polam bridge, which spans the North River. The point at which this bridge has been built, is an exceedingly beautiful one. It is a kind of gorge, through which the river finds its exit from the great Chang-chou plain, on the opposite side of the hills. The hills at this place, rise very high on both sides of the river, which, of course, add much to the grandeur of the scene. As there are no villages, and no inhabitants, in the immediate vicinity, the scene around the bridge is one of quiet beauty.

The first notice that we have of any bridge at this place, is at the beginning of the Sung dynasty. In the year 1190, a floating bridge was erected, which did service for 35 years, when it was replaced by a permanent wooden one. This was burnt down in the year 1265, that is 30 years after its erection. The prefect of Chang-chou headed a subscription list with five hundred thousand cash, in order to the building of a stone one. The requisite funds having been subscribed, a stone bridge was built. It was 2,000 feet long, and the distance between each of the piers, 80 feet, Chinese measurement. With very slight repairs this lasted for 300 years, when it had to undergo a thorough repairing in the year 1565. In 1590 a stone railing was built along each side of it. Two archways were also built, one at each end of the bridge. On the western one were inscribed four characters（三省通衢）, 'a public road for the three Provinces'. In the great rebellion under Koksenga, this bridge suffered very severely. In order to cut off the advance of the Imperial troops, the bridge was destroyed in four places. This happened in 1673. Soon after it was rebuilt of wood, but in 1678, one of Koksenga's generals destroyed it again with fire. In 1679, the Governor General of the Province rebuilt it of wood, but this was found so unsatisfactory for general use, that in 1685, it was rebuilt of stone by the Admiral of Amoy. During the present dynasty it has been repaired several times. This bridge is an exceedingly remarkable one. Its arches are not round, they are simply immense slabs of stone reaching from one pier to another. Some of these slabs are seventy-six feet long, eight feet in thickness, and three feet in width. Unfortunately we have no history of the builders of the bridge, or of the manner in which they laid the foundation of the piers. The river, generally, is a pretty rapid one, and during the rainy seasons there are freshets, which cause a rise of from twelve to fifteen feet. On such occasions the waters absolutely roar as they rush down upon the bridge and even over it, and yet, though these piers have, probably, been in existence since the year 1265, they appear as strong and as firm as ever.

Roads.—One of the great roads of China, that passes through the Canton, and Fohkien, provinces, runs through the plain on which the city of Chang-chou is situated, and crossing one of the spurs of the hills, passes over the bridge just described. This road is in fact the only practicable one, for commerce, which exists in all this region. The mountains are so high and inaccessible, that nothing but bye paths are found on them. The great stream of people that moves North, and South, must necessarily pass along this great road, as the only convenient one the Chinese have yet constructed.

Literary.—The prefecture of Chang-chou, has not yet attained a very high literary reputation. In this respect it ranks far below the neighbouring prefecture of Chin-chew. The number of scholars that assemble for the literary examination, cannot be less than 11,000, but of course comparatively few of these could, by any possibility, obtain their degree at any one examination. The number that can pass each time is absolutely fixed. Of the seven heens, or districts, within the prefecture, five are allowed twenty each, and the remaining two, fifteen each. In addition to these the city of Chang-chou, has the privilege of having twenty of its scholars graduate at each examination. Although the prefecture does not stand high in a literary point of view, it still is not absolutely without some celebrities. One graduate from Chang-chou, succeeded in obtaining every degree the empire could confer. He passed with distinction the examinations at the Hanlin college, and finally became a member of one of the Six Boards. He was on a visit to Chang-chou, in 1864, when the rebels took the city, when he was unfortunately murdered by them. Another from the town of Punan（浦南）, has been equally successful in attaining the highest literary honours, His name stood the first among the candidates for the Doctor's degree. Chang-t'ai（长泰）similarly can boast that one of its citizens has risen to the same proud position. This fact is perpetuated in one peculiar feature of their idolatrous worship.

In all this region the worship of a particular idol named Wang yeh is very widely celebrated. This idol, besides having a regular place in some of the temples, is brought around at certain periods in a gaily painted boat. Wherever this boat approaches, it is received with the greatest honour and ceremony, and there is the most unbounded faith in its efficacy to heal diseases, drive off evil spirits, &c. The city of Chang-t'ai is an exception to all this. There this idol is held in the lowest possible estimation, and it is never mentioned without the vilest epithets being launched against it. Usually the Chinese are terribly afraid of saying anything against their idols, but in this case they seem to be unrestrained by the remotest feeling of dread. The reason of this is as follows: This Wang-yeh before he was deified, was simply a Chin shih（进士）, that is a scholar of the third literary degree, Ch'ang-t'ai in the mean time, however, had produced a man who had gained the highest degree, the Chuang-yuen（状元） in the empire. Wang-yeh must therefore, in point of position, be far inferior to their celebrated townsman. Officially, therefore, he has no standing in their town. The spirit of their townsman, they believe to be presiding over their district, and can it be supposed that one who is his inferior, would presume to come in to exercise an authority, which rightly belongs to his superior. They have no dread of his power, since a stronger than he stands by to defend them. We have in this fact, a singular illustration of how the Chinese believe that there is an exact analogy between the present world, and the world of spirits, and that the same gradation of rank, &c., prevails equally in them both.

The only really world wide celebrity that the prefecture can boast of, is the famous Chu-wĕn-kung（朱文公）.

This man is the celebrated commentator of the Chinese 'Four Books'. His family really belong to the province of Honan, but as he was born in this province, he is claimed as one of its worthies. He was prefect of Chang-chou and died there."

三、行政区划

漳州府

从厦门取水路往西南方向走，经过一座岛屿，因其顶端有一片危如累卵的断壁残垣而名曰宝塔岛（Pagoda Island），进入大陆和小岛之间的一处航道，呈现在眼前的是一派足可媲美苏格兰高地一些地方的秀丽景色。这是一个长方形的大海湾，大约6英里长、4英里宽，岸边是繁华美丽、绿树成荫的村庄，村旁是开垦程度非常高的平地，其中大部分是填河造地而来的，一直绵延到或蓝色或灰色的山脚下。这个季节，海湾一带鹅、水鸭、野鸭以及其他各种各样的鸭类、鹈鹕、白鹭等禽类成群出没，是厦门打猎爱好者喜欢光顾的好去处。九龙江的两条支流以及北溪都汇入这个海湾。沿着漳州河的航道前行大约3英里，来到一座筑有城墙的名为海澄县的大城镇，继续往前两英里外是另一座更大、更热闹、更繁荣的城镇或城市，当地方言将其称为石码（Chioh bei）。这里岸上人口稠密、水上舟船络绎不绝，该地通过厦门与国内外保持着密切、繁荣的贸易往来。

蜿蜒穿过迷人、兴盛、人口稠密的乡间，随处可见玉米、水稻和甘蔗，山冈和平原绵延不绝，再往前航行十英里就到了漳州府。

漳州府下辖七个县级行政区，即龙溪县、漳浦县、海澄县、平和县、诏安县、长泰县以及南靖县。

府城漳州位于北纬24° 31’ 12”，东经117° 59”，即北京以东1° 24”。往漳州的道路要经由几条宽阔平坦、部分地段用砖石铺砌的马路，再穿过一座长度约750英尺长的大桥。这座桥总共有25座高25英尺、相距约30英尺的桥墩。一根根沉重的木头从一座桥台铺设到另一座桥台，横向摆上若干小一点的木头，用泥土盖上，最后再铺上砖块和石板，一些石板长度超过四十英尺。

整座大桥属于最原始的结构类型，大桥的两端开设了一家家兜售廉价劣质商品的店铺，这些店铺大概占大桥长度的四分之一。

顺河而下，漳州府位于厦门正西方向 24.5 英里以外的九龙江两岸。漳州肯定是一座非常美丽的城市，四周筑有固若金汤的城墙。城内街道用花岗岩铺成，一些石板宽度达 12 英尺。现在这里是一幅惹人厌恶的荒凉景象，简直就是一堆瓦砾和烧焦的废墟。1864 年这座城市落入长毛起义军手中的时候，据说有 20 万到 25 万人死于屠杀或疾病，价值约 2,000 万元的银元和财宝被起义军夺去。1865 年 5 月起义军撤走以后，在接下来的七年里，人们投入了应有的精力来修复和重建府城沿江的一条长街。和漳州府的许多其他地方一样，这一带风景非常优美。因此，洛里先生（Mr. Lourie）在《中国丛报》第 11 卷第 506 页中恰如其分地做出这样的描述：

想象一座长 30 英里、宽 20 英里的圆形剧场，其四面环绕着光秃秃的山峦，一条河流横穿而过，我们脚下是一座巨型城市，有稻田、甘蔗地、参天大树和数不清的村庄，它们从四面八方延伸到远方。它的宏伟和美丽超出了我们对中国风景的任何想象。我们脚下所站立的这座城市，它的形状几乎是正方形的，沿河岸有些许弧度，房屋鳞次栉比，城里和周边有着数量惊人的参天大树。向导说，前朝时期，漳州有 70 万居民，他认为现在有 100 万，这个数字也许比实际数值大得多。周围的村庄也吸引了我们的注意。我试着数一数有多少个村庄，但数了眼前不到半片田地内清晰可见的 29 个大村庄后，我放弃了尝试。肯定可以这么说，在这片广阔的平原范围内，至少有 100 个村庄，其中一些村庄很小，但是许多村庄拥有数百甚至数千居民。

漳州沦陷之前，这座城市以食糖、冰糖、作坊产品、茶叶、丝绸、丝绒、丝棉制品以及炼铁而闻名，是附近最富庶和最重要的城市。

这里驻有道台、同知、龙溪县令、镇台、参将以及其他武官。北部以及东北部地区是长泰（本地话发音为Tiohto'a），当地有大量未经开发的煤炭资源。我们看到的样品质量都很差，毫无疑问，其根本原因是朝廷只允许人们使用表层容易获取的那些煤炭，却不允许他们开矿。大量装在篮子里的煤炭被带到石码销售，很多煤炭也被卖给本地的铁匠。

西北面是南靖县。海澄县介于龙溪和海岸之间，县城位于海岛上。沿海地区的话，离长泰最近的是漳浦，隔壁就是云霄，诏安则位于最南端，其北面是平和。

漳州府占据福建省的南部地区，呈三角形，北面为汀州府、龙岩直隶州以及泉州府，南面为海岸，广东省潮州府位于其西面。该府的海岸线从南澳一直延伸到厦门。

江东桥

龙溪县这一带的一个奇妙景观是江东桥。江东桥又称浦南桥，大桥距离厦门十九英里半，是所有运送茶叶往厦门市场销售的必经之路。江东桥坐落在北溪一处三角洲的风景秀丽地带，北溪流经这个地段的时候，水流像被什么东西堵住了一样，形成水流湍急、怪石嶙峋的峡谷。连接大桥的道路绵延几里都是令人陶醉的风光，肥沃的冲积平原上长着禾苗、小麦和甘蔗，颜色特别鲜明，古榕树群环绕的大村庄星罗棋布，从四面八方映入眼帘，一派繁荣景象。远处平原缓缓隆起，一直延续到景色旖旎、色彩斑斓的群山脚下。

江东桥长354步，宽6步，大桥中间有一座小亭子。这座石桥由20个桥墩支撑着，三个桥墩一组形成两个小拱洞，第四个桥墩则安放在比其他桥墩相距接近三倍远的地方，形成一个跨度相当大的拱洞。这些桥墩上面横向铺设了粗略加工而成的巨大花岗岩，大部分花岗岩的长度介于54英尺到66英尺之间，厚度介于3英尺到6英尺之间。我们粗略测量了一下，最大的一块花岗岩重达八十吨，很难想象这些巨大的石板是通过什么手段安装就位的。尽管经历了七个世纪的脚踩鞋磨，桥面仍旧像原来一样有很多凹凸不平的地方。船形桥墩的两端边缘因中心承受了巨大的重量而向上翘，两块交叉放置的巨石已经从两端支架的一边滑入水中。

以前，大桥的防御依赖南端修建的一座坚固石炮台以及一座圆形石头堡垒，后者位于大约350英尺高的陡峭悬崖顶部，底部覆盖着漂亮的山毛榉、榕树、龙眼树以及其他树木，到处点缀着艳丽的红色攀缘植物。现在，大炮已经从这些防御工事里撤走了。大桥驻有一名下级武官，设有征税机构，两端都有几间极其简陋的商店和破败的房子。在我们一行到访的时候，男女村民都频频打手势告诉我们：大老虎经常在夜里穿行过桥，一年可能多达40到50次。两天前的晚上，一只老虎从我们背后的房子里叼走了一只狗，不久前，有人在不远的地方被老虎咬死了。他们急切地恳求我们前来射杀老虎，为此，他们把一座小庙留给我们使用，还把一只小山羊拴在庙旁，试图通过它的叫声来吸引老虎。

他们还说附近的山上有野猪。

浦南镇

距离这座桥10英里远的地方是浦南镇，由江东巡检司①管辖，驻有武官。据估计，浦南镇的居民人数有两三千人，主要商品是附近和周边县区生

①原文为“Chiang-tung-ss'u 江东司”。译者注。

产的产品，即茶叶、蔗糖、纸张、芦柑和柚子，后两者因其独特的美味而闻名，并成为每年进献给皇帝的贡品。在被起义军占领之前，据说此地约有1万个居民，现在却成了一片废墟，曾经质量优良的仓库再也没有重建过，该镇的大部分地方仍然荒无人居。

距离浦南25英里开始进入茶叶产区。这个地方至少有70个陡坡，树木繁茂的高地景色对我来说美到极致。我还没有机会去探索这一区域，如果有机会的话，这里将成为我另一篇文章的主题。

马高温牧师对漳州府的有趣描述让我受益匪浅：

以这个名字命名的地方早在前2169年至前1766年夏朝①时期就已经为人所知了。在那个年代，这里是一片荒凉的未开垦区域，主要为当地土著居住地，他们和台湾的土著一样，完全处于未开化状态，靠打猎为生。那时候，很少有汉族人涉足此地。我们可以假定他们是那个时代一群英勇无畏、富有冒险精神的人，他们作为拓荒者向南方的荒芜之地和未知区域开拓前进。

这些早期的历史肯定极其模糊不清，有关记载不多，而且还与神话传说混杂在一起。因此，我们不能过多地依赖这些记载去深入了解那个时期万事万物的样子，或者这个本地王国最终灭亡的过程。不过，我们可以肯定的是，华夏族人年复一年持续不断地向南方扩张，压缩当地土著的生存空间，直到秦朝（前243—前201年）②建立时，我们知道华夏族人已经占领了漳州这一区域。此时，大量的土著已经退居到更远的南部和西部，而他们当中的许多人则屈服于征服者，并默默地承袭着征服者的风俗习俗。官员是由朝廷任命③，所以这一地区实际上成为秦朝的一部分。这种状况一直持续到西汉武帝

① 中国史学界一般认为夏朝起止时间约为前2070年至前1600年。译者注。

② 秦朝起止时间为前221年至前206年。译者注。

③ “《东越传》云：闽越王无诸、越东王王摇，皆勾践后。秦已并天下，皆废为君长，经其地为闽中郡。《集解》：徐方曰：今建安侯官是，今福建闽侯县。”转引自吕思勉：《秦汉史》，江苏人民出版社，2020年，第13页。闽中郡地理范围，包括今浙南、福建全境、赣东南和粤东地区，据有关史料，闽中自秦时就弃而不属，自然不会派官治理。参见卢美松等：《福州通史简编》，福建人民出版社，2017年，第27页。译者注。

（前 81 年）[①] 时期，当时管治模式发生了变化。漳州民众和大多数居住在边疆的民众一样桀骜不驯而又独立自强，他们与原住民不断发生的激烈冲突必然使他们形成了一种不服管治的精神。此外，当时这一地区情况与现在完全不同，很多区域仍未平定，相对于其他地方来说，当地没有采取什么措施去开发本地资源。人们认为，当地的土壤贫瘠，难以育果，这片土地开发水平低下，没有生产出像现在一样支撑着数百万人生计的丰硕果实，甚至还没有人觉察到这里居然潜藏着丰富的资源。由于民风强悍，再加上当地岁入几近为零的情况，汉武帝决定放弃自己对当地的直接管治，他挑选并敕封当地一位名门贵胄为王，命令他统治福建和广东，允许他完全控制两省的领地。因此，除了向皇帝朝贡称臣外，他实际上是一个独立的君王。

这位受敕封的诸侯王很快就表现出野心勃勃、肆无忌惮的一面。不到几年时间，他不仅开始无视对皇帝效忠的承诺，而且还制定了一个入侵帝国领土的大胆计划，以便伺机取而代之。当皇帝获悉他的计划后，立即召集军队，将其彻底击溃，随后粗暴地迁走当地至少十分之六的民众。他把这些人分散到自己领土的各处地方，之所以这么做是因为当地民众完全目无王法。皇帝认为，除了彻底减少这个封地的人口外，没有什么办法能确保自己帝国领土的安全。那些从此次大规模抓捕行动中逃脱的民众躲进了山林里，那是汉武帝的军队找不到的地方。征讨军队离开后，民众壮胆从他们的藏身之处走了出来，再次回到他们以前的家园，当然一切已所剩无几：他们的房子被烧毁，他们的财物被掠夺或摧毁，他们的亲人朋友被无情地带走，此生再见希望渺茫。当地被破坏得很彻底，事实上，朝廷以为已经彻底迁移走封地的所有民众，于是放弃了对当地的管治，让它自生自灭。那些躲过劫难的为数不多的民众，由于免受外界的干扰，又开始生生不息、茁壮成长起来。在随后的两个朝代，

① 汉武帝生卒时间为：前 156 年？至前 87 年。汉武帝建元六年（前 135 年），汉廷立“无诸孙繇君丑为越摇王，奉闽越先祭祀”，并立“余善为东越王”。同上，第 33–34 页。译者注。

即东汉（30—226年）[①]和后汉（226—260年）[②]，有关此地民众的真实记录极其稀少，但是无论谁统治这个地方，肯定都是民众推举出来的结果，因为上述两朝都没有皇帝宣称得到当地任何形式的效忠。

西晋（260—313年）[③]初期，此地的重要性与日俱增，居民人口不计其数，以至于朝廷认为再次吞并此地有利可图。皇帝在占领本地区以后，便委派合适的官员前来掌管当地政府。在这期间以及随后的朝代，此地一直默默地服从最高皇权，没有发生任何值得历史学家关注的情况，因为除了关于其内部规章的简单记录外，我们找不到任何其他记载，而一般读者对此也并无兴趣。

唐朝（622—897年）[④]开始的时候，我们发现这里整个地区都卷入了内乱。这场战争是在正统汉人和业已开化的本地土著之间展开的。这场战争持续了三十多年，各有胜负。最终，汉人开始发现他们对付不了这些半开化的敌人。情急之下，他们奏请唐太宗（654年）[⑤]委派得力干将，授权该官员结束这场内战，并通过其聪明才智，恢复区域的和平与安宁。皇帝同意并敕封陈政为王[⑥]，赋予其与汉朝时期分封的第一任闽王同等的待遇和同等的权力。陈政果然才智过人、意志坚定。内战终告结束，区域内部资源在他的英明领导下逐渐开发起来。他赢得了民众的真心拥戴，当地的最高统治权自然牢牢地掌握在陈政家族手中。在长达三百年的时间里，他的子孙后代亦在该地为王。[⑦]此后，由于陈政家族后代极度无能和腐败，民众推举其他家族为王。统治者的更迭开

---

① 东汉起止时间为25年至220年。译者注。

② 东汉之后为三国时期，故这里所指应为刘备建立的蜀汉（221—263年）。不过，三国时期，漳州属于孙权建立的东吴（222—280年）领地。而中国历史上的后汉（947—950年）是五代十国时期由刘知远建立的王朝，都城河南开封府。译者注。

③ 西晋起止时间为265—317年。译者注。

④ 唐朝起止时间为618—907年。译者注。

⑤ 唐太宗李世民生卒时间为598—649年。654年为唐高宗永徽五年。译者注。

⑥ 总章（唐高宗李治年号）二年（669年），朝命王钤卫左郎将陈政为岭南行军总管，统率府兵五千六百名入闽，镇守绥安（隋废县）。参见朱维幹：《福建史稿》（上），福建教育出版社，1985年，第113页。译者注。

⑦ 陈氏自陈政起，四世守漳（州）。武后垂拱二年（686年）置漳州，自陈政之子元光起，其子孙三代除任岭南行军总管外，还兼任漳州刺史。译者注。

始引起纷争，这一地方逐渐出现了政治性的团体。一些最有权势的家族理所当然认为他们应该和最近刚被推举为王的人拥有同样的统治权。纷争导致民心涣散，社会状况惨不忍睹。

宋朝初年（950—967 年）①，适逢陈洪进在本地割据一方，一场争斗在所难免，他不得不向虎视其版图的政治势力低头，遂向朝廷献出其所有领地。陈洪进上奏朝廷称，这些领土不应该独立于朝廷之外，而应由朝廷直接管治。皇帝接受了这一提议，给予陈洪进官复原职，使其拥有与安抚使②类似的权力，当地立刻重新恢复和平。各方势力看到他们现在必须对抗整个朝廷，就悄无声息地解散了。在接下来的两个朝代，这一地区没有发生什么重要的历史事件。在归顺宋朝以后，之前是一座不设防城市的漳州，也立起了一堵方圆 4 里的泥土城墙。150 年后，泥墙已经破烂不堪，取而代之的是石头城墙，不管是出于防御还是日常所需，这肯定是对旧土墙的巨大改进。

直到本朝（1643 年）③初年，漳州没有发生什么非同寻常的历史事件。当时，郑成功割据厦门及其周边地区，公开反抗新王朝的统治。顺治十二年（1655 年），郑成功挥师漳州，轻松克敌。然而，他注定坚守不了多久。听说朝廷从福州集结大批军队朝他奔袭而来。自知无力拒敌，郑成功拆毁了城墙，据说他还把建造城墙的石头丢弃到海里。次年，朝廷重修城墙，并且规模比以前大得多。旧城墙方圆只有 4 里，新城墙扩展至 9~10 里之间。十二年后，郑成功再次围攻漳州，然而，他却已经无法在当地留下任何可记之笔。本朝的早期将士尤其擅长城池防守战，他们成功地守卫住了漳州府的两三处地方，这似乎证明了他们在这方面的声誉是当之无愧的。据说，在这最后一次围城中，城内至少有 70 万人死于饥饿。我觉得这些数字被过分夸大了，尽管如此，这种夸大却说明了此次交战给当时的人们带来了前所未有的痛苦，造成空前数

① 宋朝建立于 960 年。译者注。
② 宋朝时期路（相当于省）的军政长官。译者注。
③ 清朝（1636—1911 年），1643 年为顺治帝继位年代。译者注。

量的死亡，要不然也不会留下这样的说法。

历史的车轮再次滚滚向前。1864 年，漳州的繁华景象因为长毛起义军[1]的占领再次受到了意料之外的冲击。在沦陷期间，起义军似乎杀气腾腾，无所不毁。寺院庙宇、公共建筑和官员府第首当其冲，府城的大部分地区变成了断壁残垣。据估算当时城里有 40 万人口，全部四处逃散，被屠杀者不计其数，整个城市的商业贸易彻底停摆。这个城市要恢复往日的繁荣景象将会是旷日持久之计。即使是现在（1872 年），漳州城的许多地方仍然是一堆瓦砾废墟。以前的居民不是被杀了，就是太穷了，没有能力重建家园。只有商业化程度较高的区域，才有一些迹象来表明城市又恢复到起义军占领之前的样子。

面积。就漳州府的面积来说，很难给出一个精确的数字。可以这么说，漳州府长约 70 英里，周长 240 英里。然而，这个地方的大部分区域都不适合种植谷类作物，其四面八方均被连绵不断的群山所贯穿，有些山的海拔相当高，有很多山区的土壤非常贫瘠，所以对土地所有者来说价值相对不大。剩下的则专门种满各种树木以备砍伐下来作为柴火在整个地区销售。如果是后一种情况的话，这片群山就是许多人收入的丰富源泉。

物产。总的来说，漳州府的民众似乎比域外民众要富裕得多。在附近的泉州府，人们要比他们更受上天眷顾的邻居贫困得多，生活也更加艰难。毫无疑问，这是因为漳州地区是一个物产富饶的地方。绝大多数最重要的日常消费品都产自此地，出售这些物品所得的收入为社会的广大成员带来了财富。其主要产品有：大米、小麦、茶叶、糖、食用油、姜、蜂蜜、麻、烟草、纸张、清漆、染料、樟脑、木材、木炭。水果种类非常丰富，盛产荔枝、龙眼、芦柑、西瓜、香蕉、柿子、桃子、梨、橄榄、枣、葡萄、桑葚、柚子、石榴等。

人口。整个地区的人口估计在 300 万到 400 万之间。

历史古迹。在漳州府，有价值的历史古迹非常稀少。事实上，历史遗迹

① 即“太平天国起义军”。译者注。

寥寥无几正是中华帝国的一个显著特征。人们似乎不会重视保存任何有关古老习俗来龙去脉的记录或实物，或者保护任何有助于说明这个国家悠久历史的特定事实或特征的证明。在漳州，我们似乎完全看不到宋朝以前的任何遗迹。那些仍然保存完好的东西之所以没有正常地腐烂、破败，是因为它们对整个社会来说是必不可少的，因此必须保存下来。我指的是城市以及桥梁。任何对公众来说可有可无的东西都可以任其破败、腐烂。任何有趣的或不寻常的东西均交给私人保存，其结果都是灾难性的。漳州府唯一值得一提的古迹是横跨北溪的一座质量一流的大桥，桥的名字叫做江东桥，或称浦南桥。这座大桥建造在风景极其优美的峡谷地带，河流流经此地时从群山对面的漳州大平原奔腾流出，而河流两岸的群山则高高耸立，无疑使这一带的景色更加壮丽。由于附近没有村庄，也没有居民，大桥周围的景色呈现出一种静谧之美。

我们注意到这个地方首次建桥是在宋朝初期。1190 年[①]，这里架设了一座浮桥，总共使用了 35 年，取而代之的是后来建造的一座永久性的木桥。1265 年[②]，也就是建成后 30 年，此桥遭火焚毁。漳州郡守倡议集资并带头捐献五十万钱用以建造石桥。所需资金筹集到位后，终于建成石桥。按中国计量单位计算，该桥长 2,000 尺，桥墩间隔 80 尺。除了非常细微的维修以外，这座桥连续使用了 300 年，直到 1565 年才进行彻底维修。1590 年，人们沿着大桥两侧各修建了一条石栏杆，两端各建造了一座拱门，在西端的拱门上镌刻着“三省通衢”四个字。在郑成功全面对抗清朝期间，这座大桥遭受了非常严重的损坏。为了切断清军前进的道路，他们在大桥的四个位置进行了破坏，这是发生在 1673 年的事。不久以后，人们又重新架起了一座木桥，但是 1678 年，郑成功手下的一位将军再次将其焚毁了。1679 年，福建总督以木材为原料重

① 1190 年为南宋绍熙元年。“南宋绍熙年间（1190—1194 年），郡守赵遂伯在社里以联艘建造浮桥，开此处造桥历史的先声。”参见林国平、邱秀端：《福建历史文化博览》下册，福建教育出版社，2017 年，第 298 页。译者注。

② 南宋嘉熙元年（1237 年），桥毁于火，知州李韶……乃捐私币 50 万，多方筹集善款……于翌年二月动工，至淳祐元年（1241 年）告成。同上。译者注。

新建桥，但发现木桥不足以应付日常需要。1685年，厦门提督再次修建了石桥。本朝期间，大桥历经数次维修。这座大桥着实非比寻常，它的桥拱不是圆形的，而只是从一座桥墩连接到另一座桥墩的巨大石板，有些石板长达七十六英尺，厚8英尺，宽3英尺。遗憾的是，我们没有大桥建造者的记载，也不知道他们铺设台墩的办法。通常情况下，这条河流相当湍急，雨季时河水猛涨，水位从12英尺上升到15英尺。在这种情况下，当水流冲向大桥甚至越过大桥时，发出的声音绝对是咆哮怒吼。尽管这些桥墩可能1265年以来就存在了，但是它们看起来仍然一如既往地坚固结实。

道路。这是中国最好的一条道路，它途经广东和福建两省，贯穿漳州城所在的平原，翻过一处山麓，跨过前面所说的那座大桥。这条道路实际上是整个地区唯一的一条具有实际商业价值的路。区域里的山高不可攀，除了小路以外，什么也没有。南来北往的熙攘人群必然要走这条中国人修建的唯一一条康庄大道。

科举。漳州府在科举方面并未获得很高的声誉，这方面的成就远远低于邻近的泉州。参加科举考试的士子数可能不少于11,000千人，当然每个等级的考试只有少数人能够通过并取得功名。每次考试录取的人数是绝对固定的。在漳州府所辖的七个县级行政区中，有五个县各允许录取20人，其余两县各允许录取15人。除此之外，漳州府城享有每次考试录取20人的特殊待遇。虽然从科举的角度上看该府表现并不突出，但也不是绝对出不了名人。有一位漳州士子①顺利通过朝廷所有级别的考试，并以优异的成绩通过了翰林院考试，最终在六部的其中一个衙门任职。1864年，正值此人返回漳州期间，起义军占领了该城，他不幸惨遭杀害。另外一位来自浦南镇的士子同样顺利获得最高级别的功名，他在所有参加殿试的考生中排名第一。长泰也有一位县

① 应指简逢泰（1815—1864），漳州南靖人，清道光十八年（1838年）考中第七十三名，殿试为二甲二十名进士，钦点户部主事。丁父忧后移居漳州，同治三年，太平天国侍王李世贤入漳后被捕杀害。译者注。

民[①]取得了同样引以为傲的功名，这一真人真事作为该县偶像崇拜的一个特殊内涵得以世代流传。

在整个地区，人们普遍信奉一位叫做“王爷”的特殊神明。“王爷”神像除了固定供奉在一些寺庙以外，在某些时候也被请到绘有华丽图案的船上巡游四方，“王爷”船所到之处都受到最高的敬意和最热烈的欢迎，人们对“王爷”治病消灾等方面的灵验有着无比的信心。七县之中，唯独长泰县没有这种信仰。长泰人并不把“王爷”放在眼里，一提到他，人们尽是说些最恶毒的话来藐视他。通常中国人完全不敢说出任何亵渎他们神灵的话，但是在这件事情上，长泰人似乎没有一丝一毫的恐惧。原因如下：这位“王爷”在被奉为神明之前，只是一个进士，亦即第三等级的功名。然而，长泰此时已经有人取得了朝廷最高等级的功名，即状元，从地位上来说，“王爷”一定远不如他大名鼎鼎的老乡。因此，从官方的角度看，“王爷”在该县的分量不够。县民们认为，他们老乡的精神已经深深地烙在了县里的每个角落，难道一个地位不如他们老乡的人，会贸然前来行使一种理所当然属于他们老乡的权力？他们不惧怕王爷的法力，因为有一个更强大的人站在身边保护着他们。这个例子说明了一个奇特的事实，那就是中国人相信现实世界和精神世界是平行共存的，相同的等级秩序等在两个世界中同样存在。

漳州府唯一真正享誉世界的名人就是著名的朱文公[②]，他因注释中国四书而闻名于世。朱文公的家族实际上来自河南省[③]，但是由于他在本省出生，故被列为该省名人。朱文公曾任漳州知府并在那里逝世[④]。

---

①林震（1388—1448），漳州府长泰县人，明宣宗宣德五年（1430年）庚戌科状元，授翰林院修撰。译者注。

②即朱熹。译者注。

③应为安徽省徽州府。译者注。

④朱熹逝世之地为福建建阳。译者注。

Chüan chou fu

The prefecture of Chüan-chou-fu（泉州府）, Chin-chew local dialect, lies to the north east of, and is distant by sea, 60 miles, and by land, 40 miles, from Amoy. It possesses five districts, or Hsiens namely Chin-chiang（晋江县）, Tung-an（同安县）, Nan-an（南安县）, Hui-an（惠安县） and An-chi（安溪县）. It is bounded on the south and east, by the sea, on the north by Hsing-hua-fu（兴化府）, on the northwestby Yung-ch‘un-chou（永春州）, and on the west, by Chang-chou-fu（漳州府）. It is on a narrow tract of land, exceedingly well watered by several rivers. Its chief city is called Ch‘üan-chou-fu（泉州府）, and is built on a plain on the northern bank of the Chin-chiang, about 10 miles from its mouth, on a cape, in lat. 24°56’12” N. and long. 118°47’40” E. of Greenwich or 2°22’40” E. of Peking. An-chi（Ankoi）, known for its teas, lies due west from the chief town of the department, and is reached by road, and by an extremely narrow river, fed by mountain streams, called the Pei-chi（北溪）.The district of Hui-an, is situated to the north-east from Ch‘üan-chou; and Nan-yan to the north westward. Tung-an, and Machiang-ting, lie to the southwest, forming the southern portion of the department. The islands of Chin-mên (Quemoy), Hsia-mén (Amoy), and Kulangsu, fall within the jurisdiction of Tung-an.

The Revd. W. T. Swanson, has favoured me with most of the following account of this prefecture.

“A mass of myth and fable, surrounds the early history of most Chinese cities, and in consequence it is exceedingly difficult to ascertain anything definite regarding their founding, and almost impossible to eliminate the real from the mythical. This seems to be specially the case in regard to the city of Chin-chew. It is a prefectural city, and its inhabitants are very proud of its beauties, and are much given to talking of its eminence. To those who know anything of China, and the Chinese, the fact just stated, will be seen to increase the difficulty of ascertaining definitely and exactly, the facts of the early history of the city. It is stated that it was certainly in existence during the Tung dynasty, but all that can be gathered about its history, in the remote past, seems to be shadowy in the extreme. It appears certain, however, that during the reign of Sun-te, the first Emperor of the Ching dynasty, the city was much enlarged and its wall almost entirely rebuilt. The wall was then made 20 feet broad at the base, and 23 feet high. These are its present dimensions, and it looks as strong to-day, as when it was first built. Its circuit is 20 li, or about 6 English miles. The people say that it is somewhat more than the circuit of the city wall of Fuhchow, and that it was made so, that Chin-chew might excel even the capital of the province.

This magnificent wall encloses a large space, which has not been, hitherto, entirely occupied by buildings, and there seems little prospect of its ever being so. At the north and northwest corners of the city, inside the walls, there is a considerable space of ground which has never been built upon, and is constantly under cultivation. Between the south gate and the river, a distance of one mile, there is a densely populated suburb. The approach to the city from the south, is over a massive stone bridge spanning the river, which, at this point, appears, as nearly as can be judged, to be over 300 yards wide. The city, itself, is for a Chinese city, remarkably clean. The streets are wide, and well paved with granite slabs. The street leading from the south, to the west, gate, seems to be the only busy one in the city. The others are remarkably quiet with few, if any signs, of business being done in them.

There are no manufactures of any importance, and from reasons of state policy, the traffic that naturally should have passed through the city, has been diverted to other channels. At present retired mandarins, the acting government officials, and an innumerable host of literary men, or rather aspirants to office, and their dependants, form a very large proportion of its inhabitants. The existing house accommodation is by no means fully occupied, and, in consequence, house property in Chin-chew, is cheaper than in any other part of this region. Chin-chew was at one time the provincial city, it is now the residence of a prefect, a general and of the magistrate of Chin-chiang. Its population, together with that of its suburbs, number between 200,000 and 250,000 persons.

The celebrated Koxinga, after obtaining possession of Quemoy, Amoy, and Tungan, in the Chin-chew prefecture, and of Hai-têng, in that of Chang-chow, pressed on to the gates, of Chin-chew, but he failed to take the city, and was forced to fall back upon what he had already won; and of these places, he held possession for years. Inability to get supplies ultimately compelled him to evacuate them, and he went to "Formosa" and took it, the Manchus quietly coming, and occupying what he left.

The 'small knife' rebels never approached nearer to Chin-chew than Tungan, which place they held for only a few days. Chin-chew has produced many officials of ability and note. Among the latest is Huang-tsung-han（黄宗汉）, at one time Governor General of the two Kwang. He, and seven other mandarins, were appointed guardians of the present Emperor. At the time of Prince Kung's *coup d'état*, two of these were executed, and Huang-tsung-han, with others, was disgraced.

"The usual number of women have had memorial arches erected to them for their chastity, filial piety, and devotion to deceased husbands.

At Tang-chioh（东石）, a small port lying at the head of Hui-t'ou bay, there is a brisk trade in salt, carried on in junks, with Fuh-chow, the return cargoes are poles, charcoal, and bamboos. At Siong-si（祥芝）, a port at the mouth of the Chin-chew river, and on its southern bank, there is a large trade with 'Formosa'. Rice, in considerable quantities, is carried over from Takao, in 'Formosa', and transhipped at Siong-si, for Chin-chew, Amoy, and other places. A similar trade, but not by any means so extensive, is carried on at Eng-leng（永宁）, and Chim-ho（深沪）, two ports a few miles to the south of Siong-si. Before the opium ships were allowed to anchor in Amoy harbour, one or more of them were stationed at Ch'uan- t'ou, an anchorage near the mouth of the Chin-chew river, and on its northern side. From the districts of Ankoi, there is a large export of Tea. The other productions, are salt, peanut oil, and sugar. From Tungan district, there is a small export of indigo. In this district, during late years, there has been a considerable cultivation of the poppy, and it is stated, that it is annually on the increase. There are extensive granite quarries, about 10 miles above Chin-chew, and quite close to the river. The stones are of a superior kind, and are used all through the prefecture.

The great road from Peking, to Canton, passes through the Chin-chew prefecture. From Hui-an, it goes to Chin-chew, and thence through Tung-an, to Chang-chou, and the South. Over this road there is an immense traffic. An endless concourse of passengers, from the highest mandarins, to the lowest coolies, are constantly using it. It is kept in a fair state of repair, and there are inns, of the ordinary Chinese kind, at regular intervals. For a long time this road was so infested with robbers, that travelling for ordinary passengers had become almost impracticable. But about six or seven years ago, General Lo, was appointed T‘e-tu. He was an old Taiping, and a man of great energy and resolution. He rested neither night nor day, till he had cleared the whole district of these pests. He burnt their villages, and killed their inhabitants, whenever, and wherever, he could lay hands upon them. This vigorous action was soon followed by the most beneficial result. There are no robbers on the great road now, and even the bye roads, are perfectly safe. General Lo has been removed, and his successor does not seem to possess either his activity, or his resolution, and it is said that there are indications that would lead one to infer the possibility of a recurrence to the old state of lawlessness.

From the five districts of the prefecture, the numbers of literary candidates, and graduates, are, approximately, as follows :

Chin-kang	about 2,500
Lam-an	about 1,800
Hui-an	about 2,500
Tong-an	about 1,800
An-khoe	about 1,200

The fixed number of graduates for the whole prefecture is 180. Amongst the most notable objects in this prefecture is the bridge of Wu-hai, which is over a mile long, and most substantially built of granite."

Tea plantations

The spots where the Tea is cultivated at An-chi（安溪，An-koi）in the Ch‘üan-chou prefecture, are scattered over a great part of the country, but there are no hills appropriated entirely to its culture. The ground of the Tea plantations is not terraced, but formed into carefully tended beds, each little plantation, being surrounded by a low stone fence and trench. There is no shade, but the places selected for cultivation, are generally in the hollow of hills, where there is a good deal of shelter on two sides, and the slope comparatively easy. The highest plantation is computed to be 700 feet above the plain, but those at half, and even less than, that height, appear to be more thriving, probably from better soil, although the best is little more than mere sand. No manure is, however, used, nor are the plants irrigated. The plant is not cultivated on an eastern exposure, although it is sufficiently hardy to bear a severe amount of cold. Hoar frost is common here in the winter months, and snow falls occasionally, but does not lie long, nor to a greater depth than three or four inches.

The seed now used for propagating the plant, is all produced on the spot, though the original seed was brought from Woo-e-shan （武彝山）. Several seeds are put in a hole three or four inches deep, and the sprouts appear three months afterwards, they are subsequently transplanted, and as the plant grows, the earth is gathered up a little round the root; the leaves are taken from the plant when they are three years old, and there are from most plants, four pickings in the year; the green leaf yields about one fifth of its weight in dry tea, and each shrub may yield about a tael of dry tea annually （about the 12th of a pound）, and a mow of ground may contain about 300 or 400 plants. The plant attains its greatest sizes in 6 or 7 years, and thrives from 10 to 20 years. It is sometimes destroyed by a worm which eats up the pith, and converts both stem and branches into tubes, and by a grey lichen, which principally attacks very old plants. Some of the plants are but a few inches in height, yet are so bushy that the hand can scarcely be thrust between their branches, they are thickly covered with leaves about ¾ of an inch long. In the same beds are other plants with stems four feet high, far less branchy and with leaves 1½ to 2 inches long. The produce of great and small is said to be equal. The distance from centre to centre of the plant is about 4½ feet, and the plants average about two feet in diameter.①

The other productions of this district, are salt, peanut-oil, and sugar.

① Abridged from a memorandum of an excursion to the An koi Tea districts in the Chinese Repository, by Mr. G. J. Gordon.

泉州府

泉州府（本地方言发音为 Chin-chew）位于厦门东北方向海路距离 60 英里、陆路距离 40 英里的地方，下辖五个县级行政区，即晋江县、同安县、南安县、惠安县和安溪县。泉州府南面和东面临海，北面接兴化府，西北面接永春州，西面则与漳州府接壤。泉州府坐落在一片狭窄的土地上，流经此地的几条河流为其提供了充足的水源。府城泉州建在晋江北岸平原离河口大约十英里的岬角上，即北纬 24° 56’12”，东经 118° 47’40”，也就是北京以东 2° 22’40”。以茶叶出名的安溪位于府城正西方向，从陆路或者经一条由山涧汇集而成的名为北溪的狭窄小河可以到达该县。惠安县位于泉州府城的东北方向，南安县位于西北方向。同安以及马巷厅位于西南方向，是该府的南部地带。金门岛、厦门岛和鼓浪屿归同安县管辖。

承蒙斯旺森（W.T. Swanson）牧师惠赐，以下是有关该府的情况介绍：

丰富的神话和寓言传说与大多数中国城市的早期历史相伴而生。因此，想弄清楚任何有关城市建立的确切信息是极其困难的，从神话传说中剥离出历史的真实面貌更是几乎不可能的事情，泉州城的情况似乎也是如此。泉州城是府城，居民皆以其城市之美为荣，也非常喜欢谈论其显赫历史。那些对中国和中国人有所了解的人们认为，以上所述事实进一步确证了试图清楚准确地查明该城市早期真实历史的难度。据说泉州城早在唐朝时期就已经存在了，但是人们所能收集到的有关这个城市的古老的历史资料似乎都鲜为人知了。然而，可以肯定的是，在清朝的第一位皇帝顺治[①]在位期间，泉州城大

①顺治（1644—1661 年），清朝第三位、清军入关后的第一位皇帝清世祖爱新觉罗·福临。译者注。

规模扩建，其城墙几乎全部重建。当时建造出来的城墙基底有二十英尺宽，二十三英尺高，现在的尺寸也是如此，看起来和城墙刚完工的时候一样坚固。城墙周长二十里，即大约六英里，当地人说这比福州的城墙还要长一些，人们还说，建成这个样子，泉州就可以超越省城了。

气势宏伟的城墙围起很大一块土地，迄今为止，这块土地上还没有完全建满房子，而且看起来以后也没有建满的可能。墙内城里的北面和西北角有一片相当大的空间，上面从来没有盖过房子，倒是一直当作耕地使用。从南门到河边一英里的地带是人口稠密的郊区。从南面进城得穿过一座横跨河流两岸的巨大石桥，据判断，这座石桥此时看起来似乎有三百多码宽①。就中国城市来说，泉州城本身是非常干净的，花岗岩石板铺就的街道既宽阔又平坦。从南边通向西门的街道似乎是这座城市里唯一一条繁忙的街道，其他街道非常安静，几乎没有任何商业活动的迹象。

这里没有什么重要的作坊加工行业，而且由于朝廷政策影响，本来应该穿过这个城市的道路被改道了。目前，泉州城的居民有很大一部分是退休官员、现任朝廷官员、为数众多的文人，或者更确切地说是志在仕途者，以及他们的家人。现有已经建好的房子仍有闲置的，因此，泉州的房地产比这个地区的其他任何地方都要便宜。泉州曾经是省会所在地，现在是知府、将军和晋江知县衙门所在地，包括郊区在内，人口在二十万到二十五万之间。

大名鼎鼎的郑成功在占据泉州府的金门、厦门、同安以及漳州府的海澄之后，又兵临泉州城下。郑成功未能攻下这座城市，只能转而退守业已夺取的其他几座城市，并坚守这些地方多年。由于缺乏补给，郑成功又被迫从这些城市撤离，进军并攻克台湾。满洲人则一声不响地乘虚而入，占领了他留下的一切。

① 指“顺济桥”。清朝道光年间《晋江县志》卷十一载：“顺济桥，在德济门外，笋江下流，旧以舟渡。南宋嘉定四年（1211 年）郡守邹应龙造石桥，长一百五十丈余，翼以扶栏。以近顺济宫（即天后宫），因名顺济。” 1 码约等于 0.914，4 米，此处之宽度有误。译者注。

小刀会起义军进军泉州时所到达的最远之处是同安，不过也只是守了几天而已。泉州培养了许多能力卓绝、享负盛名的官员。时间上最近的一位是曾任两广总督的黄宗汉[①]，他和其他七名官员被任命为顾命大臣[②]。恭亲王发动政变时，其中两位顾命大臣被处死，黄宗汉和其他人则均被贬黜。

针对女性的老一套做法是为她们立牌坊，以示她们的贞洁、孝顺和对亡夫的忠诚。

东石是围头湾湾头处的小海港。在那里，食盐用帆船运到福州，返程时运回杆枝、木炭和竹子，相互之间的贸易往来活跃。祥芝是位于泉州河口南岸的港口，与台湾保持着非常频繁的贸易交往。台湾高雄运抵的大量大米从祥芝转运到泉州、厦门和其他地方。祥芝以南几英里外的永宁和深沪二港也有类似的贸易，但是规模没有这么大。鸦片船获准在厦门港停泊之前，已经有一艘或多艘停泊在靠近泉州河口一处名叫泉头（Chuan t'ou）[③]的锚地以及河的北侧。安溪县出口大量茶叶，其他农产品包括盐、花生油和糖。同安县有少量的靛蓝类染料出口，同时，近年来当地的罂粟种植量相当大，据说每年都在增长。在泉州以北大约十英里处，离河流很近的地方有大片的花岗岩采石场，这里的石头可是上等货，整个泉州府都在使用它。

从北京到广州的大马路贯穿泉州，具体路线是：从惠安到泉州，再从泉州经同安到漳州，最后到达南方。这条道路的交通极其繁忙，从位居极品的高官到最底层的苦力，人来人往，川流不息。道路养护工作相当到位，并且每间隔一段距离就有中式客栈。很长一段时期，这条道路上强盗横行，普通

① 黄宗汉（1803—1864 年），泉州人，清道光十五年进士，官至两广总督兼通商大臣。译者注。

② 1861 年咸丰帝病死后，慈禧太后联合恭亲王奕䜣发动了辛酉政变，此次政变打倒了顾命八大臣势力，黄宗汉被劾为八位顾命大臣之一的肃顺之党羽，革职永不叙用，但黄宗汉本人并非顾命大臣之一。参见南炳文：《清史》（下编），上海人民出版社，2020 年，第 168-170 页。译者注。

③ 应为大坠岛。该岛位于泉州湾入海口，据记载，大坠岛曾作为英国人运输鸦片的中转站，再通过洛阳、陈三坝及洛江区河市等处运往外地销售。译者注。

旅客几乎无法出行。不过，六七年前，罗将军①被任命为提督。他带兵多年，精力充沛、意志坚定。罗将军夜以继日加紧剿匪，终于清除了整个地区的匪患。他烧毁盗匪聚居的村庄，杀死村内居民，无论何时何地都绝不手软。这些强有力的行动很快产生了巨大的效益，这条大马路上现在已经没有强盗，甚至连小路都非常安全。罗将军已经调任他处，他的继任者似乎既不像他那样主动作为，也不如他那般意志坚定，据说现在的种种迹象使人们推断出道路有可能再次恢复以前混乱的老样子。

泉州府所辖五县的应考士子和录取人数大致如下：

晋江	约 2,500 人
南安	约 1,800 人
惠安	约 2,500 人
同安	约 1,800 人
安溪	约 1,200 人

全府固定录取 180 人。本府最具盛名的建筑之一是五海桥②。这座桥全长一英里多，由花岗岩建造而成，极其坚固结实。

茶　园

泉州府安溪县的茶叶种植园分散在乡间的大部分地方，不过并不是整座山丘都被完全开辟出来种植茶叶。茶场的园地不是梯田状的，而是被精心划分成不同的区块，每个小区块都被低矮的石墙和沟渠分隔开来。茶园往往无

① 罗将军即罗大春（1833—1890 年），字景山，原名大经，贵州省施秉县人。清朝将领，曾任福建陆路提督、福建船政轮船统领、署福建水师提督，四十六岁任湖南提督。光绪十七年（1890 年）病逝在福建建宁总兵任上，终年 59 岁。参见刘琳：《福建戍台名将列传》，福建美术出版社，2010 年，第 583-586 页。译者注。

② 原文为“the bridge of Wu-hai”，泉州并无“五海桥”，推测应为“安平桥”，又称五里桥、安海桥、西桥。安平桥始建于南宋绍兴八年（1138 年），绍兴二十二年（1152 年），安平桥竣工投入使用，是福建省泉州市境内连接晋江市和南安市的一座桥梁，是世界上中古时代最长的梁式石桥。译者注。

遮无盖，只不过开辟出来的种植场一般都在山谷之中，这样的话两边的群山就能为其提供足够的遮蔽，同时山谷的坡度也相对较缓。据计算，最高的茶园位于平原之上七百英尺，但是那些海拔只有一半高度，甚至更低的茶园似乎更加枝繁叶茂，可能是因为那些地方的土壤更加肥沃吧，尽管最好的土壤也比沙子好不了多少。然而，茶树既不用施肥，也不用灌溉。虽然茶树足够耐寒，能够抵挡住严寒的天气，但却不是朝东栽种。在这里的冬天，霜降很平常，偶尔会下雪，但持续时间不会很长，降雪厚度也不会超过三四英寸。

现在，繁殖茶树所需要的种子都是现场培育，尽管最早的茶种是从武夷山[①]带过来的。把少量种子播撒到一个三四英寸深的孔穴里，三个月后长出嫩芽，随后进行移栽。在茶树生长的过程中，要把根部周围的泥土稍微聚拢起来。茶树种植三年后就可以采摘茶叶了，大多数茶树一年可采摘四次，干茶重量为茶青的五分之一，每株茶树每年可产出约一两（约为十二分之一磅）干茶，一块地可能有约三百或四百株茶树。茶树种植六到七年后个头长到最大，并有十到二十年的盛产期。有时茶树会毁于病虫害，一种是病虫啃食枝干髓心并将茎和枝都蛀成中空，还有一种灰色的地衣专门侵袭年迈的老茶树。有些茶树只有几英寸高，但是叶子非常茂密，手从叶子之间伸进去也几乎不能触碰到树枝，这是因为它们被大约四分之三英寸长的紧凑浓密的树叶覆盖着。在同一个茶树区块里还有其他茶树，茎有四英尺高，树枝少得多，叶子有一英寸半到二英寸长。大茶树和小茶树的产量据说是相等的。茶树中心点之间的距离约四英尺，茶树的平均直径约为二英尺。[②]

该县的其他产品是盐、花生油和糖。

①原文为“Woo-e-shan 武彝山”。译者注。

②节选自戈登（G. J. Gordon）著《安溪茶叶产区之旅备忘录》（*A memorandum of an excursion to the An koi Tea districts*），原载于《中国丛报》。作者注。

Tung-an-hsien

Tung-an-hsien,(同安县 , local dialect Tung-oa) containing another somewhat important city, is situated at the bottom of an inlet about 30 miles to the northwest of the island of Amoy. I am indebted to the Revd. William McGregor for the following particulars:

"This hsien extends southwards to the island of Wu-sew（浯屿）, near the foot of the Tai-wu-shan（太武山）, and includes the belt of islands that guard the entrance to Amoy harbour, the islands of Quemoy, little Quemoy, Amoy, and Kulangsu. Inside the island of Amoy, a shallow creek runs up to Tung-an city. The hsien thus consists of a border of mountains towards the north, a strip of level ground, indented by creeks along their base, and a large bay containing a number of islands. An extensive range of mountains bounds the district towards the north, separating it from Ankoi, and on the northeast from Nan-an. The extreme spurs of this range to the eastward, are the Hun-chien shan（鸿渐山）, and the Chi'chi-shan（崎髻山） laid down in the Admiralty charts as West Peak and Hast Peak. A road passes from Tung-an to Ankoi, through the intervening mountains, and thence down the river to Chin-chew, but it is not much frequented. The teas grown on the Ankoi hills, either go down to Chinchew, or come to Amoy, by the North river. The high road from Chang-chou to Chinchew, passes through Tung-an city. As there is an alternative road by water from Chang-chou to Amoy, and thence to Chin-chew, over Amoy island（joining the other road at Sha-chi 沙溪）, this one is not so much frequented as it otherwise would be. The road from Tung-an to Chinchew was, up to a recent date, much infested by robbers; the villages in the neighbourhood levying blackmail on all passers, but the number of northern soldiers at the disposal of the mandarins, during the rebel occupation of Chang-chou in 1864-5, enabled them to suppress this brigandage, and from that date the road has been free from danger.

The city is said to date from the time of the Southern Sung（南宋）, but the first notices of it which seem to possess any historical value, do not go further back than the Mongol dynasty（元朝）. Under the Mongols it was known as Ta-lun（大轮）, a name derived from a wheel shaped hill in its neighbourhood, now generally called Han-tien-shan（梵天山）. During the conflict between Coxinga and the present dynasty, the city of Tung an, changed hands several times. On one occasion its inhabitants were all massacred by the Manchus, and on another the city wall was demolished by Coxinga. Hsü-sun-chi（许顺之）, a disciple and assistant of Chu-hi（朱熹）, the celebrated commentator on the Confucian writings, is said to have been born here under the Southern Sung; and also Lim-hi-goân（林希元）, the author of a commentary on the Yih-king（《易经存疑》）, who flourished under the Ming dynasty. The only man of note that this district has of late produced, is So-ting-yueh（苏廷玉）, who, some forty years ago, in the reign of Taukwang, was viceroy of Szchuen. In his old age he retired to Chinchew, where members of his family still reside. Of persons, not natives of the district, who have lived in it, the most noted is Chu-hsi（朱熹）, who, in his younger days, held office in Tung-an as "主簿" under the Southern Sung.

In character the natives of Tung-an, are more energetic and violent, than their neighbours of the Chang-chou prefecture, to the west. This applies especially to the people of the villages on the Tung-an creek, and on the coast inside Quemoy, and Amoy, Islands. These villages were, up to a recent date, more or less nests of pirates. On the coast of the mainland, inside Quemoy islands, a considerable quantity of salt is manufactured, but of the ordinary products of the country, rice, sugar, indigo, &c., this hsien does not produce more than is required for local consumption; indeed the rice crop is never sufficient for local necessities. Of late years, however, there has been a considerable cultivation of the poppy for the manufacture of opium, and it is stated that this is annually on the increase. At Shih-hsien（石浔，Chioh jeim local dialect）, the sea port of Tung-an, there is considerable local traffic."

As compared with the Chang-chou prefecture, Tung-an stands high in regard to literature, but its reputation in this respect is quite eclipsed by Chin-kang-hsien（晋江县）, in which is situated Chinchew city, which, as a literary school, is inferior to few in the empire. Up to the time of the small knife rebellion（小刀会）, in the third year of Hsien-Féng（咸丰）, the number of literary graduates was fixed at 22. The number for the various hsiens in the prefecture, being Chin-kang（晋江）32, Tung-an（同安） 22, Nan-an（南安） 22, An-koi（安溪） 22, Hui-an（惠安） 22; but on account of the large contributions in money raised by Tung-an, (including Amoy) to put down the local rebellion, the number of graduates was for one year made 72, and afterwards fixed at 32, which still continues to be the fixed number. The addition to the number of graduates at that time, gave an impulse, to education, which is to some extent still felt. The number of candidates attending the examination is about 1,600, or 1,700, of these, the number that really write essays, is about 500 or 600, and the number of those so proficient as to have a chance of success, is about 100, or 150.

Some villages in this hsien, have a curious custom of going out to the fields on or about the 15th of the first moon, and then pelting each other with stones, lumps of earth, sticks, or whatever comes to hand. One clan "叶", residing at "领下叶", regularly set thus to maul each other at the close of a feast in the ancestral hall. The idea seems to be that a certain amount of suffering is fated to fall on the clan, or village, during the year, and they prefer to take it in the form of broken heads, lest otherwise it may come in the shape of fever, cholera, or famine. The same custom prevails at Chioh-bei (石码，Shih-ma) in the Chang-chou prefecture. Throughout the whole of this district there is during the latter half of the 7th moon and the first half of the 8th, a great pilgrimage to a temple called Tung-shan-sen（铜山汛）in the district of Nan-an（南安）.

This temple is at the grave of a certain sacred King Kwoh（郭圣王）— who seems to have done nothing remarkable during his life, (he died when only 13 or 14 years of age), but whose grave has somehow become famous. As his birthday approaches (in the 8th moon) pilgrims arrive from north and south, to the number of several hundreds of thousands, attracted by the fame of this grave, from the province of Canton on the one side, and from Cheh-kiang, on the other; and at such times the roads in the neighbourhood of Chinchew, get quite populous with pilgrims in companies of from 10 to 40, marching gravely along, distinguished from ordinary travellers by their carrying a number of small flags, and having a small idol tied in front of their persons. Large numbers also pass through Amoy, crossing from the south by boat. Some add to their pilgrimage (which seems in many instances to be undertaken in fulfilment of a vow) other hardships, such as kneeling down once every three or ten steps of the journey. The temple at the grave contains a large number of priests, who improve the occasion of the pilgrimage to carry on a flourishing trade in small flags, lamps, candles, incense sticks, &c.

同安县

泉州府辖区内另一个颇为重要的城邑是同安县（当地方言发音为 Tung-oa），该县位于厦门岛西北约三十英里处的一块三面环海的陆地底端。承蒙麦格雷戈牧师惠赐，以下是有关同安县的详细资料：

该县南至靠近太武山①脚下的浯屿②岛，包括扼守厦门港入口的岛屿带、金门岛、小金门岛、厦门岛和鼓浪屿。在厦门岛上，有一处浅浅的小溪③向北流向同安城，因此，该县的地貌特征为北部耸立着一座山脉，有一小块狭长的平地，陆地底部地带是蜿蜒的小溪，还有散落着若干岛屿的大海湾。该县北部和东北部的连绵山脉分别把同安县与安溪县和南安县分隔开来。这条山脉最东端的支脉是鸿渐山和崎髻山，它们在航海图上被标注为西峰和东峰。从同安往安溪的道路先是穿山而过，然后顺河而下到达泉州，但走的人不多。产于安溪山上的茶叶，要么经北溪往南运到泉州，要么运来厦门。从漳州往泉州的大马路穿过同安城，因为另外有一条水路从漳州通往厦门，穿过厦门岛再抵达泉州（在沙溪与另一条道路衔接），所以走这条路的人并不多。直到不久以前，从同安到泉州的道路上还是强盗出没，附近的村庄向所有过路人敲诈勒索。但是 1864 年至 1865 年太平起义军占领漳州期间，朝廷官员统率的北方士兵人数众多，他们顺利镇压了这股匪徒，从那个时候起，路上再也没有危险了。

据说同安城的历史可以追溯到南宋时期，但是最早从元朝开始，人们才

①福建有两处太武山，此处指“南太武山”，金门岛上的是“北太武山”。译者注。

②原文为“Wu-sew 活屿”。译者注。

③指“浔江”。厦门人经常用“江”来称呼厦门岛周边的海域，比如此处厦门岛和同安之间的海域称为“浔江”，又如厦门岛和鼓浪屿之间的海域称为“鹭江”。译者注。

首次注意到这个地方似乎具有一定的历史意义。元朝时期，此地被称为“大轮”，这个名字源自该县附近一座车轮形的小山，现在一般被称为梵天山。在郑成功和本朝官府交战期间，同安县几经易手。有的时候居民全部被官军屠杀，有的时候城墙全部被郑成功摧毁。据说南宋时期，著名的儒家著作评注者朱熹的弟子兼助手许顺之就出生在这里。《易经存疑》的作者林希元[①]在明朝时期名声显赫一时。该县近来唯一出名的人物是苏廷玉，在大约四十年前的道光年间，他曾任四川总督[②]。晚年时，苏廷玉告老还乡回到泉州，他的家人现在仍然住在那里。在那些曾经居住在这里的外地人当中，南宋时期的朱熹名气最大。朱熹年轻的时候担任同安主簿。

同安人的性格与他们西边的邻居漳州人相比要更加激进和粗暴，这种情况对于居住在同安沿海地区以及厦门和金门岛海边村庄的人来说尤为明显，这些村庄直到不久以前还几乎都是海盗窝。大陆的沿海地带以及金门岛内盛产盐。除此之外，农村的常见物产有稻米、蔗糖和靛青等，本县出产的这些产品仅够本地消费，事实上，水稻从来都无法满足本地需求。不过，近年来，当地大量种植罂粟用以生产鸦片，在同安的海港石浔，本地的航运交通非常繁忙。

同漳州府相比较而言，同安人在科举方面的成就很高，但是他们在这方面的声誉与泉州府城所在的晋江县相比就黯然失色了。从科举成就来看，晋江县并不比帝国的其他地方逊色多少。小刀会起义之前的咸丰三年，同安县固定取士 22 名。泉州府内各县的人数是：晋江 32 名，同安 22 名，南安 22 名，安溪 22 名，惠安 22 名。但是由于同安（包括厦门）为平定地方叛乱筹集了

---

① 林希元（约 1480—约 1560），字茂贞，号次崖，福建同安县人。明正德十二年（1517 年）进士。林希元一生著作颇丰，主要有《易经存疑》《林次崖先生文集》《四书存疑》《更正大学经传定本》等著作。《易经存疑》主要讲述对《周易》的经文、传文逐字逐句十分详细的解释。参见富路特等：《明代名人传》，北京时代华文书局，2015 年，第 1250-1253 页。译者注。

② 苏廷玉（1783—1852），福建同安人，嘉庆十九年（1824 年）进士，道光十八年（1838 年）秋，苏廷玉署（代理）四川总督、加兵部侍郎衔。译者注。

大笔捐款，有一年的取士人数为 72 名，后来固定为 32 名，并且这样延续下来。那时候，录取人数的增加促进了教育的发展，某种程度上来说，这种促进仍然在发挥着作用。参加考试的考生人数有 1,600 ~ 1,700 人，真正完成答卷的有五六百人，而饱读诗书有机会金榜题名的有 100 ~ 150 人。

本县的一些村庄有一种非常奇怪的习俗，比如村民们在正月十五日当天或前后会来到田地里，然后互相投掷石头、土块、树枝或任何随手可拿的物件。因此，居住在岭下叶的叶氏宗亲规定族人在定期举办的宗祠庆典结束时互相攻击。这个想法似乎意味着，一年中总会有不幸的事注定要降临到宗族或村庄，他们宁愿以头破血流的方式来化解这种不幸，否则，不幸可能会以热病、霍乱或饥荒的形式出现。同样的习俗也在漳州府的石码盛行。在七月下旬和八月上旬，全县很多民众会前往南安县一座名为凤山寺[①]的寺庙进香朝拜。

这座寺庙位于郭圣王坐化处，他终其一生似乎也没有做过什么了不起的事（他只活了十三四年），但是他的坐化处不知道为什么却出名了。受坐化处的名气所吸引，农历八月他的诞辰临近，成千上万的香客从远在南边的广东和北边的浙江赶来进香朝拜。这个时候，泉州附近的道路上挤满了十到四十个人为一队的香客团，他们表情庄严，齐步并行。与普通旅客不同的是，他们举着一些小旗子，身前绑着一尊小佛像。也有很多人乘船经厦门从南边渡海而来。有些人在进香之旅中增加了一些难度（许多情况下，进香似乎是为了还愿），比如每三步或十步一跪。这座建在坐化处的寺庙里有为数众多的僧人，他们充分利用进香的时机，出售小旗、灯火、蜡烛、香等物品，生意做得红红火火。

① 原文为“Tung-shan-sen 铜山汛”。凤山寺，原名郭山庙，又名将军庙、威镇庙，位于福建省南安市诗山镇西北角凤山麓，建于五代后晋天福初年（936—947 年），供奉郭圣王。译者注。

Quemoy

To the eastward of Amoy, and separated from it by a channel of from five to seven miles wide, in the middle of which is little Quemoy island, is situated in lat 24°20’30” N. long 118°16’30” E, the island of Chin-mên（金门） or Quemoy, on which is a city of the same name, carrying on a small native trade, and containing, it is said, about 10,000 inhabitants, This island forms the south western side of a harbour （having the mainland on the north east of it） called the bay of Quemoy.

Ts‘ai-ching-hsien（蔡青献）, a man famous in history for having held high office in the reign of the Ming Emperor（嘉靖）, as ruler over five of the thirteen provinces into which the empire was then divided, was born at Quemoy.

金 门

金门岛位于厦门以东、金门湾西南部（陆地位于海湾的东北部），即北纬 24° 20’30”，东经 118° 16’30”，隔一条 5—7 英里宽的水道与厦门相望，中间是小金门岛。金门岛上是与之同名的金门城，据说人口大约 1 万，本地贸易规模小。

蔡清宪[①] 出生于金门，因为他在明朝嘉靖年间身居高位而成为历史名人，他曾经主政过明朝所有行政区划十三个省中的五个。

① 原文为“Tsai-ching-hsien 蔡青献”，实际应为“蔡复一”，“清宪”为其谥号。据记载，蔡复一（1577—1625），字敬夫，号元履，明代同安县翔风里 17 都刘浦保蔡厝（现属金门县）人，明万历二十三年（1595 年）19 岁中二甲第七名进士，是同安科举最年轻的进士。他官至右副都御史，总督贵州、云南、湖广军务，兼巡抚贵州，谥号“清宪”，追赠“兵部尚书”。译者注。

4.Animals

Fauna

The fauna, with the exception of the tiger, in this and the regions around, is but little known to foreigners, and my investigations on this subject, enable me to add but slightly to the information already possessed.

It consists, so far as I have been able to ascertain, of tigers, leopards or panthers, called by the natives pah, an animal, I believe, to be the lynx; and in the large natural forests at Yung-ch'un（永春）, wolves are stated to be found. The rocky hills or mountains, extending from Polam, and forming the highlands of this vicinity, are said to contain wild pigs. In nearly all the hills, foxes, wild cats, badgers, armadillos, porcupines, hedgehogs, stoats, rats, guinea pigs, etc., are more or less numerous.

Formerly, tigers confined their depredations to the sparsely populated neighbourhoods of their rock fastnesses amidst the hills. Of late, they have become so numerous and daring, that scarcely a week passes without some account reaching us, of attacks made on natives, on the cultivated and peopled plains, sometimes two or three hours after daybreak. Such is the terror that they have inspired, that the inhabitants of one small hamlet, at the foot of the hills, have deserted it, and sought the safer shelter of a populous village; and it is significant that the little matsheds, formerly on the ground, in which the Chinese lie to watch their growing crops at night, are now all raised many feet above it, on bamboo poles. When moving about, or travelling at night, torches, and braziers full of lighted wood, are carried.

I am informed by several gentlemen, whose duties as Missionaries, constantly take them into the surrounding districts, that, on an average one man in five days, is killed by these ferocious beasts, while goats, pigs and dogs are continually being carried off, by them. Last year the Rev. W. McGregor, at early morning, was unable to leave his Chapel for some two hours, owing to a tiger, which had apparently "set" his coolie, when outside, prowling and roaring round it.

I have before me, several instances of men, and women, being attacked by these animals, some instances occurring only a few days, or weeks since. The first, is the death of a military mandarin of low rank, and the wounding of two men near Chang-chou, in their endeavour to kill a tiger; the beast escaped. The second refers to the finding of his wife dead, and in such condition as may be supposed, by a husband on his return from work. The murderer was still in the room with his victim, and assistance being procured, was subsequently despatched, from the roof. Two men are reported to have been mauled by a tiger at the stone quarry village, near Haimên, on the mainland opposite Kulangsu. A man is reported to have been seized by the shoulder, in the presence of his wife, and others, she with great courage and devotion, flew to his aid, and seized the tiger by the ears, and tried to pull him off; it instantly turned on her, and bit her also in the shoulder. It was surrounded by the villagers, and killed. In a populous neighbourhood, at the back of the island of Woo-seu （the entrance to the outer harbour）, two tigers were lately seen, their lair, a cave, was marked, the entrance blocked up, and the tigers smoked throughout the night; next morning two men went in, expecting to find the animals suffocated, they were however alive; the men fired killing one, the other retreated further into the cave, and was not followed.

A man on the top of a hill, or bluff, a few weeks since saw *three* tigers （probably a tigeress and her cubs） advancing parallel to a field, in which a man was working. He shouted to the man, without at first attracting his attention, at length he was heard, but too late for escape, for one tiger had turned off into the field and made at the man. In utter desperation he stood his ground, and met the attack with a swingeing blow from the heavy hoe shaped pick he was working with; the tiger is said to have come at the man four times, when the latter by a providential blow, succeeded in laying him dead at his feet.

Next follows a dreary story of a woman being taken from her own door, in the gloaming, and horribly mangled, within a short distance. In this case the tiger was also killed. A place called K'he be（坑尾）, about fifty miles distant, is said to be infested with them; and it may be that, owing to this region being devastated and nearly depopulated, by the Tai-ping rebels, in 1864, and 1865, they have so increased, as to be driven by want of food, thence to this neighbourhood. Certain it is that they have been met with near Peh-

Chui-ya, Wo-seu, on the Nan-tai-wu, near Hai-mên, and at other places, where they have rarely, if even, been seen before. Tales of their depredations at Hai-tsang（海沧）just at the head of the inner harbour, are also common. I have, myself, on several occasions tracked the foot prints of tigers, along the damp sandy beds of the nullahs, among the inner range of mountains at this place, and also found their excrement. There are some caves said to be their lair, near, but I never found a guide who could, or who would, point them out.

That tigers are numerous may safely be inferred from one, two, and sometimes three, of their cubs, being brought here, occasionally, for sale. The animal is described as being marked in the same manner as the Bengal tiger, but longer in the legs, and shorter in the body. Judging from one which I have seen, and from a cub, I once possessed, I should say that this description is generally correct.

四、动物资源

动物群落

除了老虎以外，外国人对厦门和周边地区的动物群知之甚少，而我对这个问题的研究使我能够对人们已经掌握的信息作一些补充。

据我所知，厦门的本地动物包括老虎和豹（当地人称为 pah），但是我认为这是一种名字叫做猞猁的动物。在永春广袤的天然森林里据说有狼出没。从浦南绵延而来的丘陵和山峦在附近形成高地，据说那里有野猪。几乎所有的山上都有狐狸、野猫、獾、犰狳、豪猪、刺猬、白鼬、老鼠、豚鼠等，数量难以统计。

以前，老虎的活动范围仅限于大山里面的岩石洞穴附近，或是在人烟稀少地带捕杀猎物。近来，随着族群数量的大量增长，老虎变得大胆无畏起来，几乎每个星期我们都会收到老虎在田地或人来人往的平地上袭击当地人的报告，有时候袭击就发生在天亮后两三个小时。老虎的出没引起了人们的恐慌，以至于山脚下有个小村庄的村民们不得不抛家舍业，搬到人口稠密的村庄寻找安全的避难所。以前中国人在地面上搭建起以便夜间躺在里面看护庄稼的凉棚，现在不得不用竹竿将凉棚撑离地面几英尺高，这就很能说明问题。当人们夜间四处走动或者赶夜路的时候，得带着火把和烧着满满柴火的火盆。

几位因传教而经常到周边地区的牧师告诉我，平均每五天就有一人被这些凶猛的野兽杀死，而山羊、猪和狗经常被叼走。去年的一个清晨，麦格雷戈牧师被困在他的教堂里约整整两个小时，因为有一只老虎显然已经在外面

“盯上了”他的苦力，于是便围着教堂徘徊、咆哮。

我手头上有几个男男女女被这些野兽袭击的例子，有些就发生在几天或者几周之前。第一个例子发生在漳州附近的打虎行动中，一名下级军官被老虎咬死，还有两个人受伤，老虎却逃脱了。第二个例子，正如人们所想象的那样，丈夫下工回家时发现妻子已经死亡，此时“凶手”和死者还在屋子里面，于是人们前来相助，随后从屋顶上将“凶手”杀死。据报告，两名男子在鼓浪屿对岸的陆地上，也就是海门附近一个开办采石场的村庄里被老虎咬伤。另据报告，一名男子被老虎抓住肩膀，他的妻子以及其他人也在场，她鼓起极大的勇气、做好牺牲的准备，飞奔过去帮忙。她抓住老虎的两只耳朵，试图把它拉开。老虎立刻攻击她，也咬住她的肩膀。于是村民们把老虎围住，然后杀了它。在浯屿岛（外港的入口）后面一个人口稠密地带，最近有两只老虎出没。人们在老虎的洞穴上做了记号，堵住了入口，用烟往洞里熏了一整个晚上。第二天早上，两人进了洞穴，希望这两只老虎已经窒息而死，可是却发现它们还活着。于是人们开了枪，打死了其中一只，另一只则往洞穴的深处里逃窜，人们就不再往下追了。

几个星期以前，有人在山顶上或是悬崖边看到三只老虎（可能是一只母老虎和它的两只幼崽）齐头并进走向一位独自在地里劳作的农民。他赶紧朝那人喊叫，起初没有引起农民的注意，最后农民终于听到了，但是来不及逃跑了，因为一只老虎已经跑进了田里，向那人扑去。在走投无路的情况下，那人挺身而上，抄起手上沉重的扁嘴镐头猛烈反击。据说老虎四次扑向那位农民，结果那人有如神助般的一击，把老虎打死在他的脚下。

接下来是一件令人悲伤的事，一位女子黄昏的时候被老虎从自己的家门口叼走，在离家不远的地方被撕扯到面目全非。在这起事故中，老虎也被杀死了。据说在离此地约 50 英里外的坑尾，老虎成群出没。这可能是因为 1864 年和 1865 年太平天国起义军摧毁了这一地区，导致人口几乎被清空，老虎数量急剧增加，只能跑到这一带寻找食物。可以肯定的是，人们曾经在白嘴崖附近、浯屿、南太武山上、海门附近和其他地方看到过老虎，这在以前是极其罕见甚至是不可能的。老虎在内港顶端的海沧袭击民众的传言也经常有之。我自己也曾经几次在本地的深山老林中沿着山涧潮湿的沙床追踪到老虎的脚印，也看到过它们的排泄物。据说附近有一些山洞是老虎的巢穴，但是我从来没有碰到过一个能够或者愿意指出这些巢穴的向导。

老虎数量众多，我们完全可以从偶尔被带到这里出售的一只、两只、甚至三只幼虎中推断出来。人们都说这种老虎与孟加拉虎有着相同的特征，但是腿更长，躯体更短。从我见过的一只成年老虎以及一只老虎幼崽来看，应该说这个描述大体准确。

Birds

There are in the interior, pheasants, a kind of partridge, called by the Chinese, Chuh Chi, or Bamboo fowl, quail, pigeons, snipe, geese, duck of almost every description, curlew, pelicans, herons, and an endless variety of water fowl, including, as I have now and again seen, the sea eagle. Amongst the birds which are not game, are most of those varieties, from the rook down to the sparrow, common alike in China and England. One beautiful bird, rare and valuable with us, the Hoo-poo, is found here in numbers; kites, hawks, minas, and the hwa-me-chéao, or painted eyebrow'd thrush, are also here, as elsewhere in China.

鸟 类

内陆地带有野鸡，这是山鹑的一种，中国人称之为雉鸡或竹鸡。还有鹌鹑、鸽子、沙锥、鹅、鸭、杓鹬、鹈鹕、白鹭，以及各种各样的水禽，包括我经常看到的海鹰。非猎禽的鸟类主要是乌鸦、麻雀及其各类亚种，它们在中国和英格兰都很常见。美丽的戴胜鸟，对我们来说稀有而珍贵，在这里却随处可见。正如中国其他地方一样，这里也有鸢、鹰、八哥和画眉鸟。

Fishes

Of fish, and shell fish, I am informed there are nearly one hundred varieties sold in the Amoy market. Within the last month, or so, a curious circumstance has been noticeable. Large numbers of fish, have been found floating on the surface of the water in the outer harbour, either dead or dying. At first this was difficult to account for, but latterly it has been discovered that a kind of leech has been the cause. In many instances these leeches have been found attached to the fish. After sucking the blood of the fish, they detach themselves from it, to go in pursuit of other prey. This leech, when at rest, is about an inch and a half in length, but it has the power of elongating itself to fully twice that length. In addition to its mouth, it is provided with a sucker at the other extremity, with which it holds on to its prey with great tenacity. The presence of this creature is looked upon by the uneducated classes, as an inauspicious omen to the reigning dynasty.

鱼类病虫害[①]

人们告诉我，在厦门市场上销售的鱼类和贝类有近百个品种。大概从上个月开始，人们注意到一个奇怪的情况，大量的鱼漂浮在外港的水面上，这些鱼要么已经死了，要么奄奄一息。起初人们找不出原因，后来发现罪魁祸首是某种水蛭。在很多情况下，人们发现这些水蛭吸附在鱼的身上，在吸完鱼的血液后，它们脱离宿主去寻找其他猎物。这种水蛭静止不动时大约有一英寸半长，但是它却能把自己的身体拉长到整整两倍的长度。除了嘴以外，它身体的另一端有一个吸盘，这个吸盘可以非常牢固地吸附住猎物。这种生物的出现被没有受过多少教育的民众视为统治王朝的不祥之兆。

① 此标题为译者根据内容所拟。原文标题翻译为“鱼类”。译者注。

Reptiles

The reptiles consist of snakes, some specimens of which have been killed, and found to be six, and even eight, feet, in length. They are mostly harmless. A small whiplike snake, and a particular variety of the water snake, of which there are great numbers in these seas, are said to be venomous, as is also a snake, called by the Chinese from the shape of its head, the spoon headed serpent (probably the cobra) , and another known as the banded adder. The centipede, and the scorpion, are common.

爬行动物

爬行动物包括各种蛇。从被人们杀死的一些品种来看，这些蛇 6 英尺、7 英尺，甚至 8 英尺长，它们大多是无害的。有一种像鞭子一样的小蛇，也有一种在这里的海洋中数量众多的水蛇，据说是有毒的。另外有一种蛇，中国人根据它的头部形状称之为“饭匙倩”（可能是眼镜蛇），最后还有一种被称为带状蝰蛇。蜈蚣和蝎子很常见。

Part III

Trade

General sketch of its history under the Sung, Yuan, Ming, and Tartar dynasties. First arrival of European vessels. Superintendency of Revenue on oversea trade, entrusted to Commandant of coast guard. Institution of a tariff. Amount of collection. Misappropriation by Superintendents. Control transferred to Nai-chien, or bureau charged with control of the Eunuchs in Imperial Palace. Given to the local authorities. First establishment of Custom House at Amoy. Institution of present system, whereby Superintendency of Customs, devolves on Tartar General at Foochow. Early tradal relations with European nations. Interesting memorial by Minister on this subject. Hast India Company's tradal relations with Amoy district. Trade with foreign countries prohibited. Amoy reopened by treaty of Nanking.

Trade under the foreign Inspectorate. Values of Import, Export, and Re-export trade 1862-1872. Dues and Duties collected during same period. General remarks on trade. Tea Trade between Amoy and "Formosa".

第三部分
贸易篇

宋、元、明、清朝时期的对外贸易概况——欧洲船舶首次抵华——朝廷授权海防同知监管对外贸易税收——关税制度——收费金额——负责人挪用税银——控制权转移到内监——移交给地方当局——厦门第一个海关机构的设立——在目前的制度下，海关监管权移交给福州的清朝将军负责——与欧洲国家的早期贸易关系——给事中傅元初关于开放洋禁的有趣奏疏——东印度公司与厦门地区的贸易关系——朝廷禁止海外贸易——《南京条约》使厦门重新开放。

外国人监管下的贸易情况——1862—1872年输入、输出和再输出贸易量——同期收取的税费和关税——贸易的总体情况——厦门与台湾的茶叶贸易。

General sketch of its history

It is difficult to fix a precise date to the opening of trade at Amoy with foreign countries, but Dr. Williams, in his Middle Kingdom, p. 418-9, writes, "The first recorded knowledge of the Chinese, amongst the nations of the West, does not date further back than Ptolemy, the celebrated geographer, who seems also himself to have been indebted to a Tyrian author, named Marinus. Previous to this period, however, the account of the existence of the land of Confucius, and an appreciation and demand, for the splendid silks made there, had reached Europe. It is a difficult, and almost profitless, endeavour, to attempt to identify the names of the places mentioned in these early records. The emporium called Cattagara, may have been Canton; it may also have been Fuhchou, or Amoy, for the places are all natural entrepots."

Sir John Davis, p. 19, says, "Abundant evidence is afforded by Chinese records, that a much more liberal, as well as enterprising, disposition, once existed in respect to foreign intercourse, than prevails at present. It was only on the conquest of the empire by the Manchus, that the European trade was limited to Canton." He further speaks of Chinese junks being seen as far West, as the coast of Malabar, about the end of the 13th century; and adds, that even before the seventh century, it appeared from native records, that missions were sent from China, to the surrounding nations with a view to inviting mutual intercourse. The earliest attempt at intercourse between Great Britain, and China, was in the year 1506, when three ships, bearing letters from Queen Elizabeth, to the Emperor of China, were despatched, but they were lost on the way, and the project was not then renewed; and the oldest record of the East India Company at Canton, is dated the 6th April, 1637. It is, however, certain that tradal relations have existed from a remote period, between Amoy, the Philippines, the Dutch and English settlements of Batavia, Sourabaya, the Straits of Sunda, Padang, Sumatra, and in fact with the entire Malay Peninsula, the Gulf of Siam, the coast of Borneo, and even as far as Timor, in the far east of the Sunda Islands, and Dutch possessions.

At this date, it appears that the port of Amoy was at Haitêng (Haitien) , a large town up the Nanchiang, or Southern river, about fourteen miles from the present port, for in the Hsia-men-chih (Chinese History of Amoy) , the following passage occurs: Before the opening of Amoy as a port of trade, junks from seaward, on entering, passed the island of Taitan, and proceeded to Haiteng, where, after reporting to the District Magistrate, they were allowed to move up to Shih-ma (Chioh-bei) , when compliance with the port regulations being secured, by certain native hongs, they were allowed to discharge, and load cargo. Of the nature and value of this trade, no authentic record is obtainable. The silting up of the estuary below Chioh-bei（石码）, and Haiteng, probably necessitated the removal of the port to Amoy.

The notices of this region contained in Chinese histories, topographical works, and itineraries, which alone form the source of the information, historical, and geographical, possessed by occidentals, for the ages preceding the visit of the Roman Catholic propagandists, shew that the existence of Amoy, as an emporium of trade, dates but from a, comparatively, recent period, some 190 years. The maritime and foreign trade, for which this portion of the empire has been so preeminently distinguished, was, prior to that date, divided between the two prefectural cities of Chang-chou, and Chuan-chou.

During the reign of Yuan-yu, 7th emperor of the Sung dynasty, (from 1085 to 1100 A.D.) , the province of Fuhkien, was first opened to foreign, or oversea, trade, and an official was appointed to superintend (as is evident from his title, 市船提举司) the collectionof duties upon, and other matters relating to, the commerce in, goods brought from abroad. The trammels by which this branch of trade had been confined, having been now removed, the people found a new, exciting, and, though dangerous, highly profitable, means of gaining wealth. They flocked to it, intercourse increased, and traders came in such numbers, that this single official, was quite unable to maintain anything like a useful surveillance. To remedy this state of things, the government entrusted the examination of goods, to the ordinary local officials at the various ports of entry (viz. the 知州，通判，知县监官）, who acted under the supervision of an officer specially appointed to watch the transport and shipment of goods, whose title was “转运司”.

The trade appears to have gone on developing in much the same manner, under the succeeding dynasty of Yüan. And about the commencement of the 13th century, ① it had attained such proportions that the local authorities found it impossible, while attending to their own duties, to superintend the collection of the revenue, and legislate on the matters incidental to such extensive commercial transactions. They were, therefore, relieved of this burden, and replaced by a staff of seven officers, specially appointed to take cognizance of all such matters.

Under the Ming dynasty, owing probably to the depredations committed on this portion of the seaboard, in the first instance, by the Japanese, and subsequently by Chéng-chih-lung, and his son Chêng-kung (Koxinga), this trade appears to have declined. For the three superior officers of the staff, established by the preceding dynasty, were dispensed with, and three subordinate officers were found sufficient to maintain an effective control. And when an entire cessation of trade was caused by these troubles, this small staff was removed to Fuchow, from Chüan-chow-fu, known to foreigners as Chinchew, to which it was originally appointed.

It is stated in the Tung-hsi-yang-káo, a sort of compendium of notices of Foreign countries, that it was the custom under the Sung dynasty, to send an official on board every vessel leaving the port, whose duty it was to see her beyond its limits. An inscription was then cut upon some rock in the neighbourhood, giving the vessel’s name, date of departure, her destination, &c. This practice would seem to have been maintained under the two succeeding dynasties, but gradually fell into desuetude.

The first notice of the arrival of an European vessel, would appear to date from about the commencement of the fifteenth century. As it is stated that, during the reigns of Chêng-hua (成化), and Hung-chih (弘治), the 8th, and 9th, emperors of the Ming dynasty, whose reigns dated from 1465-1486 and 1486-1506, respectively, amongst the foreign vessels that arrived, some were observed of an immense size. Aided by the natives, who were of course

① The exact date is not known. The Pa-min-t‘ung-chih, or “Universal gazeteer for the province of Fuhkien” fixes it at 1316, while the Chüan-chou-li Kuan-chih, or “Category of officers who have held appointments with the prefecture of Chüan-chou,” gives the date at some time between 1298 and 1309.

the chief gainers, the supercargoes of these vessels, appear to have carried on an extensive system of smuggling, till the outbreak of troubles with Japan put a stop to the collection of all revenue. Soon afterwards the prohibition of oversea trade, was promulgated afresh.

The first notice of their arrival, expressly stating them to be European vessels, does not appear, however, until some years later. In 1548 (26th year of Chia Ch'ing, the 11th emperor of the Ming dynasty) Frankish vessels arrived with foreign merchandise at Wu-hsü, an island situated some 7 miles seawards of Amoy, at Chuan-chou-fu, and Chang-chou-fu. A brisk trade sprung up with the natives, but it was looked upon with unfavourable eyes by the officials, who, it would appear, conceived the idea that these attempts on the part of foreigners to effect an opening for their commerce, were but the prelude to further and more forcible designs of possessing themselves of the country, and therefore, determined to crush it in embryo. A force was, therefore, despatched by Ho-chiao（柯乔）, the Hsün-hai-tao, or Intendant commanding the Coast guard contingent, to put a stop to the trade; but as this produced no result, a censor named Chu-wan（朱纨）, seized over 90 of the merchants, and struck such fear into the mercantile body, generally, by their summary execution, that all commercial operations were suspended, and trade brought to a stand still. It was, however, merely a temporary cessation, and we find about twenty years later, the native officials, themselves, awakening to the importance of international commerce, and of the advantage to be derived from it. In 1567 Tu-shih-min（涂泽民）, a Censor, and Governor of the province, addressed the throne praying that the prohibition restricting the coast-landers from the free use of the sea, be abolished, and commerce with all foreign nations, Japan alone excepted, be legitimised, The request was granted, and a large trade was again created, which appears to have been carried on viâ Meiling, in Nanchao（南诏之梅岭）, until the frequent piratical depredations compelled a change of course to Hai-têng. The new port prospered so rapidly, with this fresh influx of trade and wealth, that, say its chronicles, in 1564, a Tung-chih, a magistrate, of very subordinate rank, it is true, but still the superior of any the district had yet been able to boast of, was added to the staff of collectors, and two years later Hai-têng was erected into a Hsien, or district town.

The collection of duties on the foreign trade, does not appear to have been entrusted to any regular branch of the Civil Service, prior to 1573, but to have been handed over to a set of officials, appointed, certainly, for this express purpose, but now under the control of one chief, and now of another. In this year, however, a Custom House, charged with the collection of these duties, was established by Lo-ching-hsiao（罗青霄）, the Prefect of Chang-chou, and its superintendence handed over to the subprefect commanding the Coast guard.

This addition to the duties of Commandant of the Coast guard, had been made six years earlier, in consequence of a proposal made by Wang-chi-tsung（王起宗）, the then controller of Customs, to establish a branch office at Kuia-hsü（圭屿）, a small island lying nearly opposite Hai-têng. This change appears, though such is not stated to be the case, to have been decided upon, partly, to avoid the expense of maintaining another establishment in such close proximity to that of Hai-têng, but chiefly, from a desire to ensure, as Superintendent of Customs, by the appointment of an officer holding a military command and entrusted with the disposal of troops, a person not only whose interest it would be to put a stop to the smuggling, always prevalent in this district, and to clear the approaches of the port from the piratical craft which infested it, but who would, at the same time, have the means at his disposal for effecting these ends, which hitherto with divided authority and conflicting interests, it had been impossible to secure.

In 1576, it was decided, at the proposal of the Governor, Liu-jao-hui（刘尧诲）, to devote the shipping duties, to the payment of the troops. In order then, to bring the total collection as much as possible under control, and to fix a sum, upon the receipt of which they could depend, the authorities drew up a sort of tariff, consisting principally of three descriptions of duties. Amongst these, first comes the license fee, which is subdivided into two classes, according as the license includes, or not, the right to trade with the northern "Formosa" ports of Tan-shui, and Chilung (Keelung). For a license to trade with any foreign port, a fee of 8 taels was levied. Were it desired to include the two ports of Tan-shui, and Chilung, as well, an endorsement to this effect was made on the original document (both documents being the same in the first instance), and an additional fee, of 2 taels, collected.

The most important of these duties, as returning the largest sums to the treasury, are the Export duty（水税）, and Import or Inland tax（陆税）. It is exceedingly difficult to trace, accurately, the nature of these taxes after the lapse of so many years, and with the sparse records kept in statistical works. But as far as can be judged. the Export duty would appear to have been levied upon the owner, or charterer, of the vessel, and to have been computed according to her size, so that, as far as the manner of levying be regarded, it would correspond more nearly with our Tonnage dues, than Export duty. Import duty, on the other hand, was levied on the salesman, and the amount proportioned to the quantity of goods disposed of. It would thus seem probable, that a lump sum was levied roughly, on each vessel leaving, or entering, the harbour, the dues in the former case, to be paid by the charterer alone; and in the latter, by the purchasers of goods, in proportion to the amount purchased.

An "Additional tax"（加增饷）, of 150 taels, would appear to have been levied on every vessel, probably, though I have been unable to discover whether such is the case or not, upon her entering and leaving the port, in addition to those above mentioned, in order to recoup the government, for the loss they would, otherwise, have sustained from impurities, or alloy, in the Philippine, and Japanese silver, which had to be received in payment of duties from vessels coming from those countries, just as, previous to the ratification of the treaty of Tientsin in 1860, a meltage fee of 1.2 per cent, was levied on the total amount of duties, from the foreign merchants established in China.

The amount of duties to be accounted for annually, was, at the same time, fixed at 6,000 taels: four years subsequently, this sum was raised to 10,000 taels, and in 1594, this latter amount, was almost tripled, and the collection fixed at 29,000 odd taels. This system of a fixed return, gave rise, however, to an immense amount of embezzlement; for the collector, after paying the amount required annually, into the treasury, instead of reporting any surplus there may have been, to the higher authorities, retained it as his own perquisite. With an extensive and flourishing trade, this was a very considerable amount, and in all probability, the sum which the collection might by law attain, was but a small portion of the actual total receipts. For, in spite of the fact that this sum was, on one occasion, increased to three times what it had previously been, the enormous fortunes amassed by the collectors, proved such a public scandal, (which culminated during the holding of Ying-so 嬴缩) that the authorities found themselves compelled to insist upon the literal execution of a law, passed to regulate the appointment to the post of collector, many years previously, but which had been allowed to fall into disuse, whereby the Superintendent was to be changed annually; and it was decided that, in future, a sub-prefect should be elected from some one district within the province, annually, to fill the post.

It seems probable that when the proposal made by Liu-jao-hui to apply this revenue to the maintenance of the troops, was acceded to, the sum collected by the Hai-têng Custom House, alone, was devoted to meet the expenses of the troops under the orders of its superintendent, the Commandant of the Coast guard. For mention is made in the local records, that some time subsequently, when the military treasury of Chüan-chou became exhausted, a proposal was made by the Intendant of the circuit of Chang-chou-fu, and Chuan-chou-fu, to establish an officer meanway between the two places at Chung-tso-so（中左所）, as Amoy was then called, whose duty it would be to determine whether the vessel came from the Eastern sea, i.e. Japan, or from the Western, i.e. Manila, or one of the many islands in the Malayan archipelago, which maintained tradal relations with this port. In the former case the duties were to be received by the Chüan-chou treasury; in the latter by that of Chang-chou.

But this was, of course, found to be impracticable, so matters remained in *statu quo* until 1600, when a general enquiry and examination was instituted by the Emperor Wan-li, throughout the empire, into the manner of conducting public business, as then followed by the officials. One of the eunuchs attached to the palace, a body who throughout this dynasty, and especially during the later reigns, enjoyed posts of vast influence and great emolument, named Kao-ts'ai（高斋）, was commissioned by Imperial decree to inspect the Superintendencies of Customs, both Inland and Maritime. A man of considerable ability, he laid bare a number of the abuses, which had of late disgraced the system. He proposed, and carried, some radical changes, but as he had the aggrandisement of his own order more at heart, than any patriotic desire to serve his government, or ameliorate the condition of the people, the abuses continued in much the same state as previously, the only difference in result, being, that the eunuchs, instead of the local officials, enriched themselves at the expense of the revenue. The principal changes effected were, reversion of the collection upon all the natural produce of the province, and of the sea, to the Nai-wu-fu, a metropolitan office charged with the direction of all matters of the Imperial household; and the transference of the control of the revenue derived from foreign, or oversea, trade, to the Nai-chien, or bureau charged with the control of the eunuchs belonging to the Imperial Palace. This officer lost no time in despatching members of his own class, to take up the appointments throughout the province. The system, however, did not enjoy along life. Fourteen years after, Kao-t'sai fell into disgrace, and with him collapsed the supposed reform, whose real end, it was now seen, had been little else than to extend the power of the eunuchs. The Nai-chien was deprived of its control of the revenue, which was simultaneously reduced to one third its previous amount, and entrusted to an officer, to be appointed yearly, from among the ordinary local authorities. All matters of particular importance, however, he had to refer to his superior, the prefect, for decision. So matters continued till near the close of Chung-chën's reign, the last emperor of the Ming dynasty, when Chêng-chih-lung commenced his harassing descents upon this portion of the empire, as has been detailed above, seized upon the revenues, and in short caused an entire cessation of commerce.

When in the 22nd year of Kang-hsi, 1683, "Formosa" was incorporated with the fifteen provinces, and the Imperial authority firmly established on the mainland, the local magistrate, through the medium of the Board of Works, pointed out to his Majesty, the advantages the people were deprived of, by the maintenance of the old prohibitions against oversea trade; and prayed that the province of Fuhkien might be opened to this trade, as, three years earlier, had been done with that of Shantung. In consequence of these reports, the prohibition was withdrawn, and the sea opened up to the coastlanders, for both fishing and commercial purposes. This necessitated the establishment of another port, for, during the troublous times that were just finished, the alluvial deposits brought down by the river Lung, had so shoaled its bed as to render its navigation by vessels of such a size, as had previously frequented it, impossible. Amoy, situated just at the mouth of the river, and possessing admirable harbour accommodation, was, notwithstanding its political insignificance, its paucity, in fact, almost absolute want of commercial resources, the spot fixed upon, and a Custom House was opened there the same year.

The same spirit of adventurous daring, which had always distinguished the inhabitants of this portion of the empire, coupled with the necessity of seeking an escape from the calamities caused by famine, and the ravages of buccaneers, induced considerable emigration to Manila, and the islands of the Malayan archipelago. A large and flourishing trade arose in consequence, indeed, the dimensions it attained, in so short a space of time, are quite remarkable, and shew how lucrative it might have been, had it been properly fostered and looked after. But after flourishing and increasing for thirty-six years, official opposition again interfered with its usual baleful influence, and put a stop to it, on the ground that cargoes of rice were, in violation of the trade regulations, being smuggled away to Manila, and Batavia.

During the next few years, deprived of their means of gaining a livelihood, and harassed by failure of crops and other distresses, the people were forced to resort to brigandage and robbery to escape starvation. Recognising the fact that the only means of alleviating the distress, was to find some new occupation for the idle and destitute; and that the removal of the oversea trade prohibitions, by finding a profitable outlet for native produce, by the employment of large numbers on the shipping, &c., and by the stimulus it would afford to local manufacture and emigration, would be most calculated to attain this end, Kao-chï-cho, governor of the province in 1727, prayed his Majesty to legalise this branch of commerce. His request was based upon two reasons, first, that the wealth of the people would be greatly increased, and the provincial treasury filled with the revenue derived from it; and, secondly, because rice, to compensate the constant failure of crops, might be obtained from abroad. His prayer was granted, and from this date sprung up a flourishing and lucrative trade with the South, which has not, except by such indirect means as excessive taxation, and extortionate fees, been since interfered with.

The collection of the Revenue, was, as has been stated, entrusted to the local officials subsequent to 1614, and it would appear, continued to be so (if indeed the collection was attempted at all, during this unsettled period; it certainly was not during the latter portion), at the time of the reduction of "Formosa", and the establishment of a Custom House at Amoy in 1683. The following year, however, in Fuhkien and Shantung, the two provinces, in which oversea trade had been legalised, two Superintendents of Customs, one Manchou, and one Chinese, were appointed to control the collection: but in 1729, after the prohibition, issued in 1719, had been rescinded at the instance of the governor, it was entrusted to him.

This arrangement continued up till 1788, when the General commanding the Tartar garrison of Foochow, was appointed Superintendent of Customs for the whole province, and deputies, appointed by him, had control of the subordinate posts. This is the system, which obtains at the present time.

对外贸易概貌

想要确定厦门开展对外贸易的准确日期是一件困难的事。不过，卫三畏博士（Dr. Williams）在他撰写的《中国总论》第418–419页中这样写道：“西方国家有关中国人的书面记载最早可以追溯到著名的地理学家托勒密（Ptolemy）①，他似乎也受到提尔②作家马里纳斯（Marinus）③的启发。然而，在此之前，欧洲已经流传着有关孔子故乡以及人们对那里所生产的华丽丝绸的赞美和渴求的描述。试图确定这些早期记录中所提到的地名是困难的，而且几乎毫无益处。名为卡塔加拉（Cattagara）的贸易港口可能是广州，也可能是福州或者厦门，因为这些地方都是天然的转运口岸。”

约翰·戴维斯（John Davis）④爵士在其所撰著作的第19页中写道：“中国的历史记载充分证明了过去中国人在对外交往方面过去比现在的主流模式更具自由、进取的特性，只是在满洲人征服帝国以后，与欧洲之间的贸易才被限制在广州。”他进一步谈道，大约在13世纪末，中国帆船已经出现在远如西方的马拉巴尔（Malabar）⑤海岸。他还补充道，从本国的记载来看，甚至在7世纪以前，中国已经派遣使团到达周边国家以建立双边交往关系。英国和中国之间试图进行交往的年份最早可追溯至1506年。当时，英国派遣

① 托勒密（约90—168）是古希腊天文学家、地理学家、地图学家，其著作《天文学大成》创立了地心说，其另一部著作《地图学指南》主要论述地球的形状、大小、经纬度的测定以及地图投影的方法。译者注。

② 提尔（Tyre，又译推罗、泰尔、提洛、苏尔）是位于黎巴嫩南部的古腓尼基城市。译者注。

③ 马里纳斯（70—130），出生于腓尼基的著名港口提尔，是最早了解如何绘制海图的人。译者注。

④ 约翰·戴维斯（1543—1605），英国探险家。他曾经进行3次北极地区航行，试图寻找西北航道，即由格陵兰岛经加拿大北部北极群岛到阿拉斯加北岸的航道，并详细记录了航行经历。1605年，他于苏门答腊岛海岸外被日本海盗杀害。译者注。

⑤ 马拉巴尔位于印度西南海岸。译者注。

了三艘船只，携带着伊丽莎白女王致中国皇帝的信函驶向中国，可是船队却在途中迷路了，于是计划就此搁浅。有关广州东印度公司的最早活动记录是1637年4月6日。然而，可以肯定的是，在很久以前，厦门就和以下地区存在着贸易往来：菲律宾、巴达维亚的荷兰和英国定居点、苏拉巴亚[①]、巽他海峡、巴东、苏门答腊，事实上还有整个马来半岛、暹罗湾、婆罗洲[②]海岸，甚至远到帝汶岛、巽他群岛遥远的东部地带，以及荷兰属地。

这一时期，厦门的港口似乎在海澄，一个南溪上游的大城镇，离现在的厦门港口大约十四英里，因为在《厦门志》里有如下记载：厦门未开放通商口岸之前，从海上驶来的船只入港前必须经大担岛抵达海澄，向县令报告后，方可驶往石码，经当地商行担保符合入港要求后，方可装卸货物。[③]关于这种贸易的性质和价值，我们没有可靠的记录。也许是石码和海澄以下河口的淤积使得港口不得不迁到厦门。

在罗马天主教宣教士们造访之前的很长一段时间里，中国历史、地理著作和游记中有关本地区的记载是西方人了解本地历史和地理信息的唯一来源。这些记载表明了厦门作为贸易中心的时间只能追溯到距今较近的约一百九十年前。在此之前，本地的海上贸易和对外贸易由漳州和泉州二府共同分担，如今这些贸易早已闻名遐迩。

宋朝第七位皇帝元祐年间（1085—1100年）[④]，福建省首次开放对外贸易，即海外贸易，并任命一名官员掌管关税征收以及其他与进口货物贸易有关的事宜（从其官职名称“市舶提举司”中便可见一斑）。摆脱了束缚这一行业的枷锁，人们找到了一种前所未有、激动人心，虽然危机四伏但又利润丰厚的致富途径。他们纷纷涌入这一行当，对外往来增加，商人数量剧增，以至

① 苏拉巴亚（Sourabaya）现为爪哇岛上的印尼城市“泗水”。译者注。

② 婆罗洲（Borneo）系加里曼丹岛的旧称。译者注。

③ 据道光《厦门志》卷五之二十七：“厦门未设口之先，各船驶进大担口，直抵海澄石码，行保在焉。”进口由海澄查验。译者注。

④ 元祐（1086—1094年）是宋朝第七位皇帝哲宗赵煦的第一个年号。译者注。

于单凭一位官员已经无法有效掌控住局面了。为了弥补这种不足，朝廷委任各入境口岸的普通地方官员（即知州、通判、知县、监官）检视货物。这些官员在一名专门负责检视货物运输和装运的官员，即转运司的监督下行使职权。

在随后的元朝时期，对外贸易似乎也以同样的方式继续发展。大约到了13世纪初[①]，对外贸易份额已经达到非常庞大的规模，地方官员发现他们已经不可能在履行自己份内职责的同时，还能监管关税征收，还要颁布律令以规范如此庞杂的商业交易活动所附带的各项事宜。因此，朝廷为地方官员免除了这项负担，专门任命七位官员[②]来负责所有这些问题。

到了明朝，先是日本人，后来是郑芝龙和他的儿子郑成功在这部分沿海地区进行劫掠，可能是出于上述原因，对外贸易似乎已经萎缩了，于是朝廷撤免了前朝设立的三个职位较高的官员，认为三位下级官员[③]就足以维持有效的管控。当这些动荡导致贸易完全终止的时候，这个小衙门就从泉州府迁到了最初设置时的所在地福州。

《东西洋考》[④]是一部介绍外国概况的汇编，里面写道：宋朝规定，对于每一艘出港的船只，官府要委派一名官员上船，其职责是送船驶离自己的管区，随后在附近岩石上刻上船只的名称、出发日期、目的地等信息。这种做法似乎在随后的两个朝代中得到沿袭，但是后来逐渐消失了。

欧洲船只首次到达此地的记载似乎可以追溯到大约15世纪初。据称，在

① 确切日期已无从知晓。《八闽通志》确定为1316年，而《泉州历官志》给出的时间介于1298年至1309年。作者注。综上所述，此处应为十三世纪末、十四世纪初。译者注。

② 据道光《厦门志》卷七之一，这七位官员是：市舶司提举二员，同提举、副提举各二员，知事一员。译者注。

③ 据道光《厦门志》卷七之一，明朝任命的官员是：市舶提举司提举正、副各一员，吏目各一员。译者注。

④《东西洋考》为明代张燮撰写的介绍东西洋列国以及明朝海外贸易的著作。该书卷七与此处相关的记载为：宋时，发舶海上，郡国有司临水送之。尝登泉山，见刻石纪岁月甚伙，尔时典綦重云，闽在宋元俱设市舶司，国初因之，后竟废。《厦门志》卷七之一的相关记载为：又按《东西洋考》，宋时，发舶海上，郡国有司临水送之。登泉山刻石记岁月，元明因之皆设官，后竟废。译者注。

明朝第八位皇帝和第九位皇帝时期，即在位年份分别为成化 1465—1486 年[①]和弘治 1486—1506 年[②]的两位皇帝时期，人们发现有些抵港的外国船只体型巨大。在作为主要受益者的当地人帮助下，这些商船货运员似乎经营着庞大的走私系统。直到与日本人的战争爆发后，税收的征收工作才宣告停止。不久之后，朝廷重新颁布海外贸易禁令。

然而，直到几年后才第一次有欧洲船只到达的明确记载。1548 年（明朝第十一位皇帝嘉靖二十六年[③]），佛朗机[④]船只载运外国商品到达位于泉州府和漳州府之间、距离厦门大约七英里海路的浯屿岛[⑤]，与当地人的贸易立刻红红火火地开展起来。但是官府对此却心怀成见，他们认为这些外国人的到来表面上是为了开拓贸易市场，实际上这是他们使用更加暴力的手段进一步将帝国占为己有的序曲而已。因此，官府决心将对外贸易扼杀于萌芽状态，巡海道副使柯乔[⑥]派兵前去制止贸易，但是无功而返。于是，都御史朱纨[⑦]就抓捕了九十余名商人并将他们全部从速处决，这给商家带来普遍的恐惧，以至于所有商业陷于停顿，贸易停止。然而，这只是暂时的中断，我们发现大约二十年后，本地官员便意识到国际贸易以及从中获取利益的重要性。1567 年，都御史兼福建巡抚涂泽民上奏请求废除限制人员上岸的海禁政策，允许当地与除日本以外的世界各国开展商业贸易。这一请求得到了批准，一个贸易王国再一次呈现于世人面前。贸易似乎先是通过南诏的梅岭[⑧]进行的，后因海盗

---

① 成化为明朝第九位皇帝明宪宗朱见深的年号，起止时间为 1465—1487 年，共二十三年。译者注。

② 弘治为明朝第十位皇帝明孝宗朱祐樘的年号，起止时间为 1488—1505 年，共十八年。译者注。

③ 嘉靖是明朝第十二位皇帝明世宗朱厚熜的年号，嘉靖二十六年为 1547 年。译者注。

④ 佛朗机，又译“佛郎机”，是明清时期中国人对葡萄牙、西班牙的泛称，有时也指欧洲。译者注。

⑤ 据道光《厦门志》卷七之一：“嘉靖二十六年，有佛朗机船载货泊浯屿，漳泉贾人往相贸易。”译者注。

⑥ 据道光《厦门志》卷十六之一：“（嘉靖）二十六年佛朗机番船泊浯屿，巡海副使柯乔发兵攻之不克。”柯乔（1497—1554），明南直隶（现安徽省）池州府青阳县人，嘉靖二十五年（1546 年），柯乔升任福建按察使副使、巡海道副使，专理海道。译者注。

⑦ 朱纨（1494—1550），江苏苏州人，据《明史·卷二百五·列传第九十三》，朱纨于嘉靖二十五年（1546 年）擢右副都御史，巡抚南赣。嘉靖二十六年（1547 年）改提督浙、闽海防军务，巡抚浙江，防御倭寇。译者注。

⑧ 即漳州市诏安县梅岭镇。译者注。

频繁劫掠被迫改道海澄。新的港口迅速兴旺起来，贸易量剧增，财富大量涌入。据县志记载，1564 年[①]，征税官队伍里增设一名同知，虽然这实际上是个级别很低的地方官，但也是此地级别最高的了。两年后[②]，海澄被设立为县，或称县治。

1573 年[③]以前，对外贸易关税的征收似乎不是由常设的专门衙门负责，而是交由专门任命的一套官员班子负责，只不过主管官员时常更换。然而，就在这一年，漳州知府罗青霄设立了督饷馆[④]负责征收关税，由海防同知负责税收的监管工作。

这次海防同知职责的拓展源于六年前[⑤]，时任督饷通判王起宗上奏朝廷，提议在海澄对面的一座小岛——圭屿[⑥]设立饷馆。虽然朝廷没有明说，但是之所以决定改变现行体制，部分原因是为了节省开支，避免在海澄附近的地方开设另一个性质相同的衙门，更主要是因为朝廷希望通过任命一位握有兵权的武官来掌管征税，这样他不仅肩负扑灭本地历来猖獗的走私行为的职责，又能驱离侵扰港口的海盗船只，同时又可便宜行事来实现这些目的，这在目前权力分散和利益冲突的情况下是无法保证实现的。

1576 年[⑦]，巡抚刘尧诲提议，征收船舶税以支付兵饷。当时，为了尽可能地征收所有税款并确定征税金额以满足他们的需求，官府拟定了关税种类，

① 应为 1563 年（即嘉靖四十二年）。据道光《厦门志》卷七之一：“《海澄县志》：嘉靖四十二年，增设同知，镇抚海澄。”译者注。

② 即嘉靖四十四年（1565 年）。据道光《厦门志》卷七之一：“（嘉靖）四十四年设海澄县治。”译者注。

③ 应为 1572 年。据道光《厦门志》卷七之一：“（隆庆）六年，漳州郡守罗青霄议征商税及贾舶，以海防同知为政。”隆庆六年为 1572 年。译者注。

④ 明代初期设市舶司，后期设督饷馆，实质上是近代海关的前身。据道光《厦门志》卷七之一：“隆庆间，改海防馆为督饷馆。”隆庆是明朝第十三位皇帝明穆宗朱载垕的年号，起止时间为 1567—1572 年，共六年。译者注。

⑤ 指嘉靖四十五年（即 1566 年）。译者注。

⑥ 据清顾祖禹《读史方舆纪要》第九十九卷漳州府海澄县“云盖山”条下：圭屿“在海澄县东海中央，状如龟浮水面，俗呼龟屿。亦曰鸡屿”。现为福建厦门鸡屿岛。译者注。

⑦ 应为 1575 年。据道光《厦门志》卷七之一、之二：“万历三年，巡抚刘尧海请税舶以充兵饷。”万历三年为 1575 年。译者注。

主要有三种类型的税收。首先是许可费[1]。根据是否拥有台湾北部的淡水港和鸡笼港[2]的贸易权，许可费被细分为两类。与任何外国港口开展贸易，要征收银 3 两的许可费。如果要把淡水和鸡笼这两个港口也包括在内，就要在原始单据[3]上作批注（这两种单据起初都是一样的），并收取银 2 两的额外费用。

这些关税中最重要的是进口税和出口税，即水税和陆税，因为它们在上交国库的税款中数额最大。由于年代久远，再加上统计数据的不足，很难准确地查明这些税收的性质。但据判断，出口税似乎向船东，或者船只的承租人征收，并根据船只的大小来计算税额。所以，就征收方式来看，它更接近于我们的吨位税，而不是出口税。另一方面，进口税是向商户征收的，其金额与所购货物的数量成正比。因此，似乎有可能对每艘出入港口的船只一次性征收一笔大概的总额，前一种情况下的税款由船只的承租人单独支付，在后一种情况下，税款由货物的购买者根据购买数量按比例支付。

除了以上提到的税收外，虽然我一直无法确定情况是否如此，但官府似乎还会在每艘船进出港时征收银 150 两的“附加税”，即加增饷，目的是补偿因菲律宾银和日本银中含有杂质或合金而给官府带来的损失。这笔费用以关税的形式附加给上述国家的船主，就像 1860 年《天津条约》[4]批准之前，官府向在中国经营的外国商人征收 1.2% 的银两熔铸折耗费[5]一样。

当时[6]，每年征收的关税数额定为银 6,000 两。四年后，这一数额被提高到银 1 万两，到了 1594 年[7]，关税数额几乎又增加了 2 倍，征收额定为银

① 即“商引”。译者注。
② 即台湾基隆港。译者注。
③ 即“文引”。译者注。
④ 清政府和英国关于“倾熔银两”的有关规定请参见《中英通商章程善后条约》（即《中英天津条约》的补充）第九款。译者注。
⑤ 即“倾熔之费”。译者注。
⑥ 指万历三年，即 1575 年。译者注。
⑦ 应为 1593 年。据道光《厦门志》卷七之二：“（万历）二十一年，溢至二万九千有奇。”万历二十一年即 1593 年。译者注。

29,000 多两。然而，这种固定税额制度导致了严重的贪污。税务官员在向国库上缴了每年所定的金额后，没有向上级报告盈余情况，而是把这部分作为自己的额外收入截留下来。随着贸易的蓬勃发展和壮大，被截留的款项达到非常可观的数额，而且通过依法征收而获得的税额极有可能只占实际总收入的一小部分而已。事实上，尽管依法征收的税额曾经增加到以前的三倍，但税务官员所积累的巨大财富表明了截留款项是一个人尽皆知的丑闻（这种丑闻来自于对税银赢缩[①]的操纵），以至于朝廷不得不严格执行一项多年前通过但是已经被废弃的律令，以规范税务官员的任命。根据律令，主管官员每年更换，同时规定，以后将每年从全省各府选择一名佐官[②]担任主管。

当刘尧诲提出用关税收入以维持军队的建议被采纳时，海澄督饷馆很有可能奉其最高长官即海防官之命将征收来的款项用于支付军队的开支。因为地方志上有记载，不久以后，当泉州兵饷匮乏时，漳泉道提议在两地之间的中左所，即现在的厦门，设置官衙以决定船只来自东洋，即日本，或者是来自西洋，即同该港有贸易往来的马尼拉或马来亚群岛。在前一种情况下，关税由泉州收取，后一种情况则由漳州收取。

但是，这种做法显然不切实际，所以朝廷只能维持现状。1600 年，万历皇帝下令对全天下官员的政务作风开展广泛调查和检查。在整个明朝，特别是明朝后期，皇宫里的宦官是个身居高位、领取高俸的群体，其中有位名叫高寀[③]的宦官奉圣谕检查市舶司的水税和陆税情况。高寀精明能干，他揭露了近年来许多使整个官场蒙羞的滥用职权行为，提出并实施了一些激进的变革措施，但是由于他的所作所为本意是为了强化自己的统治秩序，而不是出于报效国家或者造福于民的爱国之心，这些滥权行为与之前相比几无任何改变，

① 赢缩即盈亏。译者注。

② 佐官此处指“同知”。译者注。

③ 原文为“Kao-ts'ai 高斋”。据道光《厦门志》卷七之二：“（万历）二十七年大榷天下，命宦官高寀入闽。”万历二十七年为 1599 年。译者注。

唯一不同的是，这次是宦官而不是地方官员以贪污关税收入之利来中饱私囊。这次变革的主要措施是：本省和海上物产税费的收取归内府[①]（京城掌管所有皇家事务的衙门）；外国或海外贸易的关税征收则交由内监（宫廷宦官的管理机构）来负责。高寀不失时机地委派同党到全省各地任职。然而，这些措施并非“长命百岁”，十四年后[②]，高寀失宠了，随之而来的是所谓的变革失败。现在看来，改革的真正目的不过是为了扩大宦官的权力。内监被剥夺了税收控制权，同时税收也减少到原来的三分之一，征税主管交由当地官府每年委派一名普通地方官担任，如遇重大要事，则需交由上级，即知府决断。此后，这种体系得以延续到明朝最后一位皇帝崇祯统治的末期，后来郑芝龙开始上岸骚扰明王朝的这部分地区，正如前面已经详细说明的那样，他侵吞了关税收入，最终导致了商业的完全停顿。

康熙二十二年（1683 年），台湾被纳入清朝十五个行省[③]的版图，皇权统治在大陆牢固确立。由于延续了明朝的海禁政策，当地民众的生计无以为继，地方官员通过工部向皇帝上奏，请求福建能像三年前的山东那样开放海禁。朝廷议覆的结果是取消海禁，允许沿海百姓出海捕鱼和贸易。这就需要建设一个新的港口，因为在刚刚结束的动荡时期，九龙江带来的冲积物使河床变得非常浅，以至于那些以前经常光顾的大型船舶已经无法通航了。尽管政治意义不大，而且商业资源稀少，甚至可以说是完全匮乏，但是厦门就坐落在河口，并且拥有优越的港口住宿条件，所以地点就这样选定了，同年，海关也在此地开设了。

① 原文为“Nai-wu-fu”，即内务府。但内务府是清朝的官署名，掌宫廷事物，其并非宦官机构。明代内府是明代宦官伺奉皇帝及其家族的机构，内设十二监、四司、八局，统称二十四衙门。据道光《厦门志》卷七之二：“闽山海之输半搜罗以进内府，而舶税归内监委官征收矣。”译者注。

② 即 1613 年。据道光《厦门志》卷七之二的“（万历）四十一年撤高寀”，万历四十一年为 1613 年。译者注。

③ 在行省设置方面，清朝初年基本沿袭了明代所置的两京与十三布政使司，共 15 行省。康熙七年（1668 年），形成了“内地 18 省”的格局，分别为直隶、江苏、安徽、山西、山东、河南、陕西、甘肃、浙江、江西、湖北、湖南、四川、福建、广东、广西、云南、贵州。康熙二十三年（1684 年）设台湾府，隶属于福建省。译者注。

帝国这一地区的民众向来具有与众不同的英勇无畏和富于冒险的精神，加上逃荒逃难以及躲避海盗蹂躏的需要，民众大量移居到吕宋以及马来亚群岛，庞大而繁荣的贸易就此发展起来。事实上，贸易在如此短的时间内达到相当大的规模，表明了如果得到恰当的培育和悉心的经营，这将是个非常有利可图的行当。但是在经过三十六年[①]的繁荣发展后，官府以海外贸易一向具有弊端为由对其进行干涉，他们提出了反对意见并严禁继续通市，理由是大米被走私到吕宋和巴达维亚的行为违反了贸易规定。

在接下来的几年时间里，民众失去了谋生的手段，同时又饱受农作物歉收和其他苦难所困扰，只能通过偷盗和抢劫来填饱肚子。朝廷意识到减轻苦难的唯一办法是为无所事事和一贫如洗的人谋取新的出路，而取消贸易禁令乃是最为万全之策，它不仅能为本地物产寻找到一个有利可图的销售渠道，还能通过航运等行业的发展创造大量就业机会，又能通过海外贸易刺激当地的制造业和移民产业。1727 年，巡抚高其倬奏请开洋通商，原因有二：其一，可以大大增加民众的财富，不断充盈该省的税收收入；其二，可以从国外运回米粮以弥补农作物持续歉收所造成的粮食短缺。他的奏折得到了批准，从这一天起，除了过度的税收和过高的收费等间接手段以外，与南洋的贸易蓬勃发展起来了，它不但为人们带来了丰厚的利润，而且再也没有受到任何干扰。

如前所述，从 1614 年[②]到 1683 年清朝收复台湾以及厦门设立海关之时，税款的征收都是由地方官员负责的，而且政策似乎一直都是如此（如果在那个动荡的年代里他们真的想收税的话，当然后一段时期[③]他们根本没有想到征税的事）。但是，第二年，在海外贸易已经合法化的福建省和山东省，朝

① 据道光《厦门志》卷七之二：“（康熙）五十六年，因愚民私聚吕宋、噶喇吧（即今之印尼首都雅加达），有盗米透露诸弊，严禁通市南洋。”自康熙二十二年（1683 年）开放海禁至五十六年（1717 年）严禁通市南洋，前后共三十五年。译者注。

② 应为 1613 年，即从（万历）四十一年撤高寀起。万历四十一年为 1613 年。译者注。

③ “后一段时期”应指清廷于 1661 年颁布迁海令后到 1683 年的这一段时期，沿海省份所有居民及其财物一律内迁，对外贸易停止，关税征收自然是无从谈成。译者注。

廷任命了满和汉海税监督各一名官员来管理关税的征收。不过，1719 年[①] 颁布的禁令被取消以后，朝廷于 1729 年应福建巡抚之呈请把税款的征收交由其管理。

这一体系一直持续到 1788 年，驻防福州的八旗兵将军被任命为福建海关税务监督，由他指派副手们控制海关所属职位，这种体系沿袭至今。

① 应为 1717 年，参见前页注释①。译者注。

First arrival of European vessels

To the Portuguese belong the honor of being the pioneers of foreign trade in China. In 1516 Raphael Perestrello, came to Canton; and in the following year, a fleet of eight ships, under the command of Fernão Peres de Andrade, arrived on the coast. Their trade spread rapidly, and at an early period they traded at the neighbouring port of Chinchew, here, and at Ningpo, for in 1545, ancient records state, that the provincial government attacked the native Christians and Portuguese at Ningpo killing 900 of the former, and 300 of the latter and that, four years later, the Portuguese were driven from their newly formed settlement at Chinchew.

The character of these early traders appears to have partaken more of the gentleman rover, or adventurer, than of the steady merchant and scrivener; and they seem to have been far more conversant with the sword, than with the peaceful ways of commerce. There was a want of prudence in their bearing towards the Chinese. They were intriguing, arbitrary, and aggressive; having gained a footing on shore, they proceeded to erect Forts, then usually followed an attempt to levy taxes, or other exactions, and otherwise they so conducted themselves, as to sow in the Chinese mind, that distrust of foreigners and their motives, which occasionally makes itself manifest at the present day. The Spanish, Dutch, and English, who followed them pursued much the same course.

Speaking of the transfer to the American people of a full share of all the suspicion, distrust, contempt, and hatred, which had been excited in the Asiatic mind by the acts of the Portuguese, Spanish, Dutch, English, &c., committed chiefly in the 16th, and 17th, centuries, the writer of an article on American influence on the destinies of Ultra Malayan Asia, in the *Chinese Repository*, 1838, Vol. 7, p. 77, says:

"It is a matter of history that Taiko, Gengin, and their successors on the Japanese throne, the sovereigns who gave its present shape to the foreign policy of that nation, were fully aware of the extent of European aggression on the soil of eastern Asia. Wherever the enterprising Japanese of those centuries, and their Chinese contemporaries, wandered, from India to Acapulco, they gathered and brought home one concurring story of European designs and conduct, varying only in the illustrations of their fraud, cruelty, and highhanded usurpations. The veil of many years is now drawn between us and those days, and the actors and their deeds are generally forgotten. But we have only to look into such records as still remain, only to look on the map, in fact, to see how true it is that scarce a spot on the then known world of the eastern Asia, entirely escaped European aggression. The weaker portions were seized on by right of discovery and conquest, sanctioned by the highest ecclesiastical authority; and where the native states were too powerful to be assailed, each trader sought to gain the same selfish ends by blackening, vilifying, and plundering, his rival of other nations. There was no restriction laid on one which had not been recommended by another. The Spanish denounced the Dutch, as the revolted subjects of his sovereign; and the Dutch told, in secret, of Cortes, Pizarro and Alva. No European people wanted an accuser while a subject of another European state was by; and had it pleased these pagan monarchs to pass sentence accordingly, none would have lacked an executioner. Such was the character of the times when Europe first came into contact with eastern Asia. Such were the impressions then made and ever since transmitted; engraven in literature, interwoven with tradition, identified with education, entering into every conception of the term, rising involuntarily at every mention of the name, European. Such is the sad entail, which is, as the Easterns suppose a part of the lawful patrimony of the Americans; under such ideas of descent they are driven from the harbours of Japan, and restricted in those of China."

The immediate result of these injudicious and high handed measures, here, was that foreigners were driven from the mainland; on which they resorted to "Formosa", Lum-pu-co, and to illicit trade on the China sea. That the value of foreign trade was fully appreciated by the local authorities, and the native traders, even at a very early date, may be gathered from what precedes, and from the following memorial to the Throne, from the censor Ki-shih-chung, which is such a liberal and statesmanlike paper, that I may be pardoned for inserting an abridged translation if it here.

In the third month of the 12th year of Chung-chen（崇祯）*, of the Ming dynasty*（1640）*the Minister or Censor, Ki-shih-chung*（给事中）*, a Foo-yuan-choo*（傅元初）*,*

memoralises the Throne for the removal of the prohibition against oversea trade, and to make an additional port of entry at Amoy, so as to legalise the traffic in the province of Fuhkien. He represents that funds must be raised for mobilizing and provisioning the army, and that already, for this purpose, agriculture is taxed to its utmost by levies in kind. He therefore recommends that what might be argued in the abstract as either detrimental, or beneficial, is not to be considered at so critical a period as the present; and that some modification in practice must be tried. With the merits of a case such as the extension of maritime trade in Fuhkien, he being a native of that Province, is well prepared to speak, and knows that he has a precedent for his action, in the memorials of the Minister Ho-Keao-yuan, who several times, urged this measure, but was always met with Imperial commands to the effect that such innovations could not be sanctioned. The information he has been able to gather of the history of this sea border traffic, is shortly to this effect.

In 1573, the annual oversea revenue of the district of Yue-keang, the harbour of Hai-têng, amounted to Tls. 20,000, being quite sufficient to maintain during a series of years its quota for local garrisons; no additional troops being required to take the field during that period of tranquility, yet no surplus funds were laid by to meet subsequent demands for the repulse of pirates, who, later on, infested the neighbourhood, carrying pillage into all surrounding districts. About the same time western buccaneers made their appearance, causing general consternation by piracy and robbing junks. The local Officials then memoralised the Throne, on this state of affairs, which led to trade being stopped, and this source of revenue had to be abandoned. Writers of books have indulged in the literary conceit of describing the Fuhkien peasantry, as a seafaring race, who look upon |the broad sea as their pasture lands, owing to their depending mainly on its products for their sustenance. Such resources in ordinary times, although precarious in their nature, might suffice, but in times of scarcity, it is distressing to witness the signs of extreme poverty amongst the people, who for relief are tempted to join gangs of desperadoes, and, utterly regardless of life, engage in piracy. These marauding forays along the coast, seem to be the immediate consequence of enforcing the prohibition against trade, for each time it is proclaimed, the people, whose ordinary sources of employment are thus cut off, and who would, otherwise, starve, are driven to resort to these desperate courses, and whole villages are destroyed by them, unresisting and helpless men and women, are cruelly murdered, the youth of both sexes carried off into captivity, and all the portable wealth of the place made away with in a remorseless manner. Since the return to allegiance of the piratical chief, Koxinga, the country has become somewhat tranquilised by the frequent defeats the rebels have sustained at his hands, and the people have had leisure to resume their ordinary occupations; yet such is the attraction of the chances of acquiring rapid gain, that they are entrapped, like silly geese, into breach of the laws by resorting to clandestine traffic with foreigners, which is either carried on at some distance from the coast, or by lurking about the "Formosa" coast, and visiting the dens established there by foreigners, since the ports on the mainland have been closed to the latter. This they are the more readily enabled to do, as the distance from "Formosa" to the principal towns of Chang-chou, and Chüan-chou, (in the Amoy district) is but a voyage of a couple of days and nights. The responsible Imperial Officers for preventing this, who reside in the south of "Formosa", at Tai-wan-foo, content themselves with announcing the prohibition, and forbidding access to their port, but wink at the Portuguese, and Frankish establishments at Keelung, and Tamsui, in the north of the Island. Thus foreign trade may have been prohibited in name, but it still exists in point of fact, owing to the connivance of petty officials, and the eagerness for gain on the part of the native traders. These facts which are well known, being the common topic of conversation in his native place, although attended at present with results much to be regretted, admit of a remedy by pursuing a different course.

(The memorialist's plan is to legalise and foster, the maritime and junk trades, the character of which he proceeds to describe, as follows:)

The character of the trade carried on with foreign vessels, and junks, from distant countries, may be thus classified: Besides the traffickers from the western seas, and the Japanese, there are also the Siamese, and Peguese, who bring products much needed, and consumed, by China; such as sapan-wood, pepper, ivory, and rhinoceros horns, whereas the Franks and Spanish, whose (chief) possessions are silver mines, bring coins very dexterously cast. Our people when trading with these different foreigners; in the one case, barter their goods in exchange for those above mentioned, whilst from the Spaniards and others, they receive nothing but silver dollars. These foreigners are well pleased to obtain our Chinese Silks, in exchange, and as in their countries they do not rear the silk-worm, they are glad to get the raw silk, with which they are able to weave the most exquisite fabrics, wherewith to adorn the person with rich garments. It is a profitable venture for them, as the celebrated silk of Hoo-chou, even here sold for its weight in silver, is, in their countries, worth double that sum. There is likewise much demand, from all comers, for the porcelain of Keang-se, and for the preserved fruits, and delicacies, produced in Fuhkien. Now here is a fine field for profitable commerce for our own people, for we possess those much coveted articles, which are readily handled, and with such we might easily go abroad and successfully compete with them, had we but a fiftieth part of the energy and cleverness of these Franks. The people are prevented from having a share in these good things, and yet have every temptation thrust in their way to misbehave, and involve themselves in all the consequences of being engaged in illicit trade. As to the remedy above alluded to, there is not wanting a precedent, （the reverse of the course now pursued,） for the Imperial sanction was given permitting external trade, shortly after the commencement of the Ming dynasty, when the people of both the Eastern and Western, seas, on being summoned to send tribute, brought it to the Capital, and gave constant evidence of their loyal and respectful feelings, without leading to any rioting or disreputable results. In fact, nothing occurred to disturb the even course of the trade thus sanctioned, even during the disastrous times when all the countries to the west, and the states of Eastern Europe, were suffering disruption, from the Tartar hords under Tamerlane.（The period when Moscow was sacked and burnt, and Bajazet, the Ottoman Emperor, was captured in 1402, appears to be the time to which the Memorialist alludes, for in his next paragraph he makes a significant allusion to troops being sent to guard the frontiers, against an expected invasion of China, for which Timour, in his capital at Samarcand, had been making immense preparations, and was actually on his way for its conquest, when he was fatally attacked by fever.）

In these times, amicable tradal communications, were uninterruptedly maintained with neighbouring states, and China incurred no embroilment with them, although she had to move armies of observation to guard her frontiers, against threatened invasion, （by the common enemy.） Subsequently, on serious complications arising in "Formosa", and on the neighbouring coast, the Ming dynasty became so apprehensive for the safety of those portions of the empire, that they prohibited all access to the coast, and the prohibition not having been since rescinded, the trade has been at the mercy of reckless people, and has become the monopoly of the freebooters of the Coast, involving a needless sacrifice of derivable revenue, to the extent of, at least, Tls. 20,000, annually; and to the great detriment of the legitimate trader. The mere loss to the state is severe enough, and that the benefit should be absorbed by the law breaking freebooter, is deplorable; but these circumstances are not so irritating, as to have to witness the acts of a horde of conniving officials, and petty officers, gloating over their share of the spoils obtained by winking at the trade, and professing, meanwhile, to ignore the tinkling of the dollars, which proclaims its existence to all others less deaf than themselves. Those who under the existing state of things are benefited, are the base illegal traders, who absorb the gains; also the corrupt officials, who, usurping authority, extort a full share for themselves; and such are the consequent evils of keeping the trade closed.

Whereas were foreign trade thrown open, with the exception of a prohibition against trading in munitions of war, sulphur and saltpetre; and the traders of Fuhkien, allowed to deal with all comers, and were other traders from Chê-kiang, and the northern provinces, encouraged to bring their silks, &c, and the porcelain dealers from Keangsi, allowed to resort here, the sum named would not only suffice for the troops, but many estimate that there would be produced T's. 50,000 to Ts. 60,000 instead, which would admit of a surplus, beyond the provincial requirements, being remitted to Peking. The poor people on the coast would accumulate funds, to enable them, in times of scarcity, to buy food, instead of being, as now, so poor that they are driven to piracy. A third benefit would arise, in breaking up the opportunities afforded these minor officials, of employing their perquisites in investments for storing contraband, of which pirates, and others, stand in need, and who are enticed and prepared to pay any prices for such articles.

To meet those changes, should it be permitted to again open the port to trade, all that would appear to be necessary, would be to issue a special Junk clearance on proceeding to sea, or else to reestablish Yue-cheang（月港）*, the port of Hai-ting*（海澄）*, as the port of entry; or to allow it to be fixed at Amoy in the Tung-ngan district. On leaving port, the junk's clearance or pass would suffice; on returning from abroad, the vessels would have to* *put into Canton, or Macao, to guard against their running their cargoes elsewhere on the coast. It would be necessary to entrust the prefects of Chang-chou-foo and Chüan-chou-foo, together with the sub-prefect of Amoy, as Maritime Superintendent, with the control of the trade. The Intendant of these prefectures, should be made the responsible head, reporting to the Lieutenant Governor the annual amount of collection; and all surplus sums, beyond Tls. 20,000, should be transmitted by him to Peking, under voucher cover to the Board of Revenue, to devote to Imperial purposes. The memorialist here makes mention （with a view to obtaining an appointment for him） of an official of his district, who has rendered meritorious services in the suppression of piracy and protection of the junk trade, and then proceeds to say that in the old times, as recorded in the local topographies of the districts, there was a government anchorage at Chüan-chou-foo for junks arriving from sea, and that there is still one in existence in the Canton waters, at Macao, in the Heang-shan district, and that, in the opinion of many others besides himself, there need be no distinction between the provinces of Canton, and Fuhkien, for all Fuhkien people, feel alike on the subject; and he respectfully solicits, that orders be given to the Fohkien Governor, and Provincial Judge, to investigate, whether, or not, it be really practical to entirely suppress maritime trade; and if not, whether there would not arise beneficial results from throwing that trade open, and that they should consult with the most enlightened amongst the traders of Chüan-chou-foo and Chang-chou-foo as to what the best regulations would be for properly legalising the trade, so as to terminate the illicit traffic carried on by the lawless; and, at the same time, husband the resources for maintaining the troops.*

There are records that, in 1651, the Dutch were trading here, and that they lent assistance to the government in attacking Koxinga at Quemoy, and Amoy. About 1664, the East India Company opened a trade at Amoy, and at "Formosa", with Koxinga's son, "but this rude chieftain had little other idea of traffic than as a means of helping himself to every curious commodity the ships brought, and laying heavy imposts on their cargoes." A treaty was entered into with him by which freedom to go unattended where they pleased, access to the King, liberty to trade with whom they pleased, and to choose their own clerks, was conceded. It was also agreed "that what goods the King buys shall pay no custom; that rice imported pay no custom, that all goods imported, pay three per cent, *after sale*; and all goods exported, be custom free." [1] In 1678, a factory was ordered to be established; and trade was continued for several years, apparently with considerable profit, though the Manchus continually increased the restrictions under which it laboured. The investments here, and at Zelandia in "Formosa", were $30,000 in bullion, and $20,000 in goods; the returns were chiefly silk goods, tutenague, rhubarb, &c.

In 1681, the Company withdrew their factory; and two years later, in the 22nd year of Kang-hi, the Marquis Hi-lang memorialized the Throne, to re-establish a Custom house. In the following year a Custom house for the collection of duties on foreign vessels, and on native junks, was established. In 1685 the Company's trade was again renewed by the arrival of the ship *Delight*. In 1689 the Supercargoes at Amoy were put in confinement, and not long after, one was chained in his own factory; heavy bribes were paid for their release. About 1702, both at Amoy, and Canton, the foreign trade was granted by the Government, as a monopoly, to a single privileged merchant. But it became so hampered with illegal exactions and extortions, that, in 1725, the Emperor Yung-ching published the first Tariff of duties, in the shape of a code, which was enjoined on the officers of all the Custom houses. The Tariff was not regarded, and "heavy duties, arbitrary, and haughty conduct towards the supercargoes, extortions and ruinous delays" were persisted in. Speaking of these improprieties "A visitor to China" writes: " Had a proper representation of these abuses been conveyed to the Emperor, there can be little doubt that redress would have been obtained. The Edict published at Amoy proved that the cabinet of that time was well disposed towards the promoting of foreign trade, and to the removal of any obstacles to its prosecution that were brought under their cognizance. The difficulty was to find means of communicating with the Court on the subject of wrongs. committed by the very parties, who were the regular channels for the transmission of petitions."

In 1701, the Company's investment at Amoy, amounted to £34,400 only; but trade was continued here, long after the greater part of it had been transferred to Canton, as, in 1723, Captain Hamilton loaded here. The extortions prevailing, together with the dangers of the "Formosa" Channel, probably induced the Company to withdraw. By 1720 the duties at Canton had risen to four per cent on all goods exported, and on imports, to about 16 per

[1] Vide Williams' Middle Kingdom, Vol. 1.

cent, besides a heavy measurement duty on ships, a present of Tls. 1,950 to the Collector of Customs, and a large fee from purveyors of provisions to ships; and, in 1728, an additional duty of 10 per cent was added on all exports, and it was not until 1736, that this impost was removed. These charges also obtained here. In 1725, the Hsia-mên-chih, speaks of the Spaniards as trading here, and paying tribute. The tribute paying is also ascribed to England, Holland, &c. In the collected statistics of the Ta-tsing dynasty, it is also stated that in the 58th year of Kien-lung, （about 1793,） Great Britain, first brought tribute, 英吉利国乾隆五十八年遗部臣入贡 .

Spain appears to have been especially favoured by China, for when the commerce of Great Britain was restricted to Canton, she enjoyed the privileges of trade, at Macao, and of access to this Port and Canton. She does not appear to have fully profited by the privileges she then, and subsequently, enjoyed; nor from the geographical positions of her fertile and beautiful insular possessions in the Philippines. With the wants of the teeming population of China within four or five days easy sail, India and the Malayan archipelago on the west and south, and the islands of the Pacific, and the rising Empire of the New World on the east, Spain possessed advantages for trade, with which few rivals should have been able to cope.

In 1734, one English ship, the *Grafton*, was sent to Amoy, but the extortions were found to be greater than at Canton; as, in addition to the regular duties, there was an extra charge of 20 per cent for the Haikwan: she therefore withdrew. In 1744, the *Hardwicke*, East Indiaman, having received intelligence that three Spanish ships were lying off Macao to intercept her, sailed away for Amoy, she was compelled by the Mandarins to deliver into their charge her arms and ammunition, and to anchor in the inner harbour, without conditions. where she remained fifteen days, when finding no disposition to trade, and that she was being subjected to intolerable exactions, she was obliged to proceed to India without a cargo, and against the monsoon. Sir John Davis, writes of Canton, at this time, p. 55-56: “The extortions increased in spite of all representations on the part of the supercargoes. The Hong Merchants used every endeavour, and at length succeeded, in preventing the access of Europeans to the officers of government, finding that by that means, they could exercise their impositions on both, with the greater success and impunity. To the foreigners, they alleged that the Mandarins were the authors of all exactions on trade;

to the Mandarins, that the foreigners were of so barbarous and fierce a temper, as to be incapable of listening to reason. The grievances suffered by our trade led to a remonstrance, in which the principal points were the delay in unloading ships; the plunder of goods; the injurious proclamations annually put up by the Government, accusing foreigners of horrible crimes, with the intent to expose them to the contempt of the populace; the extortions under false pretences of the inferior officials; and the difficulty of access to the mandarins." He adds: "It is to be apprehended that the want of union among the Europeans, had the usual effect of frustrating their attempts at redress."

It was, in those days, the practice on the arrival of a ship here, to despatch a boat to demand her name, nation, and business, an exact account of the number of her crew, and guns, her cargo, and the time she intended to stay. This being complied with, her arms, and munitions, were handed into the care of the authorities, a payment of about $1,700 for Port charges demanded, and a permit to remain in the harbour issued. The Mandarins appear to have adjudicated on matters concerning the internal economy of foreign ships, as in the case of the *Success*, in 1720, the Hai-fang-ting entertained a complaint from the sailors against her Captain, and directed the distribution of prize money as under:

Captain's share..	£1,466.10.10.
Second Captain's share..	£733.5.5.
Captain of Marines, Lieutenants of the ship, and Surgeon.................	£488.16.8.
Foremast-man..	£97.15.4.

But before compelling the Captain to this distribution of shares, "he ordered one half the cargo to be secured, for the benefit of the owners; which, in ready money, wrought silver, gold, and jewels, amounted to between £6,000 and £7,000 sterling. This he caused to be immediately put on board a Portuguese East Indiaman, called the *Queen of Angels*, Don Francisco La Vero commander. This ship was unfortunately, burnt at Rio de Janeiro on June 6th, 1722, so that of these effects the owners received no more, the charges of salvage deducted, than £1,800." A British ship from Madras, the *Ann*, having been severely squeezed by the purchasers of the major part of her cargo, (who, it is stated, were recommended by officials,) becoming bankrupt, shortly after obtaining about Tls. 1,500 worth of goods; her

Captain did not trumpet forth his wrongs, but on receiving his port clearance and his guns, loaded the latter, cleared ships, beat to quarters, and seized a Japanese Junk, worth twice the value of his cargo, and bore off with her into the bay. Some twenty or thirty boats, crowded with men, went in pursuit; but the stout Captain fired into them with his stern gun and put them to flight. This affair coming to the ears of the Emperor, the officials were ordered to be punished, and their Trade since the establishment of the Foreign Inspectorate of Customs, property confiscated, after satisfaction had been made to the Japanese owners of the Junk. This well merited severity induced, for a time, more care in their dealings with British ships.

It is unnecessary to particularise details further, and it will be sufficient to state that trade continued, with various checks and stoppages, until the issue of the Imperial edict ordering the East India Company's agents to withdraw, as all foreign trade was, in future, to be restricted to Canton. This edict was obeyed, and the port was closed against foreigners until legally reopened by the 2nd article of the Treaty signed at Nanking, the 29th August 1842.

Of the events which led to this Treaty, and subsequent Treaties with Great Britain, America, France, etc.,etc., it is not necessary here to allude. It will be sufficient to take a brief glance at the progress of trade since the establishment of the Foreign Inspectorate of Customs.

与欧洲国家的早期贸易关系

葡萄牙人有幸成为开拓中国对外贸易市场的先驱。1516年[①]，拉斐尔·佩雷斯特洛（Raphael Perestrello）到达广州；第二年，费尔南·佩雷斯·德·安德拉德（Fernão Peres de Andrade）[②]率领一支由八艘船只组成的船队抵达中国沿海。他们的贸易迅速开展起来，早期他们在邻近的泉州港、厦门港以及宁波进行贸易。根据旧文件记载，1545年，巡抚衙门派兵袭击并杀死了九百名宁波当地的基督徒和三百名葡萄牙人。四年后，葡萄牙人被驱逐出他们刚在泉州建立起来的定居点。

这些早期商人的性格特征更像是周游列国的绅士或冒险家，而不是稳重的商人和经纪人，与和平的商业方式相比，他们显然对武力手段要更为熟悉。他们诡计多端、专横武断且好斗成性，在处理与中国人的关系时缺乏深谋远虑。刚在岸上站稳脚跟，他们便开始建造堡垒，然后通常还试图向民众征税、敲诈勒索或犯下其他恶行。他们的所作所为在中国人的脑海中播下了不信任外国人、怀疑他们居心不良的种子，时至今日这种不信任偶尔还会表现出来。紧随其后的西班牙人、荷兰人和英国人也走上了同样的道路。

葡萄牙人、西班牙人、荷兰人、英国人等欧洲人在16和17世纪所做的恶事在亚洲人心中激起了猜疑、戒备、蔑视和仇恨，这些情绪一点不漏地转移到了美国人身上。《中国丛报》1838年第7卷第77页刊登的一篇标题为《美国对亚洲外马来地区命运的影响》（*On American Influence on the destinies of*

① 葡萄牙人乔治·欧维士（Jorge Álvares）于1513年到达中国广东沿海的Tamão岛（一般认为是广东台山的上川岛），是首批到达中国沿海的葡萄牙商人之一。参见林梅村、郝雨凡、吴志良、林广志主编：《澳门学引论：首届澳门学国际学术研讨会论文集》，社会科学文献出版社，2012年， 第583–606页。译者注。

② 又译“安德福”。译者注。

Ultra Malayan Asia）的文章里写到：

醍醐和光仁[①]及其日本王位的继承人，那些塑造了当今日本外交政策的天皇们，都充分意识到欧洲人在东亚的土地上侵略之甚，这是历史性的大事。那几个世纪里，有胆识的日本人和他们同时代的中国人，从印度到阿卡普尔科（Acapulco）[②]，无论他们走到哪里，都从不同渠道搜集到并带回去一个由欧洲人设计并付诸实践的共同故事，不同之处仅仅在于有关他们欺诈、残暴和专横夺权等具体行为的描述。现在，我们和那些日子之间隔着一层岁月编织的面纱，演员和他们的表演已经普遍被我们所遗忘。但是，我们只需要看看现存的记录，只需要看看地图，我们就会发现事实上在当时已经为人所知的东亚世界中，几乎没有一处地方能够完全躲避欧洲的侵略。在最高教会当局的授意下，欧洲人通过开发和征服的手段侵占弱小地区；在土邦[③]力量过于强大而无法依靠武力征服的时候，每个商人都试图通过抹黑、诋毁和掠夺他国竞争对手来达到自私的目的。没有人提出对其他人的言行进行任何限制。西班牙人谴责荷兰人是其君主的反叛臣民[④]，荷兰人偷偷控告了科尔特斯、皮泽洛和阿尔瓦[⑤]。欧洲人不想在另一个欧洲国家的臣民面前成为被告，要是这些异教徒君主乐意据此判刑，他们就不会缺少刽子手。这就是欧洲首次与东亚接触的时代特征和当时欧洲给世人留下的印象，它从此传播开来，镌刻于文学中，交织在传统里，与教育等同，渗透到与这个词汇相关的每一个概念中，一提到欧洲人这个名字就不由自主地浮现出来。这是可悲的继承，并被东方

① 原文为 Taiko 和 Gongin，但是日本历史上并无此两位天皇，最接近的发音是“Daigo”和“Konin”，即“醍醐”和“光仁”。产生此种误差的原因可能是音变的缘故，故此处取“醍醐”和“光仁”。译者注。

② 阿卡普尔科始建于 1550 年，是墨西哥一座美丽且古老的港口城市，1565—1815 年间为与菲律宾进行贸易的主要港口。译者注。

③ 原文为“native states”，即“土邦”。

④ 尼德兰（意为“低地”）包括当代的荷兰、比利时、卢森堡三国和法国北部的一小部分，古代曾由罗马统治，14 世纪至 16 世纪中期，通过中世纪的王朝婚姻关系和王位继承，尼德兰成为西班牙的一部分。为摆脱西班牙的专制统治和宗教迫害，西属尼德兰与西班牙帝国于 1568 年至 1648 年期间爆发战争，西班牙帝国称之为低地国叛乱。战后尼德兰联省共和国独立，建立“荷兰共和国”。译者注。

⑤ 此三人均为西班牙航海家、殖民者。译者注。

人假定为美国人合法遗产的一部分。在这种“出身论”的影响下，美国人被驱逐出日本的港口，被限制在中国的港口地区。

这些浅薄的高压措施导致外国人被赶出了大陆。为了解决这个问题，他们只得转向台湾和琉球，在中国海上进行非法贸易。然而，当地官府以及本地商人早已充分认识到对外贸易的重要性，这可以从下面这份给事中[①]上报给皇帝的奏疏或者此前的其他奏章里找到证明。这是一份思路非常开阔、充满政治家风范的奏疏，诸位请原谅我在此插入这份奏疏的部分节译[②]。

明崇祯十二年（1640年[③]）三月，给事中傅元初就开洋禁一事上疏，奏请增开厦门口岸，以使福建海上贸易合法化。他提出必须筹集资金以充兵饷，为达此目的，农业征税已达极至。因此，他建议在目前这样的关键时期，不宜抽象地考虑开洋禁有害或者有益，而是应该根据实际情况做一些变通。鉴于福建先前开洋市带来的利益，作为福建人，他已经准备好对此加以分析说明，同时他知道在此之前尚书何乔远曾经多次上疏，敦促开洋互市，但朝廷多次下了敕令，大意是此种变革不可实行。目前为止，他所能收集到的关于此地海上贸易相关信息的大意是如此。

万历年间[④]，开洋市于漳州府海澄县之月港，一年得税二万有余两，以充闽中兵饷。海上久安，武备废弛，遂致盗贼劫掠，兼以红毛番时来倡夺船货，官府以闻，朝廷遂绝开洋之税。然语云：海者，闽人之田，海滨民众，生理无路，兼以饥馑荐臻，穷民往往入海从盗，啸聚亡命。海禁一严，无所得食，则转掠海滨。海滨男妇，束手受刃，子女银物，尽为所有，为害尤酷。近虽

① 给事中，全称为六科给事中，据《明史》卷七十四《职官三》：给事中执掌“侍从规谏、补阙、拾遗，稽察六部百司之事”，实际上是专司谏言、监察方面的官职。译者注。

② 此处为奏疏的节译，回译参考了《清一统志·台湾府》附录之崇祯十二年三月给事中傅元初《请开洋禁疏》，其中斜体字为英文原作者添加的内容，小括号内为作者向西方读者所做的解释。译者注。

③ 应为1639年。译者注。

④ 英文原文为1573年，即万历元年。译者注。

郑成功[①]就抚之后，屡立战功，保护地方，海上颇见宁静。海滨之民，惟利是视，走死地如鹜，往往至岛外区脱之地曰台湾者，与红毛番为市，红毛业据之以为窟穴。自台湾两日夜可至漳、泉（州之厦门地区）内港，驻扎于台湾南部台湾城负责执行禁令的官员满足于宣布禁令以及阻止民众进入港口，对吕宋佛朗机于岛屿北部之鸡笼、淡水建立定居点熟视无睹，因下层官员之默许，致使有禁洋之名，未能尽禁洋之实，此臣乡之大可忧者，如今之计，唯有另外寻找解决办法。

给事中上疏的目的是促进开洋互市的合法化并促进其发展。他接着描述了开洋贸易的特征，如下所述：

盖海外之夷有大西洋，有东洋。大西洋则暹罗、柬埔诸国，其国产苏木、胡椒、犀角、象牙诸货物，是皆中国所需。而东洋则吕宋[②]，其夷佛朗机也，其国有银山，夷人铸作银钱独盛。中国人若往贩大西洋，则以其产物相抵；若贩吕宋[③]，则单得其银钱。是两夷者，皆好中国绫缎杂缯。其土不蚕，惟藉中国之丝到彼，能织精好缎匹，服之以为华好，是以中国湖丝百斤值银百两者，至彼得价二倍。而江西瓷器、福建糖品、果品诸物，皆所嗜好。佛朗机之夷，则我人百工技艺有挟一器以往者，虽徒手无不得食。民众虽然被禁止参与有利可图之事，然而他们受到诱惑而行不端之事，结果造成违法贸易。至于前文所提之寻找解决办法一事，朝廷已有先例可循，只需恢复以前的做法即可。因为国朝初期先后招徕，东西二洋入贡之夷恭谨信顺，与狡悍不同。事实上，朝廷所批准之贸易平稳发展，未受任何干扰，即使西洋以及东欧各国饱受帖木儿[④]鞑靼游牧部落的侵扰。（1402年莫斯科遭洗劫以及奥斯曼帝国苏丹巴

① 英文原文为“Koxinga”，即“国姓爷”。译者注。

② 英文原文为“Spanish”，即“西班牙人”。译者注。

③ 英文原文为“Spaniards”，即“西班牙人”。译者注。

④ 帖木儿帝国（1370—1507年），是中亚河中地区的西察合台蒙古贵族帖木儿于1370年建立的帝国，帝国的鼎盛时期横亘从小亚细亚到印度德里的西亚、中亚和南亚和费尔干纳盆地，北起锡尔河和咸海，南及阿拉伯海和波斯湾的大帝国。译者注。

耶赛特被活捉[①]似乎发生在上疏者所提及的那段时期，因为在奏疏的下一段落，他特别提到朝廷派遣官军卫边，抗击即将入侵的来敌，原因是帖木儿在都城萨马尔干紧锣密鼓准备出征，事实上他在征讨途中死于热病。）

在此期间，中国与邻国的友好贸易不受干扰持续进行，与他们并无任何纠纷，虽然另得派兵戍边，观察敌军动向以防止他们共同敌人的入侵。随后，台湾及周边海域局势复杂起来，明朝开始为这部分国土的安全感到忧虑，于是决定禁绝开洋，禁止令迄今仍未废止，而利乃归于奸民矣。夫利归于奸民，而使公家岁失二万余金之饷，犹可言也。利归于奸民，而使沿海将领、不肖有司因以为奇货，掩耳盗铃，利权在下，将来且有不可言者。窃谓洋税不开，则有此害。若洋税一开，除军器、硫磺、焰硝违禁之物不许贩卖外，听闽人以其土物往，他如浙直丝客、江西陶人，各趋之者当莫可胜计，即可满足兵饷需求，或有云可至五六万，而即可省原额之兵饷以解部助边；一利也。沿海贫民多资以为生计，不至饥寒困穷，聚而为盗；二利也。沿海将领等官，不得因缘为奸利，而接济勾引之祸可杜；三利也。

倘以此言可采，则今日开洋之议，洋税给引，或仍于海澄县之月港，或开于同安县之中左所。出有定引，归有定澳，不许窜匿他泊；即使漳、泉两府海防官监督稽查，而该道为之考核，岁报其饷于抚臣。有出二万余之外者，具册报部，以凭吊用。上疏者此处提及其乡弁[②]屡立奇功，希望加升赏，其继续写到，市舶司实置在泉州，载在旧制可考。广东香山澳亦见有税额。闽、广一体耳，此非臣一人之言，实闽省之公言也。伏乞下闽省抚按，查洋禁果否尽闭？开洋果否无害有利？广询泉、漳士民，着为一定之规，庶奸利可杜、兵饷可裕矣。

① 1402年春，帖木儿动员14万左右的军队，进攻奥斯曼帝国。7月20日在安卡拉战役大败奥斯曼帝国，俘其苏丹巴耶塞特一世，使其帝国疆域成为从印度德里到小亚细亚、美索不达米亚的大帝国。译者注。

② 奏疏原文系“臣乡弁郑芝龙”。译者注。

据记载，1651 年，荷兰人在厦门从事贸易活动，并帮助官府在金门和厦门两地攻打郑成功。大约 1664 年，东印度公司在厦门和台湾两地与郑成功的儿子进行贸易，“但是，这位粗鲁的首领除了搜罗夷船带来的各种奇珍异宝供自己享用，并对他们的货物征收重税以外，心思几乎没有放在同他们互市上面”。双方签订了条约，允许荷兰人自由地前往任何地方而无需当地派人陪同，可以随时面见郡王，可以自由地与任何他们愿意交往的人进行贸易，自由地雇用职员。双方还同意“郡王购买的货物免征关税，进口大米免征关税，所有进口商品在销售后征收百分之三的关税；所有出口商品均免征关税”[①]。1678 年，东印度公司下令开办了一家工厂，双边贸易持续开展了几年，尽管在满人不断加码的限制措施下艰难发展，但公司显然也获得了可观的利润。公司在此地以及热兰遮城的投资是现金计 3 万银元，实物值 2 万银元，回购的主要商品是丝绸产品、中国白铜和大黄等。

1681 年，东印度公司撤走工厂。两年后，即康熙二十二年，靖海侯施琅奏请在此地重设海关，第二年，向外国船只和本国帆船征收关税的海关成立了。1685 年，随着“欢乐号”（Delight）商船的到来，该公司再次恢复了贸易。1689 年，商船的货物押运员被集体关进厦门牢房。事发后不久，又有一人被官府用链子锁在自己的工厂里，公司花了巨额贿赂才将他们赎了出来。大约 1702 年，朝廷把厦门和广州的对外贸易作为一种垄断经营权授予了一位特权商人，由此导致的非法敲诈勒索已经严重阻碍了贸易的发展。1725 年，雍正皇帝以法典形式颁布了第一次税率表，并要求所有海关官员务必严格执行，但是官员们视若无物，“沉重的关税、对货物押运员的专横傲慢、勒索和让人耗费不起的拖沓延误”仍然存在。在谈到这些不端行为时，“一位访华游客”写道：“要是有人向皇帝告发这些滥权行为，皇帝毫无疑问将会拨乱反正。

①参见卫三畏：《中国总论》卷一。作者注。

在厦门颁布的敕令证明了当时朝廷对促进对外贸易以及对他们正在审理的消除贸易壁垒的诉求持支持态度。困难在于找到与朝廷就当事官员所犯错误进行沟通的方式，而这些当事官员恰好就是传递诉状的正常渠道。”

1701 年，东印度公司在厦门的投资仅为 34,400 英镑。但是即使公司已经将大部分投资转向广州，在此之后的很长一段时期里，贸易仍然在厦门进行着，比如 1723 年，汉密尔顿（Hamilton）船长就在这里装货。猖獗的敲诈勒索加上台湾海峡的不安定因素很可能是促使公司撤出本地的原因。到 1720 年，广州对所有出口商品征收的关税已升至 4%，对所有进口商品征收的关税已升至 16% 左右。此外，广州还对船只收取高额吨位税，即向海关征税官员支付 1,950 两银子的贿赂款，对船只货物供应商也要收取一大笔费用。1728 年，对所有出口货物增收 10% 的额外关税，直到 1736 年，这一关税才被取消。这些税费也在此地收取。据《厦门志》记载，1725 年，西班牙人在此地从事贸易活动并向朝廷进贡。英格兰、荷兰等国也进献了贡物。大清朝的资料汇编也明确记载了乾隆五十八年（1793 年）英吉利国首次纳贡方物（英吉利国乾隆五十八年遣部臣入贡）。

西班牙似乎受到中国的优待，因为当英国的商务活动被限定在广州时，西班牙已经享有在澳门开展贸易以及进入该港口和广州的权利。然而，西班牙似乎并没有从当时以及随后所享有的特权中充分获益，也没有从其所占据的富饶而又美丽的菲律宾群岛的优越地理位置中占到先机。中国人口众多、需求量大，只需四五天的航行即可轻松抵达，其西面和南面分别为印度和马来亚群岛，东面为太平洋岛屿以及正在不断崛起的帝国，西班牙所拥有的贸易优势是其他竞争对手难以匹敌的。

1734 年，英籍船舶“格拉夫顿号”（Grafton）被派往厦门，它发现这里的勒索比广州还严重，除了正常的关税以外，海关还额外收取 20% 的费用，“格拉夫顿号”只能弃之而去。1744年，东印度公司商船“哈德威克号”（Hardwicke）收到情报称，三艘西班牙船只停泊在澳门外海准备对其实施拦截，于是转而驶向厦门。抵达后，当地官员强迫商船交出武器和弹药，并要求商船无条件执行停泊在内港的要求。十五天后，“哈德威克号”发现当地不仅没有进行贸易的意向，还不断对其进行敲诈勒索，只得顶着季风空船前往印度。德庇时（John Davis）爵士[①]在其当时所撰著作的第55–56页是这样描述广州的：“尽管商船押运员不断抗议，勒索仍然不断加剧。商行老板用尽一切办法阻止欧洲人面见朝廷官员。他们发现通过这种方式可以同时对双方施加影响以获取更大的利益，还能免受责罚。对外国人来说，他们认定官员是敲诈勒索的始作俑者；对官员来说，外国人是如此野蛮粗鲁、脾气暴躁、蛮不讲理。我们对在贸易上所遭受的委屈进行了抗议，主要包括延误卸货、抢夺货物；官府每年发布公告，污蔑外国人犯下可怕罪行，意图挑起民众对外国人的敌视；下级官员伺机勒索；难以面见官员。”他补充道：“人们应该意识到，欧洲人之间缺乏团结，这通常会使他们丧失补救的机会。”

在那些日子里，当一艘船只抵达此地的时候，通常官府会派一艘小船前往登记船名、船籍和所涉业务，还有船员、火炮、货物的准确数目，以及拟定停留期限等信息。各项手续都完成以后，官府要求船舶将所携带的武器和弹药交由官府保管，缴纳约1,700银元的港务费，随后颁发停泊许可证。官员们似乎还曾裁决过外籍船舶的内部经济纠纷，比如1720年海防厅受理了“成功号”（Success）水手投诉船长案，并判决奖金分配办法如下：

① 德庇时（1795—1890），又译戴维斯、大卫斯、德俾士等，英国人，1844年5月8日就任第二任香港总督，并兼任英国驻华公使，直至1848年3月21日。德庇时精通汉学，曾撰写多部有关中国的著作，包括1836年的《中国人：中华帝国及其居民概述》（*The Chinese: A general description of the Empire of China, and its Inhabitants*）以及1841年的《中国见闻录》(*Sketches of China*)等。译者注。

船长所占份额	1,466.10.10 英镑[①]
副船长所占份额	733.5.5 英镑
船上护卫队队长、小队长以及随船医生所占份额	488.16.8 英镑
普通水手所占份额	97.15.4 英镑

不过，在强制船长分配这些奖金之前，“他下令控制住其中的一半货物以确保货主的利益，这些货物以银锭、金锭和珠宝等现钱计算，价值在 6,000 英镑到 7,000 英镑之间。他立即让人把这些货物搬上弗兰西斯科·拉瓦罗（Don Francisco La Vero）担任指挥官的葡萄牙东印度公司商船‘天使女王号’（Queen of Angels）。这艘船于 1722 年 6 月 6 日在里约热内卢惨遭火灾，因此，扣除打捞费用，货主所获之利不会超过 1,800 英镑”。一艘来自马德拉斯的英国籍商船“安娜号”（Ann），由于受到其所运载的大部分货物买家（据说这些买家是官员引荐的）的严重压榨，在收购完价值约银 1,500 两的商品后不久就破产了。船长对于自己所受到的冤屈没有声张，但是却在领到出口许可证和领回枪支后，要求船员把子弹上膛。办理完离境手续后，船长立即命令船员进入战斗岗位，随后劫持了一艘两倍于“安娜号”商品价值的日本籍帆船，两船双双驶入海湾。二三十条挤满了人的各色船只连忙前去追赶，但是那位肥胖的船长用尾炮朝他们开火，追赶的人只得逃窜了。这件事传到皇帝的耳朵里，他下旨给予日本船主满意的赔偿，随后悉数惩处有关官员，还查抄了他们的家。这些措施在一段时间内促使官员们在与英国船只打交道时更加小心谨慎。

没有必要再进一步论述细节了，这些内容已经足以说明虽然受到各种各样的约束，面临各种各样的停业风险，通商互市一直在持续进行，直到皇帝下诏撤走东印度公司的代理商，因为将来仅限于在广州一地通商开市。遵照

① 即 1,466 镑 10 先令 10 便士。先令为英旧货币单位。1971 年英国货币改革前，1 英镑等于 20 先令，1 先令等于 12 便士，下同。译者注。

圣谕，本港口不再对外国人开放，直到后来才依照 1842 年 8 月 29 日在南京所签署的条约的第二款内容重新开放[1]。

这里没有必要讨论这一条约以及清政府同英国、美国、法国等国后续签订的各种条约的导火索事件，只要简单地介绍一下海关税务司署成立以来在贸易方面取得的进展就足够了。

① 1842 年 8 月 29 日清政府与英国签订《南京条约》，该条约共有十三款，其中第二款规定："自今以后，大皇帝恩准英国人民带同所属家眷，寄居大清沿海之广州、福州、厦门、宁波、上海等五处港口，贸易通商无碍；且大英国君主派设领事、管事等官住该五处城邑，专理商贾事宜，与各该地方官公文往来；令英人按照下条开叙之列，清楚交纳货税、钞饷等费。"译者注。

Trade since the establishment of the Foreign Inspectorate of Customs

Although the Treaties with Great Britain and France were signed at Tientsin in June 1858, and ratified at Peking in October 1860, it was not until the 1st April 1862, that the Customs was first opened at Amoy under the Foreign Inspectorate.

During the following nine months, a trade was carried on represented by 394 vessels, 129,677 tons, entered, and 364 vessels, 119,412 tons, cleared, conveying merchandize, which represented an import trade valued at $5,042,307, or, at the then rate of exchange, £1,177,242, and an export trade valued at $2,226,251, or £522,199. The import of Treasure amounted to $405,170; and its export, to $909,612. The total amount of duties, coast trade duties, and tonnage dues, collected, was Tls. 306,210 or £102,070. The importation of Cotton piece goods of all descriptions, was 70,593 pieces: of Woollens, 5,866 pieces; of Raw Cotton, 15,468 peculs; of Cotton Yarn 5,721 peculs, and of Metals 18,953 peculs; that of Opium amounted to 2,047 chests, or 2,384 peculs, of which 273 peculs were re-exported.

The re-export trade, the value of which was *not* at that time deducted from the gross total of the import trade, was $519,829, or £121,933. It consisted chiefly of Cotton piece goods, Woollens, Raw Cotton, Metals, Opium, and native Sundries. The principal staples exported, were black Sugar 39,921 peculs, white Sugar 8,898 peculs, Sugar Candy 46,781 peculs, Tea 5,329,283 pounds, of which Great Britain, only took, direct, 345,886 pounds, against 3,318,752 pounds taken by the United States. Paper 15,963 peculs, Chinaware 6,956 peculs, &c., &c. The most important statistics, and articles of commerce are thus briefly enumerated, as no report on the trade of the port, was made for the nine months in question.

The following tables will show more readily than words at length the values of Imports, Exports, and Re-exports, together with the amounts of Duties collected, since the opening of the Custom House, under foreign inspectorate, to the 3lst December 1871.

	IMPORTS.		EXPORTS.		RE-EXPORTS.	
	$	**£**	**$**	**£**	**$**	**£**
1st April to 31st December 1862	5,042,307	1,177,242	2,226,251	522,199	519,829	121,933
Year ended 1863	8,430,991	2,048,036	4,092,574	994,129	382,447	92,369
Year ended 1864	9,419,625	2,276,409	3,773,811	912,004	774,877	187,261
Year ended 1865	12,974,724	2,919,313	2,699,286	607,339	1,225,636	275,768
Year ended 1866	12,004,531	2,701,019	3,989,843	897,714	1,251,288	281,539
Year ended 1867	9,814,144	2,208,182	3,597,057	809,337	1,019,092	229,295
Year ended 1868	7,421,750	1,669,894	3,226,078	725,867	1,017,357	228,846
Year ended 1869	9,136,900	2,055,802	4,147,893	933,275	1,168,244	626,854
Year ended 1870	8,513,009	1,915,616	3,410,710	767,486	1,673,938	376,673
Year ended 1871	8,511,074	1,844,066	4,583,576	993,108	1,713,883	371,341

DUES AND DUTIES COLLECTED.										
	IMPORT.		EXPORT.		COAST TRADE.		TONNAGE.		TOTAL.	
	Tls.	£	Tls.	£	Tls.	£	Tls.	£	Tls.	£
1st April to 31st December 1862	126,793	42,264	150,169	50,056	13,787	4,595	15,461	5,153	306,210	102,068
Year ended 1863	184,121	61,373	237,984	79,328	29,201	9,734	19,686	6,562	470,992	156,997
Year ended 1864	219,502	73,167	206,514	68,838	26,693	8,898	22,200	7,400	474,909	158,303
Year ended 1865	245,000	81,667	167,318	55,773	27,898	9,299	31,762	10,587	471,978	157,326
Year ended 1866	252,250	84,083	224,204	74,735	34,996	11,665	21,698	7,233	533,149	177,716
Year ended 1867	243,781	81,260	212,829	70,943	25,857	8,619	20,860	6,953	503,327	167,775
Year ended 1868	235,671	78,557	158,597	52,866	17,214	5,738	14,562	4,854	426,044	142,015
Year ended 1869	230,342	76,781	283,090	94,363	23,785	7,928	19,187	6,393	556,404	185,468
Year ended 1870	229,653	76,551	229,450	76,483	18,683	6,228	20,889	6,963	498,675	166,225
Year ended 1871	223,007	74,336	26,2933	87,644	20,870	6,957	17,450	2,816	524,260	174,753

An examination of the preceding statistics of the annual value of the Import trade, since 1863 (1862 being a broken year of nine months is omitted) to 1871, does not afford so satisfactory a view of its progress, as could be desired. Although it rose from $8,048,544 net, that is deducting re-exports, in 1863, to $11,749,088 net in 1865, and to $10,753,273 net in 1866, it has gradually decreased to $8, 511, 074 in 1871.

The value of the Export trade, exclusive of Re-exports, reached $4,092,574 in 1863, from which date it fell to $2,699,285 in 1865, and since has fluctuated at between three and a half, and four and a half, millions of dollars. Its value in 1871 was $4,583,576.

It is in the value of the Re-export trade that developed between this port and "Formosa", principally that the most significant increase is apparent, it having risen from $382,447 in 1863, to $1,713,883 the largest value it has yet attained, in 1871.

The dues and duties collected, amounted to Haikwan Tls. 470,992, or £156,997, in 1863, and remained at near that amount until 1866, when the collection reached Haikwan Tls. 533,149, or £177, 716. In the next two years it had fallen to Haikwan Tls. 426,144, or £142,015; from which it rose to Haikwan Tls. 556, 404, or £185,488, the highest amount it ever attained, in 1869. In the following year, it had fallen to Haikwan Tls. 498,675, or £166,225; and in 1871 it again rose, and reached Haikwan Ts. 524,260, or £174,753. During nine years the variation between the lowest amount collected, that of 1863, and the highest, that of 1869, is only Haikwan Ts. 85, 412, or £28,471.

Having made thots few remarks on the value of trade, and on the duties collected since the opening of this Custom House, I shall confine my observations to a brief retrospect of the trade of 1871, selecting where necessary the two previous years to illustrate its increase or decrease.

海关税务司署成立以来的贸易情况

虽然清政府与英、法两国已于 1858 年 6 月在天津签订条约，并于 1860 年 10 月在北京批准通过，但是直到 1862 年 4 月 1 日，海关税务司署才首次在厦门开设[①]。

在随后的九个月中，输入、输出[②]贸易达到以下规模：394 艘船舶运载 129,677 吨货物进港，364 艘船舶运载 119,412 吨货物清关出港，输入贸易的商品价值达银 5,042,307 元，按当时的汇率换算为 1,177,242 英镑，输出贸易价值为银 2,226,251 元，即 522,199 英镑。流入的各类银元为 405,170 元，流出的银元为 909,612 元。征收的关税、沿岸贸易税和吨位税总额为银 306,210 两，即 102,070 英镑。输入各类棉布 70,593 匹；毛料 5,866 匹；原棉 15,468 担；棉纱 5,721 担；金属 18,953 担；鸦片 2,047 箱，即 2,384 担，其中 273 担被再转口到外地。

未从当时输入贸易总额中扣除的转口贸易额为 519,829 银元，即 121,933 英镑，这些货物主要是棉布、毛料、原棉、金属、鸦片和各类土产。输出的主要产品是红糖 39,921 担、白糖 8,898 担、冰糖 46,781 担、茶叶 5,329,283 磅（其中英国仅直接进口 345,886 磅，而美国则为 3,318,752 磅）、纸张 15,963 担、瓷器 6,956 担，诸如此类。因为尚无本口岸这九个月贸易情况的专门报告，我

① 清政府与英、法两国于 1858 年签订的《天津条约》之附约《中英通商章程善后条约》（亦称《中英通商章程》）中，有“任凭总理大臣邀请英人帮办税务”及“各口划一办理”等规定。根据这一附约成立了“大清皇家海关总税务司”（1912 年改称“中国海关总税务司”），名义上隶属于总理衙门或外务部，实际上是一个由外国人控制的独立机构。总税务司署设总税务司一人，掌握全国海关关税、行政及关员任免等事务。译者注。

② 本文所说的“输入”既包括从外国进口，也包括从本国其他港口输入到本地（厦门）的商品贸易，“输出”既包括出口至外国，也包括输出至本国的其他口岸贸易，“转口”则指上述输入的商品再输出到外国或本国的其他港口贸易。译者注。

们只能简要地列举出最重要的统计数据和商品种类。

与纯粹文字叙述的方式相比较而言，下表更详细地展示了自外籍官员控制的海关设立之日起至 1871 年 12 月 31 日，输入、输出和转口的货物价值以及征收的关税数额。

输入、输出和转口的货物价值①

时间	输入		输出		转口	
	银元	英镑	银元	英镑	银元	英镑
1862 年 4 月 1 日到年底	5,042,307	1,177,242	2,226,251	522,199	519,829	121,933
1863 年	8,430,991	2,048,036	4,092,574	994,129	382,447	92,369
1864 年	9,419,625	2,276,409	3,773,811	912,004	774,877	187,261
1865 年	12,974,724	2,919,313	2,699,286	607,339	1,225,636	275,768
1866 年	12,004,531	2,701,019	3,989,843	897,714	1,251,288	281,539
1867 年	9,814,144	2,208,182	3,597,057	809,337	1,019,092	229,295
1868 年	7,421,750	1,669,894	3,226,078	725,867	1,017,357	228,846
1869 年	9,136,900	2,055,802	4,147,893	933,275	1,168,244	626,854
1870 年	8,513,009	1,915,616	3,410,710	767,486	1,673,938	376,673
1871 年	8,511,074	1,844,066	4,583,576	993,108	1,713,883	371,341

① 表题为译者所加。译者注。

征收的关税和各项税费

时间	输入		输出		沿岸贸易税		吨位税		总计	
	银两	英镑	银两	英镑	银两	英镑	银两	英镑	银两	英镑
1862 年 4 月 1 日至年底	126,793	42,264	150,169	50,056	13,787	4,595	15,461	5,153	306,210	102,068
1863 年	184,121	61,373	237,984	79,328	29,201	9,734	19,686	6,562	470,992	156,997
1864 年	219,502	73,167	206,514	68,838	26,693	8,898	22,200	7,400	474,909	158,303
1865 年	245,000	81,667	167,318	55,773	27,898	9,299	31,762	10,587	471,978	157,326
1866 年	252,250	84,083	224,204	74,735	34,996	11,665	21,698	7,233	533,149	177,716
1867 年	243,781	81,260	212,829	70,943	25,857	8,619	20,860	6,953	503,327	167,775
1868 年	235,671	78,557	158,597	52,866	17,214	5,738	14,562	4,854	426,044	142,015
1869 年	230,342	76,781	283,090	94,363	23,785	7,928	19,187	6,393	556,404	185,468
1870 年	229,653	76,551	229,450	76,483	18,683	6,228	20,889	6,963	498,675	166,225
1871 年	223,007	74,336	262,933	87,644	20,870	6,957	17,450	2,816	524,260	174,753

考察前述 1863 年（1862 年只有不完整的九个月数据，故此处省略）至 1871 年年度输入贸易总值的统计数据，发现其增长情况并不像人们所期待的那样令人满意。虽然扣除转口贸易后，纯输入贸易总值从 1863 年的 8,048,544 银元增长到 1865 年的 11,749,088 银元和 1866 年的 10,753,273 银元，但是之后便逐年下降到 1871 年未扣除转口贸易后的 8,511,074 银元。

扣除转口贸易后，1863 年的输出贸易总值达到 4,092,574 银元，此后便开始减少到 1865 年的 2,699,285 银元，之后一直在 3,500,000 和 4,500,000 元之间波动，1871 年的总值是 4,583,576 银元。

最显著的增长主要来自厦门口岸和台湾之间发展起来的转口贸易，其总值从 1863 年的 382,447 银元上升到 1871 年史无前例的 1,713,883 银元。

1863 年，海关征收的税费和关税总计达银 470,992 两，即 156,997 英镑，并保持在这个数额附近，直到 1866 年，海关征收额达到银 533,149 两，即 177,716 英镑。在接下来的两年时间里，海关征收的数额减少到银 426,144 两，即 142,015 英镑，之后又上升到 1869 年的银 556,404 两，即 185,488 英镑，这是历史最高纪录。第二年，海关征收数额又回落到银 498,675 两，即 166,225 英镑，1871 年再次升到银 524,260 两，即 174,753 英镑。在九年的时间里，海关所征收税费的最低值（1863 年）和最高值（1869 年）只相差银 85,412 两，即 28,471 英镑。

在简要介绍了贸易额以及自本海关设立以来的征税数额后，我把分析限定于简要回顾 1871 年的贸易情况，必要时选取前两年的数据来说明贸易的变化情况。

Import trade

The value of this trade in foreign goods, (exclusive of Re-exports,) during 1871, amounted to $4,587,611. That of foreign Re-exports to $1,278,850. The value of the import trade in native produce, (exclusive of Re-exports,) amounted to $2,209,580. That of native Re-exports to $435,033. To take, first, the important articles of commerce here, Yarn, the import was in 1869, peculs 10,235, in 1870 it increased one half, or to peculs 15,724, and in 1871 it reached peculs 17,940. (Thus nearly doubling its import in three years. It may be worthy of remark that previous to the establishment of the Foreign Custom House, the trade in Yarn has been known to amount to 18,000 peculs per annum.) A similar increase is perceptible in Cotton Piece Goods of all descriptions. The aggregate import was in 1869, pieces 107,914; in 1870 it increased sixty three per cent, or to pieces 171,016, and it now amounts to pieces 195,160, an increase of over eighty per cent in three years.

The preceding figures will probably be contrary to the expectations of those interested in the foreign trade at Amoy, but they are carried out by the actual consumption in 1871, as shewn by sales, which when compared with 1870, give an increase in

Yarn	of 20 per cent.
Shirtings	of 10 per cent.
T-Cloths	of 45 per cent.

The importation, as will be seen, shows a much greater percentage than the above; but large stocks of unsold goods yet remain to be carried into, and form a portion of, the consumption of the year 1872.

Raw Cotton.—During the last three years, the importation of this article from India, has quadrupled itself. In 1870 it amounted to peculs 19,195, or about double that of 1869; and in 1871, it reached peculs 38,313. Of this quantity peculs 630, only, were re-exported to Chinese ports. Speaking in round numbers, the consumption may be said to have increased from 7,300 bales in 1869, to 14,600 bales in 1871. The cause of this is found in the comparatively low price of Indian Cotton, as compared with that of Chinese Cotton.

The importation of Chinese Cotton, peculs 24,872, from Shanghai, Ningpo, and Hongkong, also shows an increase, although a small one, over the importation of 1869, and 1870, namely peculs 20,191, and peculs 20,631. The entire quantity imported during the past year, went into consumption here, none being Re-exported.

Woollen Manufactures.—Consisting principally of Camlets, Lastings, and Woollen and Cotton fabrics, show also an increased importation as compared with 1869 and 1870, the two years being nearly on a par, namely 5,532 pieces imported net, and 1,708 pieces re-exported. The past year's Import was 6,113 pieces, of which 3,016 pieces were Re-exported. The consumption of the port however shows a decrease.

Opium.—The Imports, and Re-exports, during the past three years, stand thus:

	1869	**1870**	**1871**
Import	5,709 peculs	4,995 peculs	4,808 peculs
Re-exports	1,388 peculs	1,869 peculs	1,751 peculs

From the above figures, it is apparent that there is a small decrease in this branch of commerce. Deducting the Re-export to "Formosa" from the quantities imported during the last three years, the actual quantity required for annual consumption at the port, would seem to be between 3,721 and 3,057 peculs. During six years, namely from 1866 to 1871, the quantities imported only varied peculs 66,081, the largest import peculs 546,669, was in 1866, and the smallest in the year under review. The Re-export dwindled to peculs 1,091 in 1868, and attained to peculs 1,896 in 1870. The prices for Opium offered here, during most of last year, but more especially the latter part, have been below the equivalent of those at Hongkong, whence Amoy is supplied; consequently a very large stock remains unsold, and will be carried into the year 1872, (probably lessening that year's importation of the drug) to be held for a rise in price; which however is unlikely to occur until the end of March, or beginning of April.

In my report on the trade of Amoy during 1870, I wrote so fully on the action of the Le-kin taxes, upon Opium, and Cotton Manufactures, that any but a casual reference to it, must be irksome and unnecessary. It is, however, proper when reviewing commerce here, that it should be stated that, as trade in Opium has been legalised, and a fixed uniform tariff rate put upon its importation, it would be well if the same principle were applied in Le-kin taxation. The entire removal of the Le-kin impost cannot be, and is not, expected by reasonable persons. Most of the wishes that I have heard expressed, would be met by the issue of a fixed uniform and just tariff, by the Imperial government, instead of leaving the provincial authorities to impose what tax they please, limited, it would appear, not by necessity, or by any system of valuation, but by the temper of the people they govern, the highest tax being inflicted that they are likely to bear, without risk of disturbance. Thus at Swatow, where the people are turbulent and aggressive Opium is taxed to the extent of only Tls. 14.7.6.0 per chest, against Tls. 90.2.6.6, the amount imposed here, where the people are peaceful, and order loving. An uniform Le-kin tariff on the great staples of European import, and export, would, I feel convinced, be as beneficial to the Imperial Exchequer, as it would be to foreign trade.

The grain supplies imported, consisting of foreign rice, peculs 50,498, native rice, peculs 69,254 (of which peculs 3,936 only were re-exported) and native wheat peculs 36,242, are in the aggregate, much the same as in 1870. But a very considerable deficit, nearly 90 per cent, is apparent in the receipts of foreign rice. This is, however, more than balanced by an increase, of nearly 130 per cent, in Native grain. The prices of these cereals during the latter part of the year, have been slightly above the usual average, though not to the extent anticipated by Chinese, who predicted scarcity and high prices, as they now do for the present year. Beans and Peas, peculs 228,437, and Beancake, peculs 159,442, aggregated, have been used as manure to about the same extent as in 1870; but the importation of Peas shews an increase of about 55 per cent, replacing a decrease of nearly the same amount in Beancake. The former having ruled relatively cheaper in the North.

Metals are an unimportant branch of this trade. In 1871, peculs 6,273 of iron were imported, against peculs 8, 367 in 1870, and peculs 5,454 in 1869. Lead reached peculs 5,688, Quicksilver peculs 431, or nearly the same as the two. preceding years. Nail rod iron, peculs 2,879, shows an increase of ninety per cent, as compared with the importation of 1869. It should be observed that there exists a monopoly, here, of the Trade in this article.

Foreign importers find the utmost difficulty in disposing of their stocks for that reason, and this branch of trade cannot reach its limit of expansion so long as the monopoly is maintained. The increase above alluded to in Nail rod iron, does not extend to consumption, but merely to importation.

Shipping.—566 vessels, representing an aggregate tonnage of 215,651 tons, entered; and 570 vessels, representing 219,038 tons, cleared in 1871. These figures shew an increase of 9 vessels entered, and 19 vessels cleared, as compared with 1870, although in regard to tonnage there is a slight decrease both in vessels entered and cleared. The statistics in 1869, are so nearly the same that comparison is superfluous. The number of steamers visiting the port has greatly increased, and leads to the inference that were permission obtained to work the rich Coal mines of this Empire, they would soon entirely supersede sailing vessels. The supply of shipping up to about the middle of November was very large, and poor freights only, were procurable; but this supply falling off here, as appears to have been the case at other ports, at the same time, very high rates of freights obtained in December, with every prospect of their rising still higher during, at least, the early part of 1872. The Charters made were 162, against 171 in 1870. Had there been more vessels here in December, they would have been eagerly chartered.

输入贸易

1871年间，外国商品进口贸易额（不包括转口贸易）达4,587,611银元，转口贸易额为1,278,850银元。本国土特产品（不包括转口贸易）输入贸易额为2,209,580银元，其转口贸易额为435,033银元。首先说一说此地重要的商品——纱线，1869年的输入量是10,235担，1870年增加了一半，即15,724担，1871年达到17,940担（照此计算，三年内输入量几乎翻了一番。值得一提的是，众所周知，在海关税务司署设立之前，纱线贸易量每年高达18,000担）。各类棉布贸易同样也取得了显著的增长，1869年的输入总量为107,914匹，1870年增加了63%，即171,016匹，目前达到195,160匹，三年内增量超过80%。

上述数据可能与那些对厦门外贸感兴趣的人所预料的情况相反，然而，它们是从1871年的实际消费统计得来的。正如销售数据所表明的那样，与1870年相比，1871年实际消费的增长情况如下：

棉纱销售增长了20%

衬衫布料销售增长了10%

T型布料[①]销售增长了45%

我们可以看到，贸易输入的增长幅度要比上面的数据大得多，但是大量尚未售出的商品有待于1872年出售，并成为当年消费总量的一部分。

原棉。在过去的三年中，从印度进口的原棉增加到之前的4倍，1870年达到19,195担，大约为1869年的2倍，1871年则达到38,313担，其中只有

①T型布料，又译“丁字布”或“标布”，是一种优质棉品种，布身坚密，结实耐穿。译者注。

630 担被转口到中国的其他口岸。经过粗略计算，消费量从 1869 年的 7,300 包增加到 1871 年的 14,600 包，其原因在于，与中国棉花相比，印度棉花价格相对较低。

从上海、宁波和香港输入的中国棉花共 24,872 担，这也比 1869 年和 1870 年的 20,191 担和 20,631 担有所增长，尽管幅度很小。过去一年所有输入的中国棉花均用于本地消费，未被转口到其他地方。

棉毛织品。与 1869 年和 1870 年相比较而言，主要包括羽纱、强捻厚斜纹织物、毛织物和棉织物在内的棉毛制品的输入量也有所增加，上述两年的数据几乎持平，即净输入 5,532 匹，转口 1,708 匹。去年输入 6,113 匹，其中 3,016 匹用于转口。不过，厦门港的消费量呈下降趋势。

鸦片。过去三年的输入和转口的情况如下：

	1869 年	1870 年	1871 年
输入	5,709 担	4,995 担	4,808 担
转口	1,388 担	1,869 担	1,751 担

从上面的数字来看，很明显这一商品的贸易量略有下降。从过去三年的输入总量中扣除转口到台湾的数量，本口岸每年消费所需的实际数量似乎介于 3,721 担至 3,057 担之间[①]。从 1866 年到 1871 年的六年间，输入的数量各不相同，差别只有 66,081 担，最大输入量是 1866 年的 546,669 担，最少的是在我们正在讨论的年度。1868 年转口数量减少到 1,091 担，1870 年达到 1,869 担。在去年的大部分时间里，此地销售的鸦片价格尤其是下半年已经低于香港的对应价格，而厦门的鸦片是由香港供给的，由此可见当年鸦片的库存量非常大，只能留到 1872 年（该年的毒品输入量可能就会减少）进行销售以等待价格上涨，

① 上述三年中，输入和转口贸易差额最大的年份是 1869 年，为 4,321 担，最小的是 1871 年，为 3057 担. 故此处应为“介于 4,321 担至 3,057 担之间”。译者注。

不过价格不可能在 3 月底或 4 月初之前上涨。

在我所撰写的《1870 年厦门贸易报告》(*Report on the Trade of Amoy during 1870*)一文中，我全面说明了针对鸦片和棉制品征收的厘金税[①]问题，此处再次提起它不仅令人厌烦，同时也没有必要。然而，在考察本地商业贸易的时候对此加以说明是再恰当不过的了。由于鸦片贸易已经合法化，其进口关税是固定和统一的，最好把同样的原则也运用于厘金税的征收。通晓事理的人不可能也不会指望完全取消厘金税。我所听到的是大多数人希望朝廷颁布一个固定统一和公正合理的关税标准，而不是任由各省当局随心所欲地征税，而且税率似乎不是出于必要或者遵照任何评估体系，而是由他们统治下的百姓脾气所决定的，征收的最高税率是以他们能够承受而又不会引起骚乱作为标准。因此，在民众桀骜不驯、好斗成性的汕头，鸦片税率仅为每箱银 14.7.6.0 两[②]，而厦门百姓安静平和、安分守己，每箱收税达银 90.2.6.6 两。我确信，为欧洲输入和输出欧洲的主要商品征收统一的厘金税，对朝廷财政和对外贸易同样有利。

在粮食输入方面，包括外国大米 50,498 担，国产大米 69,254 担(其中只有 3,936 担被转口到其他地方)以及国产小麦 36,242 担，三项加在一起与 1870 年的数据大致相同。从外国输入的大米数量明显大幅度减少了，即减少了接近 90%。不过，本国粮食的产量增长了近 130%，远远抵消了此项不足。该年下半年，这些谷物的价格略高于往日的平均水平，但是还没有达到中国人之前预料的水平，他们现在也同样预测今年粮食将会出现短缺并且价格高昂。豆子和豌豆 228,437 担，豆饼 159,442 担，此三项全部用作肥料，其规模与 1870 年大致相当。不过豌豆的输入量大约增长了 55%，填补了因几乎等量

① 厘金税：又称厘捐、厘金税。中国旧时对通过国内水陆交通要道的货物设立关卡征收的一种捐税，因其初定税率为 1 厘(1%)，故名厘金。厘金创行于咸丰二年(1852 年)，在全国通行后，不仅课税对象广，税率也不一致，且不限于百分之一。有的高达百分之二十以上，有部分货物实行人量抽厘，这种税直到 1931 年才撤消。译者注。

② 在明清两朝，主要的货币单位是“两”，“两”以下有“钱、分、厘、毫”等。“两”以下均为十进制，故本处应可理解为“银十四两七钱六分”。译者注。

的豆饼输入减少而产生的缺口，同时由于前者在北方遍地皆是，因此也就相对便宜。

金属在输入贸易中重要性不大。1871 年，铁的输入量为 6,273 担，而 1870 年的输入量为 8,367 担，1869 年为 5,454 担。铅的输入量达到 5,688 担，水银达到 431 担，与前两年几乎持平。制钉盘条为 2,879 担，与 1869 年的输入量相比，增长了 90%。值得注意的是，此项商品的贸易存在着垄断现象。因此外国进口商在处理存货时遇到了极大的困难，只要存在垄断局面，此项贸易就无法发展到顶峰。上面提到的制钉盘条的增长，并没有延伸到消费领域，而仅仅是指输入量的增长。

航运。1871 年，共计各类船只 566 艘、总吨位为 215,651 吨货物进港，570 艘各类船只共计 219,038 吨货物清关离港。与 1870 年的数据相比，尽管进港和出港的吨位数都略有减少，但是从船舶的数量看，共增加了 9 艘船只进港，19 艘船只清关离港。1869 年的统计数据非常接近，因此拿来比较是多余的。停靠本港的蒸汽船数量大大增加，由此可以推断，如果允许开采帝国丰富的煤矿资源的话，蒸汽船将很快完全取代帆船。11 月中旬之前的船舶运力非常大，但货物却少得可怜。不过到了 12 月，厦门似乎也与其他港口一样，船只运力下降，同时运费上涨得厉害，而且到 1872 年初，运费有望进一步攀升。用于包租的船只数量是 162 艘，1870 年是 171 艘，如果 12 月份有更多船只的话，肯定很快就能包租出去。

Export Trade

The total value of the trade in native produce exported, and removed coastwise, during 1871, amounted to $4,583,576. That of native Re-exports, to $1,713,883. Of the articles of which it is comprised, it will perhaps be sufficient to enumerate but two or three. Tea being the most important export, and the one in which foreign merchants are most interested I have prepared a return of the quantities exported since the opening of the Amoy Custom House up to the present date.

The figures in the return, include the quantities exported by Chinese to the Straits, and to sundry ports; but are exclusive of the Tamsui Teas sent here for convenience of shipment to the United States.

EXPORTS.	TO FOREIGN PORTS.	TO CHINESE PORTS.	TOTAL EXPORT.
1862 Peculs	32,830:39	7,139:25	39,969:64
1863 Peculs	50,429:20	13,715:81	64,145:01
1864 Peculs	35,897:27	17,735:37	53,632:64
1865 Peculs	34,224:00	9,523:00	43,747:00
1866 Peculs	49,560:54	9,782:36	59,342:90
1867 Peculs	53,224:21	7,570:70	60,794:91
1868 Peculs	22,409:40	13,312:58	35,721:98
1869 Peculs	78,799:55	7,168:96	85,968:51
1870 Peculs	56,100:47	8,670:04	64,770:51
1871 Peculs	66,198:57	1,882:39	68,080:96
Total Peculs	479,673:60	96500:46	576,174:06

The great deficit in the export of 1868, and increase in that of 1869, arises from a very considerable portion of the 1868 crop not being shipped until 1869.

The progress of this trade will, however, be better conveyed to those interested in it, by basing my remarks on the quantities exported during the mercantile Tea season, *i.*

e. from the 30th June to the 30th June, within which period the season is closed by the shipment of the entire crop, (generally completed before the end of January) than by basing them on the Customs year, ending the 31st December, which has hitherto been the practice. I therefore subjoin another table containing the quantities exported by foreign merchants to foreign ports only, that is exclusive of the quantities exported to the Straits, &c., and removed coastwise, by Chinese.

EXPORT OF TEA BY FOREIGN MERCHANTS SINCE THE OPENING OF THIS CUSTOM HOUSE.	
Season 1862-1863	Pounds 7,856,122
Season 1863-1864	Pounds 6,224,635
Season 1864-1865	Pounds 6,918,671
Season 1865-1866	Pounds 6,979,555
Season 1866-1867	Pounds 7,284,826
Season 1867-1868	Pounds 8,006,384
Season 1868-1869	Pounds 8,691,058
Season 1869-1870	Pounds 6,763,868
Season 1870-1871	Pounds 6,823,399*
Season 1871-1872	Pounds 8,171,494*
*Including Ibs. 917,795 lost in "Taeping" and "Cengala".	

The Teas in the preceding table are almost entirely composed of Oolongs, and Congous, the only other description ever in this market being Orange Pekoe, which, when it comes at all, comes in too small quantities to be of consequence. During the last four seasons it has been altogether absent from the market.

Oolongs.—The export of this description of Tea, which had fallen in the season 1869-70 to 3,491,206 lbs. rose in 1870-71, to 5,443,593 lbs. and in the season just closed, 1871-72, it attained to 7,766,534 lbs. the largest export that has ever been made from this port. Of the entire quantity exported, the United States took 7,393,258 lbs. against 5,073,484 lbs. in season 1870-71.

The export to Great Britain was 176,665 lbs. against 380,109 lbs, in the season 1870-71. It is worthy of remark that Amoy Oolongs, price considered, are now preferred in the

New York market, to Foochow teas.

Congou.—The export of this kind of tea reached its highest amount in the season 1869-70, when some 50,000 half-chests or 2,109,232 lbs. were shipped. Since then the export has fallen to 1,216,878 lbs. in 1870-71, and to 353,514 lbs. in 1871-72. This may, in some measure, be accounted for by the fact that the teamen finding high prices ruling for Oolongs, and but a limited market for Congous, have made most of their leaf into the former tea. This, 1871-72, season's Congous, were almost entirely of good quality, and 297,91 6 lbs. were exported to the United States, leaving the export to Great Britain at 55,598 lbs. against 1,799,542 lbs. in the 1869-70 season, and 775,419 lbs. in the season 1870-71, This decrease is attributable to the quality of the commoner Congous, which has caused their expulsion from the London market, while for the superior kinds, America is a mere liberal purchaser than England. Owing, perhaps, to a small supply during the season under review, no shipment has been made to the Colonies, which received, in 1870-71, 145,790 lbs. of this tea. In the coming season the export will probably re-commence.

Amoy Teas, which, two or three years since, were unfavourably viewed on account of the large quantity of dust they then contained, are now steadily recovering their position in the American Market, (where, as has been shewn, most of them go) owing to a combination of the Hongs here in 1868, when they agreed not to purchase teas containing over 20 per cent of dust. This margin will in the season 1872-73, and in future, be still further reduced to 15 per cent. Before this combination was centered into, the teas contained sometimes as much as 60 per cent of dust, and the consequence was that Japan teas, which are singularly free from this defect, were gradually superseding them.

At the present time, Amoy teas have so far regained favour, that according to the last advices received, they appear to have been the only ones that have benefitted exporters.

Tamsui Teas, which are mostly, shipped to New York via this port, have shown a remarkable expansion.

In season 1869-70 the export to New York was	370,238 lbs.
In season 1870-71 the export to New York was	778,242 lbs.
In season 1871-72 the export to New York was	1,502,000 lbs.

And next season it will, it is expected, be much larger. The reason these teas are becoming such favorites is, that they are, in the first place, beautifully made and contain a very trifling proportion of dust (some 5 or 6 per cent); and secondly, they possess a very fine natural perfume, which probably results from the youth of the plants, and the almost virgin soil in which they are grown. The common grades of "Formosa" tea, do not pay the cost of exportation, and are chiefly used by the natives themselves.

The Export of Amoy Sugar was as under:

	1871	**1870**	**1869**	**1862** （**9 months only.**）
Brown Sugar	Peculs 155,335	Peculs 58,723	Peculs 50,733	Peculs 39,921
White Sugar	Peculs 25,553	Peculs 13,158	Peculs 13,378	Peculs 8,898
Sugar Candy	Peculs 83,519	Peculs 61,416	Peculs 60,438	Peculs 46,781

These figures are very satisfactory, showing that the export of Brown Sugar has trebled itself, that of White Sugar nearly doubled itself, and that of Sugar Candy has increased about 35 per cent, in one year. The increase since the opening of this Custom House in 1862, is noteworthy.

The export of paper, peculs 24,300, has increased 3,000 peculs, since 1870; but the increase in its export since 1862, is only about 9,000 peculs. The export of Chinaware, peculs 380,312, shews a decrease of peculs 16,000 when compared with that of 1870, and an increase of peculs 24,000, when compared with the export of 1862.

输出贸易

1871 年间，出口并沿途卸货的本国土特产贸易总值为 4,583,576 银元，转口到本国其他地区的货值为 1,713,883 银元。就输出的产品而言，也许我们只需列举两三项就足够了。茶叶是最重要的，也是外国商人最感兴趣的输出商品。我在此准备了一份自厦门海关设立至今的茶叶输出数量申报表①。

申报表中的数字包括中国人向新加坡海峡地区和其他各个港口输出的茶叶数量，但不包括为方便运往美国而在此地中转的淡水茶。

输出	到外国港口（单位：担）	到中国港口（单位：担）	输出总量（单位：担）
1862 年	32830:39	7139:25	39969:64
1863 年	50429:20	13715:81	64145:01
1864 年	35897:27	17735:37	53632:64
1865 年	34224:00	9523:00	43747:00
1866 年	49560:54	9782:36	59342:90
1867 年	53224:21	7570:70	60794:91
1868 年	22409:40	13312:58	35721:98
1869 年	78799:55	7168:96	85968:51
1870 年	56100:47	8670:04	64770:51
1871 年	66198:57	1882:39	68080:96
总计（担）	479673:60	96500:46	576174:06

1868 年茶叶输出量大幅降低以及 1869 年茶叶输出量增长的原因在于 1868 年所收成的茶叶有很大一部分直到 1869 年才被装运出港。

不过，为了更好地向利益攸关人士展示输出贸易的发展状况，最好把我

① 表中冒号前的数字指“担”，冒号后的数字指“斤”。古制一担为一百斤。译者注。

的文字分析建立在商业茶季输出数量的基础之上加以说明。商业茶季是指每年的6月30日到第二年的6月30日，在此期间，以全部茶叶作物的装运作为“茶季”结束的标准（通常在1月底之前完成），而不是基于12月31日截止的海关年，这是迄今为止的通行做法。因此，我增补了一个表格，所含数据仅为外商输出到外国港口的茶叶数量，但不包括中国人输出到新加坡海峡地区等地并沿途卸货的数量。

自厦门海关设立以来外商输出的茶叶数量

1862–1863 茶季	7,856,122 磅
1863–1864 茶季	6,224,635 磅
1864–1865 茶季	6,918,671 磅
1865–1866 茶季	6,979,555 磅
1866–1867 茶季	7,284,826 磅
1867–1868 茶季	8,006,384 磅
1868–1869 茶季	8,691,058 磅
1869–1870 茶季	6,763,868 磅
1870–1871 茶季	6,823,399 磅 *
1871–1872 茶季	8,171,494 磅 *

* 包括在“太平号”（Taeping）和“僧加剌号”（Cengala）丢失的917795磅。

上表所涉茶叶几乎全部是乌龙茶和工夫红茶，本地市场上唯一可见的其他品种是橙白毫红茶，但由于出口量太少，可以忽略不计。在过去的四个茶季中，这种茶叶甚至在市场上完全不见踪迹。

乌龙茶。这种茶叶的输出量在1869—1870茶季减少到3,491,206磅，1870—1871茶季增加到5,443,593磅，在刚刚结束的1871—1872茶季，输出量达到7,766,534磅。这也是本口岸有史以来最大的输出量。在输出总量中，美国进口了7,393,258磅，1870—1871茶季则为5,073,484磅。

输出到英国的数量为176,665磅，1870—1871茶季则为380,109磅。值得一提的是，就价格而言，厦门乌龙茶在纽约市场现在更受欢迎，而不是福州茶。

工夫红茶。这种茶叶的输出量在 1869—1870 茶季达到最高值，当时约有 50,000 个半箱装即 2,109,232 磅被装运输出。从那以后，输出量在 1870—1871 茶季减少到 1,216,878 磅，1871—1872 茶季又减少到 353,514 磅。某种程度上，这可能是因为茶农发现乌龙茶的价格很高，但工夫红茶市场有限，因此他们将大部分茶青制成乌龙茶。1871—1872 茶季的工夫红茶几乎完全是高品质的，共有 297,916 磅输出到美国，输出到英国的数量仅剩 55,598 磅。相比较而言，1869—1870 茶季为 1,799,542 磅，1870—1871 茶季为 775,419 磅。输出量的减少是因为次级工夫红茶的品质不佳，因此受到伦敦市场的排斥。而对于优级红茶，美国人出手要比英国人慷慨得多。可能由于我们正在讨论的茶季产量小，这种茶没有被装运到各个殖民地，而在 1870—1871 茶季，殖民地进口量为 145,790 磅。在即将到来的茶季，输出到殖民地的贸易可能会重新开启。

两三年前，厦门茶叶由于茶末含量高而口碑不佳，现在正稳步恢复其在美国市场的地位（如前所示，美国是大多数厦门茶的出口目的地），这是因为 1868 年本地商行联合会一致同意拒绝收购茶末含量超过 20% 以上的茶叶。自 1872—1873 茶季开始，这一比例将进一步降低到 15%。在联合会介入以前，有时茶叶所含的茶末竟高达 60%，这导致没有这种瑕疵的日本茶逐渐取代了厦门茶。

目前，厦门茶叶已经重新获得青睐。根据最近收到的意见反馈，它们似乎是唯一让出口商获利的茶叶。

淡水茶主要通过本港口运往纽约，其出口量有了显著的增长。

1869—1870 茶季出口到纽约的总量	370,238 磅
1870—1871 茶季出口到纽约的总量	778,242 磅
1871—1872 茶季出口到纽约的总量	1,502,000 磅

预计下个茶季淡水茶的输出量将会更大。这种茶叶之所以受到青睐是因

为：首先，它们制作精美，茶末含量微乎其微（约 5% 或 6%）；其次，它们散发出天然的清香味道，这可能是由于那里的茶树树龄小，又几乎全部种植在新开垦的土地上。普通等级的台湾茶叶无需支付出口费用，并且主要供当地人自己饮用。

厦门糖类的出口情况如下：

	1871 年	1870 年	1869 年	1862 年（仅含 9 个月）
红糖	155,335 担	58,723 担	50,733 担	39,921 担
白糖	25,553 担	13,158 担	13,378 担	8,898 担
冰糖	83,519 担	61,416 担	60,438 担	46,781 担

这些数字非常令人满意，说明红糖的输出量增长了 2 倍，白糖的输出量增长了近 1 倍，冰糖的输出量在一年内增长了约 35%。自 1862 年本海关开设以来，糖类输出量的增长是显著的。

自 1870 年以来，纸张的输出量增加了 3,000 担，达到 24,300 担。但自 1862 年以来，其输出量仅增加了约 9,000 担。瓷器的输出量为 30,312 担，与 1870 年的输出量相比减少了 16,000 担，但与 1862 年相比增加了 24,000 担。

Trade between Amoy and "Formosa"

The following figures will show the valuable trade that has developed between Amoy, and Takow, Tamsui, and Keelung, in "Formosa".

	1871.	1870.
Foreign Imports Re-exported to "Formosa" value	$1,127,438	$1,242,946
Amoy produce Exported to "Formosa" value	$63,459	$34,281
Native Imports, Re-exported to "Formosa" value	$14,854	$19,350
	$1,205,751	$1,296,577

In 1869 the value of this trade was 1,031,375.

The nature and extent of this trade during the past year, can be ascertained by an examination of the Tables numbered 1, 2 and 3 which follow.

No. 1—TABLE OF FOREIGN GOODS RE-EXPORTED FROM AMOY TO "FORMOSA" DURING THE YEAR 1871.

		QUANTITY	VALUE ($)	TOTAL VALUE ($)
COTTON PIECE GOODS		50,500	135,692	
SHIRTINGS, Grey	pieces.	2,926	8,132	
SHIRTINGS, White	pieces.	100	386	
SHIRTINGS, Dyed	pieces.	246	1,064	
SHIRTINGS, Dyed Figured	pieces.	4,498	8,982	
T-Cloths	pieces.	1,890	4,772	
Turkey Reds	pieces.	570	2,036	
Drills, American	pieces.	1,460	5882	
Drills, English	pieces.	100	236	
Chintzes	pieces.	61,660	——	167,122
Total Cotton Yarn	pieces. piculs.	60	2,241	2,241

		QUANTITY	VALUE ($)	TOTAL VALUE ($)
WOLLEN PIECE GOODS		660	10,485	
Camlets, English	pieces.	180	2,828	
Lastings	pieces.	1,719	13,718	
Long Ells	pieces.	72	1,874	
Spanish Stripes	pieces.			
Total	pieces.	2,631	——	28,905
OPIUM				
Benares	piculs.	1,058.40	577,914	
Patna	piculs.	234.00	134,901	
Persian	piculs.	320.40	184,257	
Turkey	piculs.	14.16	8,202	
Total	piculs.	1,626.96	——	905,274
SUNDRIES				
Flour	piculs.	78	348	
Lead	piculs.	1,976	13,454	
Window Glass	boxes.	120	447	
Various Goods	value.	——	9,647	23,996
Grand Total			**Value $**	1,127,438

No.2—TABLE OF AMOY PRODUCE EXPORTED, AND NATIVE IMPORTS RE-EXPORTED TO "FORMOSA", DURING THE YEAR 1871.

		EXPORTS		RE-EXPORTS	
		Quantity	**Value ($)**	**Quantity**	**Value ($)**
Bricks	pieces.	366,500	2,133	——	——
Earthen Ware	pieces.	1,137	1,310	——	——
Hemp Bags	pieces.	237,780	10,755	——	——
Iron Ware	peculs.	1,518	10,176	——	——
Medicine	peculs.	8	183	——	——
Nankeens	peculs.	225	13,841	——	——
Paper No. 1	peculs.	81	1,176	38	573
Paper No. 2	peculs.	156	1,089	——	——
Paper Oiled	peculs.	——	——	34	1,185
Sugar Brown	peculs.	350	1,022	——	——
Sugar Candy	peculs.	97	806	——	——
Tea Mats	pieces.	——	——	86,600	3,402
Tobacco, Prepared	peculs.	577	10,674	113	3,279
Sundries	Value.	——	10,321	——	6,415
Total value			$63,459		$14,854

The value of "Formosa" produce imported at Amoy for home consumption, and re-exportation, amounted to $515,775, in 1871, to $290,207, in 1870, and to $405,245, in 1869.

No. 3—TABLE OF NATIVE PRODUCE IMPORTED AT AMOY FROM "FORMOSA" DURING THE YEAR 1871.

	QUANTITY	VALUE（$）
Camphor	950 Peculs	13,134
Coals	25,150 Peculs	12,407
Ground Nuts	——	——
Ground Cakes	21,088 Peculs	33,109
Hemp	497 Peculs	7,850
Rice	17,301 Peculs	31,898
Seeds Indigo	100 Peculs	570
Seeds Sesamum	1,637 Peculs	6,453
Sesamum Seed Cakes	570 Peculs	951
Tea Oolong	12,290 Peculs	403,314
Hard Wood Planks	1,969 pieces	1,626
Sundries	value------	3,374
Camphor Wood Planks	726 pieces	1,189
Total value		$515,775

It should be observed that of the above imports, tea to the value of $403,314, was merely sent here for convenience of shipment, and was re-exported in due course to the United States.

In closing this sketch of trade during the past year I may be permitted to say a few words regarding its mode of conduct. For some years the system of credit extended to Chinese by Foreigners, in their dealings with them, made commerce appear very unsafe. Credits became at last so extended that, in place of advances on sales being from 25 to 35 per cent, in many instances credit was given for the entire sale, and in consequence when due date arrived, as a rule, hardly any payments to account had been made; and the time allowed for clearing the goods, two months, had generally to be doubled, and often to be allowed to exceed even that period; the purchaser, meanwhile, paying no interest on the overdue prompts. This objectionable system has of late received a check, by all the foreign merchants agreeing, and binding themselves under a penalty of $1,000, not to give credit beyond twenty per cent, and fixing the time for payment at two months' prompt.

This remedy was apparently the best that could be applied, the native dealers having too little capital to do business without a certain amount of credit; and without some credit being given the trade would have been at a standstill.

The Statistics of Treasure present an important and curious feature in the trade of the port.

Treasure Imported 1870	$1,355,395	Treasure Exported	$762,835
Treasure Imported 1871	$2,116,069	Treasure Exported	$682,738
Treasure Imported （9 months）1862	$405,170	Treasure Exported	$909,612

This enormous increase in the import of Treasure during 1871, amounting to more than three quarters of a million of dollars, has been caused by foreigners pouring it into the port, for the purpose of meeting Bills of Exchange drawn from Manila, and the Straits. But no one knows what becomes of it. Notwithstanding the receipt of the large sum shewn above, it has been found that there is every day more and more difficulty in obtaining dollars from Chinese merchants. They will give in exchange, or do anything rather than pay up in coin, yet the amount sent to "Formosa" has fallen ten per cent. It seems evident, therefore, that the whole increase must have gone into the interior, or have been absorbed here; and unless there be some at present unknown outlet for it, the supposition remains that it is hoarded by the Chinese for purposes, and in a manner, of which foreigners know nothing.

It may here be remarked that the Chinese have, at last, begun to realize the advantage of using foreign Bills of Exchange in making their remittances to Hongkong, instead of adhering to their old custom of sending treasure.

FINIS.

厦门与台湾之间的贸易

以下数据显示厦门与台湾的打狗①、淡水和基隆之间发展起来的重要商品贸易情况。

	1871 年（单位：银元）	1870 年（单位：银元）
转口至台湾的外国商品价值	1,127,438	1,242,946
输出至台湾的厦门本地产品价值	63,459	34,281
转口至台湾的本国其他地方的产品价值	14,854	19,350
总计	1,205,751	1,296,577

1869 年，此项贸易额为银 1,031,375 元。

在过去的一年中，此项贸易的性质和种类可以通过分析以下表格 1、2 和 3 加以确认。

表 1　1871 年间自厦门转口至台湾的外国产品汇总表

棉布	数量	价值（单位：银元）	总价值（单位：银元）
衬衫布料（灰色）	50,500 匹	135,692	
衬衫布料（白色）	2,926 匹	8,132	
衬衫布料（染色）	100 匹	386	
衬衫布料（染色提花）	246 匹	1,064	
T 型布料	4,498 匹	8,982	
鲜红色棉布	1,890 匹	4,772	
粗斜纹布（美国产）	570 匹	2,036	
粗斜纹布（英国产）	1,460 匹	5,882	
印花棉布	100 匹	236	
小计	61,660 匹	——	167,122
棉纱（小计）	60 担	2,241	2,241

① “打狗”（Takow）是高雄的古称。译者注。

（续表）

毛料	数量	价值（单位：银元）	总价值（单位：银元）
羽纱（英国产）	660 匹	10,485	
厚实斜纹织物	180 匹	2,828	
粗斜纹呢	1,719 匹	13,718	
染色呢	72 匹	1,874	
小计	2,631 匹	——	28,905
鸦片	**数量**	**价值（单位：银元）**	**总价值（单位：银元）**
贝拿勒斯[1]产	1058.40 担	577,914	
巴特那[2]产	234.00 担	134,901	
波斯产	320.40 担	184,257	
土耳其产	14.16 担	8,202	
小计	1626.96 担	——	905,274
杂项	**数量**	**价值（单位：银元）**	**总价值（单位：银元）**
面粉	78 担	348	
铅	1,976 担	13,454	
窗玻璃	120 盒	447	
其他货物（价值）	——	9,647	23,996
总计价值（银元）			1,127,438

① 贝拿勒斯 (Benares) 系印度东北部城市瓦腊纳西 (Varanasi) 的旧称。译者注。

② 巴特那 (Patna) 位于印度比哈尔邦 (Bihar)。译者注。

表 2　1871 年间厦门本地输出以及本国外地输入后转口至台湾的产品汇总表

	输出		转口	
	数量	价值（单位：银元）	数量	价值（单位: 银元）
砖块	366,500 块	2,133	——	——
陶器	1,137 件	1,310	——	——
麻袋	237,780 个	10,755	——	——
铁器	1,518 担	10,176	——	——
药物	8 担	183	——	——
本色棉布	225 担	13,841	——	——
一号纸	81 担	1,176	38 担	573
二号纸	156 担	1,089	——	——
油纸	——	——	34 担	1,185
红糖	350	1,022 担	——	——
冰糖	97	806 担	——	——
茶杯垫	——	——	86,600 个	3,402
熟烟丝	577 担	10,674	113 担	3,279
杂项价值	——	10,321	——	6,415
总价值		63,459		14,854

1871 年厦门从台湾输入的用于家庭消费和转口贸易的产品价值为 515,775 银元，1870 年为 290,207 银元，1869 年为 405,245 银元。

表 3　1871 年间输入到厦门的台湾产品情况表

	数量	价值（单位：银元）
樟脑	950 担	13,134
煤	25,150 担	12,407
花生	——	——
花生饼	21,088 担	33,109
大麻	497 担	7850
大米	17,301 担	31,898
靛蓝染料植物种子	100 担	570
芝麻种子	1,637 担	6,453
芝麻饼	570 担	951
乌龙茶	12,290 担	403,314
硬木板	1,969 片	1,626
杂项价值	——	3,374
樟木板	726 片	1,189
总价值		515,775

应当注意的是，在上述输入的产品中，价值为 403,314 银元的茶叶是出于运输的便利性才被运到这里，在适当的时候便转口到美国。

在结束过去一年贸易状况的简要介绍之前，请允许我就对外贸易的开展模式说几句话。多年来，在业务往来过程中，外国人把其信用制度扩展到中国人身上，这给互市贸易埋下了严重的隐患。最终，信用规则放宽到毫无底线，以至于在应该事先收取 25% 到 35% 销售预付款的交易中，买家时常赊账。因此，当结账日到来时，买家几乎不会支付任何款项。此外，尽管双方协定在两个月内结算货物，卖家往往不得不允许买家再延期两个月甚至更长时间，买家更不可能支付逾期付款利息。这个令人不快的信用制度最近受到了约束，所有外国商人一致同意，不接受超过 20% 的赊账，并把付款期限定为两个月，如有违反，就必须交纳银一千元的罚款。

这是所能采取的最好补救办法，因为当地商人如果不赊账的话就没有足够的本钱做生意，而如果不让他们赊些账的话，双方的贸易就做不下去了。

银元的统计资料展现了本口岸互市贸易的一个重要而古怪的特点。

1870 年流入银元数	1,355,395	流出银元数	762,835
1871 年流入银元数	2,116,069	流出银元数	682,738
1862 年（9 个月）流入银元数	405,170	流出银元数	909,612

1871 年间，由于外国人大量涌入本口岸，为了支付从马尼拉和海峡地区开出的汇票，流入的银元增加了银七十五万元以上，幅度巨大，但是没有人知道结果会怎么样。尽管流入了上述这笔巨款，人们发现要想从中国商人手里获得银元变得越来越困难了，他们宁可寻找其他东西或者为外国人做事来抵账也不愿意用银元来付款，可是带到台湾的银元数量却又减少了百分之十。因此，可以明确的是，增加的所有银元肯定全部都流入内陆或者就地吸收掉了，除非存在部分目前未知的流向，否则我们仍然假定这是中国人囤积的结果，而其中的方式和目的就不为外国人所知了。

因此，我们可以说，中国人终于开始意识到使用外国汇票往香港汇款的好处，而不再坚持他们寄送银元的老习惯了。